THEODORE PARKER

THEODORE PARKER

BY

HENRY
STEELE
COMMAGER

———

WITH ILLUSTRATIONS

═══════════

Boston
THE BEACON PRESS
1947

Copyright, 1947

By Henry Steele Commager

First edition, 1936
Little, Brown and Company

Second edition, 1947
The Beacon Press

august 1957

TO

SAMUEL ELIOT MORISON

PREFACE

It is just over a century now since young Theodore Parker — he was not yet forty — left the pastoral serenity of West Roxbury for the pulpit of the Twenty-Eighth Congregational Society in Boston: soon the Society moved to that great Music Hall which Parker loved so well in order to accommodate the throngs who heard him gladly. With his move to Boston Parker achieved a national platform and began to exercise a national influence. What he had to say for the next decade or so of his short life is still timely almost a century after that life ebbed out in distant Florence. For with Channing he is the most nearly timeless of American preachers: though he addressed himself, courageously, to current problems he illuminated those problems by eternal values.

Pioneer in the socialization of Christianity, in the application of spiritual standards to secular issues, he became the conscience of the North — of such men as Charles Sumner and John Hale and Abraham Lincoln, and of countless thousands of ordinary men and women who were troubled by the contrast between the faith they professed and the practices they tolerated.

He took religion out of the pulpit and went with it into the highways and byways of American life — literally in his arduous lecture tours through the North, figuratively in the subjects he embraced. He asserted the universal and eternal validity of the moral law — for week-day as for Sunday purposes, for political and business and social relationships as for religious.

He rejected the distinction between the sacred and the

profane, holding every human being sacred and requiring that every act that affected human beings — the hours of labor and the wages that industrialists fixed, the schooling that the state provided, the laws that politicians passed, the treatment that masters displayed towards slaves — conform to the moral law.

The most articulate of the Transcendentalists he insisted — what contemporaries like Ralph Barton Perry and Walter Lippmann are again insisting — that there is a Higher Law and an imperative obligation to obey it. It was perhaps an infirmity that he was unwilling to compromise, but there were compromisers enough, and it should not be difficult to forgive fanaticism when it was directed towards the maintenance of human rights and the exaltation of moral standards.

In a day when we are tempted to judge every act by its immediate political or economic consequences, and when pragmatism is invoked to justify expediency, Parker's insistence upon the timelessness of the moral law and the validity of moral judgment is peculiarly relevant.

It is ten years since I wrote this book. If I were to rewrite it now I might change it in some details, fill out some chapters, abbreviate others, add here and there from material recently made available in the writings of contemporaries. But I should not change it in any essentials. It is, after all, an interpretation, and I am content to abide by it.

H. S. C.

August 1947

TABLE OF CONTENTS

LIST OF ILLUSTRATIONS

FOLLOWING PAGE 20

Theodore Parker
Birthplace of Theodore Parker, Lexington, Mass.
Quincy Hall Market about 1830
Theodore Parker's Church in West Roxbury

FOLLOWING PAGE 52

The Parsonage
Brook Farm Buildings
Convers Francis
Samuel J. May

FOLLOWING PAGE 116

Theodore Parker
Lydia Parker
Margaret Fuller Ossoli
Elizabeth Peabody
The Old Boston Music Hall Where Parker Preached
View of Summer Street
Theodore Parker's Study
George Ripley
William Ellery Channing
William Lloyd Garrison and Wendell Phillips
T. W. Higginson, aet. 20
Theodore Parker Placard
The Marshal's Horse, with Anthony Burns, Moving Down State
    Street
Samuel G. Howe
Charles Sumner
Theodore Parker, 1859

THEODORE PARKER

CHAPTER I

LEXINGTON

THEODORE PARKER came rightly by his Yankee features and his provincialism, for his was the sixth generation of Parkers to be born on Massachusetts soil. The first American Parker, Thomas, had come to the Bay Colony in 1635; he was admitted as a freeman to the town of Lynn, moved to Reading, helped to organize the church, served as deacon, and followed the biblical injunction to multiply and replenish the earth. For threescore years the Parkers were active in the affairs of Reading. Then in 1712 Thomas' grandson, John Parker, bought "one small mansion house and sixty acres of land" in Cambridge Farms, and moved his family to that straggling village which was shortly to be known as Lexington.

For a hundred years before Theodore was born, the fortunes of the Parker family were interwoven with the history of Lexington. Johns and Josiahs, Ebenezers and Hananiahs, served as thingmen and fenceviewers, clerks and assessors, while the Sarahs and Rebeccas and Lydias married into neighboring families and bore numerous children. Parkers sat in the meetinghouse on the Common along with the Estabrooks and Russells and Tidds; they served on the school board, and trained with the militia. It was an unpretentious family; the rocky soil refused them wealth, but there was little wealth in Lexington, and the Parkers were as well off as their neighbors. None of the Parker children attended the college at Cambridge; there were no lawyers or clergymen among them. They were farmers and mechanics; they tilled the soil and raised peaches in the orchard bordering the creek that ran through their meadow, or they made barrel staves and spinning wheels and ciderpresses; with each generation they put their roots deeper into the ground.

It was Theodore's grandfather, Captain John Parker, who most deeply impressed himself upon the history of the town. He had been a sergeant in the French and Indian War, and had seen the battle on the Plains of Abraham, and the fall of Quebec. Fifteen years later, he commanded the militia on that morning of April Nineteenth when Major Pitcairn marched his redcoats down the Concord road and into Lexington village. How often Theodore heard that story; it was all very real to him, and very personal. In features and in build he resembled his grandfather, and he liked to think that he had inherited some of the Captain's courage and character. The musket that John Parker had used that day, and another that he had captured at Bunker Hill, hung always in his grandson's study; and the bold words which family tradition credited to the Captain came to have for Theodore a special meaning: "If they mean to have a war, let it begin here."

Captain Parker's son John was a boy of fourteen when he watched the skirmish on Lexington Common. That same year the Captain died, only forty-six, and John took over the farm and the carpenter's shop. He was a poor farmer, but a good mechanic, much more skillful at mending pumps than at clearing land, and the farm ran down — all but the orchard, which he tended diligently. When he was twenty-three he married Hannah Stearns, daughter of Benjamin and Hannah Segur Stearns, whose house was down the Waltham road. The Segurs came from Newton, but the Stearnses, like the Parkers, belonged in Lexington. They too had their Revolutionary tradition, and the story of Lexington seemed tame to a veteran like Ben Stearns who had fought at White Plains and at Bennington. He was a man of property and position, "Sugar Ben" Stearns, but there were eleven children in the family, and blue-eyed

Hannah had to be content with linens and pewter for her
dowry. "It was a day of small things," Theodore wrote
later of his father's wedding. "He wore home-made blue
yarn stockings, at his wedding, and brought his wife
home over the rough winding roads, riding in the saddle on
his tall gray horse, with her upon the pillion. The outfit of
furniture did not bespeak more sumptuous carriage — the
common plates were of wood; the pitcher, mugs, tea-cups
and saucers were of thick well-kept pewter. Yet a few costly
wine glasses were not wanting, with two long-necked de-
canters, a few china tea-cups and saucers, of the minutest
pattern, and the pride of the buffet, a large china bowl.
Besides, the young bride could show patch-work bed quilts
and counterpanes and a pretty store of linen towels, and a
tablecloth of the same, white as the snow, and spun, woven,
and bleached by her own laborious hands; and her father
raised the flax which her brothers pulled and rotted and
broke and swingled and hackled and combed. Hannah made
their work into linen."

Many children were born to John and Hannah Parker:
Mary and John, Lydia and Hannah, and Lydia again;
Rebecca and Isaac, Ruth and Hiram — so many, indeed,
that bibical and family names gave out, and the tenth
child, born in 1806, was named Emily Ann. Hannah Parker was forty-three when Emily Ann was born, and sister
Rebecca was old enough to sew the family tree on a
sampler. But four years later Hannah was with child again,
and the son who was born that sweltering morning of
August 24, 1810, was named by the pious parents Theodore,
"gift of God." He was the first of the family to bear that
name, and the last Parker to be born in the old house.

2

Theodore loved the old frame house, the meadow that
stretched out before it and the hills behind it, the bushes
fragrant with blossoms in the spring, and the locust trees
white in June nights. This land had been farmed for over

a hundred years, but the countryside about was still primitive and almost forbidding, and the Parkers' nearest neighbor was miles away. The house was rude and plain when the first John Parker brought his family to it, and succeeding generations of Parkers had done little to enlarge or beautify it. But in time the old house took on a gentler character, as it fitted itself, weatherworn and familiar, into its surroundings, and adapted itself to its people. The farm, too, was tamed, though the back-breaking labor of a dozen Parkers could not clear the land of all the stones that littered the fields nor make the thin soil bear good crops. The great meadow was drained, and the brook that wandered through it held no terrors for even a little boy. Apple trees brought over from England bloomed in the orchard, and the peach crop was reckoned to be one of the best in Middlesex County, in good years bringing in as much as a hundred dollars. There were barberry bushes everywhere, with their bright yellow flowers and their red berries, and on the slope behind the house there were elms and maples and oak trees, for shade and for adventure. In the field the corn stood in rows far above the head of a small boy, and when the ears were husked the cobs were playthings better than any blocks. In the spring and summer Theodore would lie in the tall grass and look up at the great yellow clouds, or he would pick the blue and white violets that grew close to rocks, or buttercups to rub on his chin; and when he was old enough to venture near the brook he could find fringed gentians along its edge and water lilies floating coldly on the shallow pond beyond. He soon learned where there were wild strawberries and huckleberries and tart cranberries, and he braved the thorns of the blackberry and raspberry bushes up in the hills. In the woods he could find walnuts and hickory nuts and butternuts, all so hard to crack. He learned to know the song of the bobolink and the whippoorwill and the chickadee, lingering through the winter months, and not to fear the snakes that slid noiselessly into the brook.

In the winter, when the snow drifted up in great banks on the hillside and against the back of the house, darkening the kitchen windows, the little boy played in the warm kitchen or in the barn, or among the chips and shavings of his father's workshop. The kitchen he liked best of all the rooms in the house; here his mother and sisters cooked and baked, made jelly or boiled soap or molded candles, while Theodore sat on the floor and played with his corncobs or with the kindling. When he was a little older he must bring wood from the shed to keep up the fire that burned always in the great fireplace with its crane and iron kettle, and he must fetch water from the well that stood at the foot of the path. In the barn there were cattle to be fed and cows to be milked, and in the loft the dry sweet hay in which a boy could hide. But best of all was his father's workshop. It had once been the belfry of the meetinghouse, and its bell had rung out the warning to all the town that morning when the British came, and it had rung men and women to church for twoscore years, and tolled many a soul heavenward. When the new meetinghouse was built, in 1794, John Parker bought the old belfry tower, and it made a fine workshop. Here he made pumps and cider presses and barrel staves and wooden bowls from maple stumps. He was a skillful mechanic, intimate with his tools, and his handiwork found its way into many a farmhouse in Lexington. Soon Theodore learned to use the hammer and the saw and the lathe; and he never lost his familiarity with tools, or his feeling for the dignity of craftsmanship.

The family, too, exerted its subtle discipline on the growing boy. It was a large family, but there were not many playmates for him. Hiram and Isaac were old enough to cut hay in the meadow, and help their father at his bench, and in the evening they courted the neighbors' daughters; they belonged to the grown-ups. Ruth and Rebecca both died when Theodore was a baby; they were buried in the Lexington graveyard among the many tombstones that spoke sedately of Parker piety. So it was Emily Ann who fell heir to the baby. She was old enough to dress him in his brown homespun petticoats and to feed him porridge out of the wooden bowl made at his father's lathe, and she read to him and taught him his letters from a bag of clippings that she had saved out of the papers, and of all his brothers and sisters he loved her best. Theodore's mother was forty-seven when he was born; when he was thirteen she died, worn out with childbearing and the drudgery of a large household, and Theodore began to understand the meaning of some of those curious inscriptions on the Parker tomb-stones: —

> Death like an overflowing flood
> Doth sweep us all away,
> The young, the old, ye middle age'd
> To death become a prey.

He remembered his mother emotionally, as one remembers from childhood, not critically. She was frail and delicate with pale blue eyes, austere, and undemonstrative, but Theodore was the baby, and she managed to spoil him a little. He remembered that for all her household tasks, she was careful, after the day's work was done, to put away the blue-checked apron of the morning for a more comely dress, and that she found time to teach him the ballads and hymns she liked to sing, and to tell him stories of his great-grandfather Nathaniel who was captured by the Indians, and at night to read to him from the Bible. She was a devout woman, much concerned with her boy's moral welfare; and Theodore never forgot how she had explained laboriously to him the meaning of conscience.

His father Theodore came to know as he grew older. He was a great, powerful man, always busy in his workshop or in the orchard, a man of some presence, silent and thoughtful. He read much, in secular as in theological literature, and his thinking was sharpened with skepticism. A man of standing in the community, well connected and respected, he chose the teachers for the local school, and was an adviser to widows and orphans. He was an exacting parent whose sternness early taught Theodore to help with the chores, to bring grain and water to the cattle, and to hold the chalk line in the workshop. Yet Theodore remembered him always with affection, and years later he wrote: "I have been cradled in his arms, fed by his hands, blessed by his prayers, and moulded by his tender care."

In an upper chamber of the house lived the widow of Captain John Parker. A stately lady of eighty years, she condescended only once in a while to join the family downstairs. Twice a day Theodore stumbled up the steep stairs to her room with a drink of flip, the iron loggerhead clinking against the side of the earthenware mug, the strong acrid smell of burnt rum suggesting indescribable delights to the small boy. He would find his grandmother knitting sweaters for her grandchildren, or reading the *Columbian Sentinel*, or the great Oxford quarto Bible bought for the price of a load of hay, or sitting idle, perhaps, keeping company with her conscience because her second marriage had turned out so badly and all but ruined the family.

Besides the family in the house there were aunts and uncles and cousins in plenty. Theodore's mother had ten brothers, who bore such names as Noah and Jeptha, Habakkuk and Nahum, Asabel and Ammi; and his father's kin were almost as many. They would come of a Sunday, bringing their younger children to play with Theodore and Emily Ann. Then dinner would be laid out in the "other room," and Grandmother Parker would descend from her chamber to take her place at the head of the table. There would be talk of the new minister, Mr. Williams, and his Unitarian doctrines, or of politics, and John Parker would lament the passing of the Federalists and the coming in of leveling principles; and afterwards, when the arguments grew heated and the gossip in the kitchen dull, the children would escape to the garden and play hide-and-seek among the lilac and barberry bushes, or go wading in the brook. At Thanksgiving and Christmas the kinsfolk would come from distant towns, from Brighton and Reading and Watertown, to exclaim over "Miss" Parker's baby and to tell about their own. Then the fine linen would be brought out and the pewter plates, and the bayberry candles would be lighted and hyson tea drunk from china teacups, and Theodore lying in his spindle-bed would hear the talk go on long after the curfew bell had tolled nine o'clock.

3

Gradually the boy's world expanded. To the discipline of the old house and the farm and the family was added the discipline of the community. The meetinghouse, the school, the taverns and the shops, the neighbors, the settled ways of village life, wove themselves into Theodore's consciousness, gave substance to his character. Sundays, weather permitting, the boy would go to Meeting with his parents, sitting in Aunt Parker's pew high up in the gallery that ran around three sides of the church. Here he could see all the neighbors and townsfolk, the Estabrooks and Russells and Whittimores and Stearnses, as they filed solemnly into their pews below, and the choir whispering in the gallery at the back of the church, and, across from him, the town paupers, and, sitting by themselves, a handful of Negroes, Prince and Candy and Patty, lifting rich voices in praise of the white man's God. He could look down at the Reverend Mr. Williams, standing in the white painted pulpit with the circular stairs on either side, the strong voice rolling on and on until the children squirmed in their pews and began twisting the spindles of the railings or snapping down the seats to accompany the "Amens." But, for all the discomforts and distractions, there was a solemnity about the great square church and the long sermons and the full-throated hymns and the bell ringing in the belfry, and the boy came to have for it all a deep affection. After the service, the women would stand in the Common and talk while the men fetched the horses from the stalls and harnessed them; and those who lived in the country would call at the post office for mail, and the children would munch the gingerbread that was their reward after Sunday Meeting.

Market Day was more fun. Then Theodore would go with Hiram or Isaac jogging down the dusty winding road to the village with baskets of the famous peaches or blueberries that he himself had picked. The town would be filled with teamsters from Lowell or Waltham or Concord, waiting while their horses were watered and fed, washing down their lunches with cider or ale, or sitting in Dudley's Tavern, swigging strong blackstrap and talking of the weather and the crops or of the hard times which had set in with the war and stayed on like a bad penny, or of the mills which were being started down at Waltham. Over at the elegant new Monument House, Theodore might see merchants and lawyers from Boston, and the talk there would be of politics: of Governor Brooks, who managed to hang on to his office even after his party had disappeared, or of Maine's demand for separate statehood, or of the coming convention to revise the Constitution. And on the way home the boys would stop, perhaps, at the Social Library, of which Mr. Parker was a shareholder, and bring home a book for reading aloud — Bishop Watson's "Apology for the Bible," or the Reverend Mr. Gordon's "History of the Revolution," or something more frivolous, such as "Charlotte Temple." Their father was getting more worldly-minded all the time: he had a habit of forgetting to say grace at meals, and he had developed this queer taste for novels.

On rare occasions, when the peach crop was harvested, Theodore would be allowed to ride in to the Faneuil Hall market in Boston. A fabulous city, Boston, already the Hub of the Universe, the gilded dome of its State House glittering in the sun, its harbor crowded with East-Indiamen and Nor'westers, unloading sandalwood and chests of hyson and souchong tea wrapped in tropical husks, its coffee-houses and taverns filled with fashionably dressed men, the great

Exchange Coffee House towering into the sky, the wonder of America, its famous churches and houses which everyone had heard about and which an adventurous boy could find. It was on one of these trips that Theodore bought his first book, with his own money earned from endless hot hours of huckleberry-picking. It was Ainsworth's "Latin Dictionary," the cornerstone of the greatest private library in America.

Schooling had already begun then, and the boy had developed a thirst for knowledge that was never to be satisfied. He began to go to school when he was six, to the little brown boxlike schoolhouse with the hip roof, down the road a mile or so. In the summertime, he could cut across the meadow and over the brook on the stones that he had placed there; if his foot slipped and he fell in it did not much matter. Farmer Wellington's daughter Patty kept this school at Smith's End; she taught Theodore reading out of Murray's "English Grammar" and she taught him figures from Adams' "Arithmetic," and added, for good measure, the "New England Primer." Many years later Theodore remembered that the Primer had filled him with "ghastly" notions of God and the Devil, and that he had often cried himself to sleep with fears of eternal damnation. But mostly school was a pleasure. The little square room with the sloping floor was hot, but Theodore could relieve tedium by reading Rollins' "Ancient History," while the younger scholars learned their letters, and when school was out he could wrestle with the other boys or go swimming with them in the pond.

It was better in the winter, though he did have to go the long way then, his overshoes squeaking on the hard-packed snow as he trudged past the Underwood place and the Cutler estate to the welcome warmth of the schoolhouse. In the winter, school was taught by a man — by Mr. Noyes, and, later, by a young student from Brown College, Mr. White. Very early Theodore began to show those traits which were later to distinguish him: a memory almost photographic, an abiding and indiscriminate curiosity, a passion for reading of all kinds, a vanity which required him to outstrip his schoolmates, a mischievous sense of humor that broke through in the most unexpected places, and a painful sensitiveness to criticism. Mr. White was interested in the shy, awkward little boy with the alert blue eyes and the snub nose who had already read Plutarch's "Lives," and Homer, and Evelyn's "Sylva and Pomona," and who could recite from memory hundreds of lines of poetry. He gave him a Latin grammar and drilled him in syntax and vocabulary, and forty years later Theodore still remembered how Mr. White had scolded him because he could not remember the meaning of the word *avello*. Mr. White stayed only two winters, and for his successor Mr. Parker chose another Brown student, Mr. Fiske. The new teacher was soon as interested in Theodore as his predecessor had been, lent him books from the college library, helped him with his Latin, and started him on Greek. Many years later Theodore was to renew his friendship with William White and George Fiske, and when he published his massive "Theism, Atheism, and Popular Theology," he dedicated it to these two teachers, "with gratitude for early instruction received at their hands."

4

And so the years rolled by, filled with the routine of the farm and the shop, the church and the schoolroom. School was confined to winter now, and reading to the winter evenings when the chores were done. There were changes in the old house on the side of the hill; Grandmother Parker no longer sat in her upper chamber reading the Oxford Bible and awaiting her toddy, and after Theodore's thirteenth year the mother too was gone, and Emily Ann kept house. Isaac and Hiram grew up and married and moved off to New Hampshire, and Emily Ann was "keeping company" with Charlie Miller of Somerville, and after a while she too married and moved away from the old house, and only Theodore and his father were left. His father was aging now, his hair gray and his great frame bent and his hearing so poor that he stayed away from church; more and more the responsibility of the farm rested on Theodore. With the help of the hired man, he plowed the cornfield and the potato patch, and mowed the hay, and picked the peaches and marketed them in Lexington or in Boston. It was hard work running a farm: up at four in the morning and working through the long hot summer days, clearing the land of underbrush, dragging stones across the fields to use for building walls, and often Theodore worked too hard even for him. Life was coming to be a very serious business, for a boy in his teens. Schooling came to an end when he was sixteen, with a brief session at the new Academy. It was the pride of the town, a large, white building with tall pillars, facing the Common; and the principal, Mr. Caleb Stetson, — one day to be one of Theodore's closest friends, — was so well known that students came from far and wide. A little later, young Mr. Parker was to come back to the Academy and deliver a lecture on "Poland," a grave young person just turned twenty-one.

For Theodore was not going to be a farmer or a mechanic. All the Parkers had been farmers, his brothers were farmers or shopkeepers, but he was destined for something different — everyone agreed on that. He thought he would like to be a lawyer and go into politics, and he would catch himself about to run his plow into a ditch while he made famous orations in the Senate. But in the end it was not the law that attracted him most; it was the ministry. This was his mother's doing, perhaps; she had always wanted him to be a minister, and in time it came to be taken for granted that Theodore was to go to the Divinity School at Cambridge, if it could be managed.

But that was a long way off; the first task was to make some money. There was no money in farming, so at the end of his short session at the Academy he began to teach. That first winter he was invited to hold the Farms District School

at Quincy. It was an exciting experience for a boy of seventeen, for here was ground no less sacred than that of Lexington Common. Here, two centuries earlier, Mr. Wheel-
wright had preached such heresies as were now being voiced
in the liberal pulpits of the church. Here, history was per-
sonified in the Quincys and the Adamses who walked the
streets of the old town, and just a year before Theodore
came, old President Adams had been buried here beside his
wife Abigail; and, as if to emphasize the passing of the
old order, the enterprising townsfolk had begun to build the
first railroad in America. A short stroll brought Theodore
to Quincy Bay and Weymouth, where the fishing smacks
were drawn up for the winter, and a brisk half-hour's walk
took him to the Blue Hills of Milton. As a boy he had often
climbed Mount Tabor, behind the farm, and looked south
toward the Blue Hills; now he could explore them, examine
the soil and the rocks and the trees, apply all his botanical
learning. Soon school was over, and Theodore pocketed his
earnings and hurried back home to pay off his substitute
and to do the spring plowing.

The next winter he found a school at North Lexington;
he could live at home and walk to and from the schoolhouse,
and there would be time to help with the farm. When the
snow was too deep on the road, there were cousins in North
Lexington to put him up for the night.

When he was nineteen he went to Concord to teach. It
was a proper place for the grandson of Captain Parker,
and after he had dismissed the children he would find time
for a visit to the Wright Tavern where the minutemen had
assembled, or for a walk along the banks of the Concord
River and over the North Bridge. On Sundays he would go
to the meetinghouse on the Common and listen to Dr.
Ripley, eighty years old but as strong and alert as a whole
class of the young men turned out by the Divinity School
now; in the evening he might visit Dr. Ripley at the Old
Manse and hear some of those famous anecdotes — hear,
for example, how each one of the nine dissenters who broke

away from Mr. Bliss's church back in the sixties had come
to some bad end. On week days there were books from the
village Library Company, or a "theatrical" at the Academy,
or a lecture at the new Lyceum, perhaps by young Mr.
Emerson, who had once lived in the Old Manse and loved to
come back to Concord.

Theodore, too, wished to come back to Concord, but
he never seemed to stay more than one winter in any one
place; perhaps he was too exacting in his demands upon the
scholars. The next year found him at Waltham, a lovely
old town on the banks of the Charles. Here, as in Quincy,
the young teacher could see the beginnings of a new America,
for cotton mills were rapidly changing the country village
into a bustling center of industry, its population swelled
by hundreds of rosy-cheeked country girls who lived in the
neat little company houses, the green Venetian blinds
pulled down demurely. On Sundays Theodore would see
them sitting in the gallery of the new meetinghouse, while
down below, in the pews, you could pick out the merchants
from Boston and New York, or a banker up from Charleston and uneasy in a Unitarian pew.

But teaching in district schools was becoming monotonous, even with an annual change of scene. If he didn't
watch out, he would bog down in this kind of thing; but
he had no money for college, or for the Divinity School.
Nevertheless, one summer day in 1830 he walked over to
the college at Cambridge, passed his examinations, and
enrolled as a non-resident student; in that way he got out of
paying tuition. He always remembered the day, and many
years later he recorded in his journal, "It is this day twenty
years since I entered Harvard College. How joyfully I went
to work again the next day." His father was a little sus-
picious of this plan, afraid that it would cost money in the
end, or that Theodore would not be able to keep up with
his classes and help out with the farm and do his teaching.
But Theodore reassured him: he could do the work of three
men, he could do anything that needed to be done.

That day was his twentieth birthday, and it marked the beginning of the last year in the old house, the last year in
Lexington. He loved the place where his roots went deep,
like those of the great elm behind the house — the church
where he had sat with his mother, the Common where he had
trained with the militia (a lieutenant, he was, one winter),
the shops and the taverns and the handsome old houses where
the rich families lived, the countryside that he knew with
such intimacy. Lexington was not like a suit of clothes to
be put away when outgrown. It was the soil in which he was
planted, and he was never really uprooted. But now he was
young and curious and ambitious, and it was time for him
to go away. When a chance came to teach at a private school
in Boston, he accepted it eagerly, and on the twenty-third
of March in 1831, he set his steps toward the city which he
came to love with such passion and which was to reward him
with such love and such hatred as few men have known.

CHAPTER II

TEACHER AND STUDENT

IT was something for a raw country boy scarcely twenty-one, and without even the dignity of a Harvard degree, to be invited to teach in Boston, and the responsibility weighed on him. Awkward and ungainly, clad in an ill-fitting suit and coarse shoes, his hands rough from the toil of the farm and the bench, Theodore found his natural shyness increased, and he sought to make up in diligence and learning for what he lacked in social grace. How much they expected of him here; he was asked to teach Latin, Greek, French, mathematics, and, just to be sure nothing had been overlooked, "all sorts of philosophy." He was weak on mathematics, and had to take instruction from Mr. Francis Grund; science fascinated him, but he knew little of it, and in all Boston there was not a copy of Newton's "Principia" to be bought. His real interest was in languages and history, and six hours of teaching left him, after all, the best part of the day for work. "I had always from ten to twelve hours a day for my own private studies out of school," he remembered later. "Judge if I did not work; it makes my flesh creep to think how I used to work, and how much I learned that year and the four next."

He had brought his books with him from Lexington: Homer and Horace and Vergil, the companions of those endless winter evenings on the farm, and a dozen volumes of history and philosophy, the pages loose from much reading. The stalls of the bookshops on Cornhill were tempting, but his salary of fifteen dollars a month did not run to book-buying. But he was not without resources: there was the new Mercantile Library, and, when he could get out there, the library at Cambridge; and the oil lamp in his little room on Blossom Street burned far into the night as he worked through his German grammar or worried over John Locke's "Essay on Human Understanding." It was all too much, by far, for even his sturdy constitution, and he lost twenty pounds that year. Nor was that the end of it. Years later, sick and prematurely old, he looked back on this experience in Boston and wrote: "O that I had known the art of life, or found some book or some man to tell me how to *live,* to study, to take exercise. But I found none, and so here I am."

It was, all in all, a lonely year, and not a happy one. There were no kin in Boston, and few friends; and the boy became moody and introspective as he struggled with his scholars and pored over his books. Then Emily Ann died, his favorite sister, who had played with him and taught him his lessons, and he hurried out to Lexington to see her buried in the old graveyard beside her mother and her sisters, and the pine trees which had once seemed so full of the promise of life looked dark and forbidding. He sought consolation in religion, and went often to the Hanover Street Church, where the great Lyman Beecher, grim with theology, thundered indiscriminately against Catholicism and Unitarianism. Did this Litchfield parson think he was a Jonathan Edwards, with his fire and brimstone theology? Even the Reverend Mr. Williams out in Lexington could do better than that, and Parker turned away from this limping Calvinism with disgust.

It was a pity that this should have been his introduction to Boston and its religion, and he never quite forgave the town. He was headed for the ministry himself; he should have listened to preaching of a different kind. The saintly Channing was at the Federal Street Church, and when you heard him say "from Everlasting to Everlasting," you had a conviction of Eternity; young Emerson, with a face like a Franciscan monk's, could be heard at the Second Church,

and at the meetinghouse on Purchase Street, eager young
George Ripley, one day to be Parker's closest friend. Occasionally he did go to hear the younger Ware, so gentle,
so seraphic, who did not argue dogmatics but seduced you
into piety. But about most of this Unitarian preaching
there was a coldness, a formality. It reached your mind,
but not your heart. Better the gospel which Hosea Ballou
was preaching at the new Universalist chapel. And had
Theodore but gone up to North Square, to Father Taylor, he
would have found a religion that neither Beecher nor Ware
ever knew, for there the great preacher "walked his pulpit like a quarter-deck" and had warmth enough to kindle
the hearts of all Boston.

Of what use the Sunday sermons and the weekday grammars? There was time enough for those later; better had he
walked the streets of this great bustling town, growing and
changing so breathlessly. There was the Faneuil Hall market place where he had come as a boy and the new Quincy
market, piled so high with merchandise that there was
little room for the countryfolk to peddle their vegetables
and fruit; and up in North Boston the slums were growing prodigiously, and the packet ships spawned Irish immigrants who cared not a whit for the dialectics of Calvinism or Unitarianism. That winter Theodore might have
heard the concerts of the Handel and Haydn Society, or he
might have seen Hackett in his Yankee rôles at the old
Federal Street Theater, or Junius Brutus Booth re-creating
"King Lear" at the Tremont. Or he might have found his
way out to the Baptist church on "Nigger Hill," just off
Joy Street, on that stormy winter night when William Lloyd
Garrison and Ellis Gray Loring and Samuel Joseph May
(how well he was to know them all, later!) drew up a constitution for their anti-slavery society. It was the beginning of a new day for Boston, and for Parker too; but the
little schoolmaster from Lexington missed it all — his eyes
searched the past, not the future.

The winter with its days of teaching and its nights of

THEODORE PARKER

BIRTHPLACE OF THEODORE PARKER, LEXINGTON, MASS.

QUINCY HALL MARKET, ABOUT 1830

THEODORE PARKER'S CHURCH IN
WEST ROXBURY

study went slowly enough, and Theodore began to long for walks in open fields and for a change from the sea smells to air fragrant with clover. His relations, too, thought it time for a change; they were worried, perhaps, at his loss of weight and fits of melancholy. Uncle Peter Clarke, in Watertown, suggested that Theodore come out there and open a school of his own; Mr. Wilder was leaving, and the schoolroom over the storehouse would be vacant. Theodore took to the idea, a chance to be his own master, and a chance to make some money, too. He had decided that fifteen dollars a month didn't get one very far; he needed to make more than that if he was ever to enter the Divinity School. And so in April, 1832, he packed up his books and his clothes and went to Watertown.

2

Watertown was a quiet old village of some two thousand people, spread out along the banks of the Charles River, midway between Cambridge and Waltham. It had been founded by Sir Richard Saltonstall, in whose ship the first Parker came to America. Many of the old families lived there still, — the Coolidges and the Wellingtons and the Bonds, tilling their ancestors' acres whose produce went into Boston, — and wealthy Bostonians were building themselves handsome new houses for summer residence. It was a proper place for the grandson of Captain Parker: in the great square meetinghouse on the Common the First Provincial Congress had met, and the General Court, and Hancock and Adams had fulminated against British tyranny.

Theodore came here in the spring, when the elms and the maple were in bud and the bushes out in Mount Auburn were flowering. He took a room at Mrs. Broad's boarding house on the Newton road, and began at once to put the schoolroom in shape. Now his skill with tools was of use as he laid a new floor and wainscoted the walls and built some rough desks for prospective pupils. Young Mr. Parker was well-connected here, his uncles and cousins recommended him to their neighbors; soon the scholars began to come, and before the year was out there were over thirty of them. They were of all ages; he taught them everything from the three R's to Latin and French, and did not neglect the moral instruction considered the duty of a teacher. In the winter mornings the young schoolmaster would be up early to chop wood and build a fire in the Franklin stove; in the spring-time there were long walks across the fields to Smooth Helmet, where the apple trees were in bloom, or past Mr. Cushing's magnificent gardens, where the children might catch a glimpse of a fabulous Chinese butler; or he would lead them along the banks of Beaver Creek and the Charles, and teach them such botany as he knew.

It was pleasant, too, at Mrs. Broad's boarding house. His room was large and comfortable, the meals generous, and Theodore had here a life far more wholesome than that of Boston. There was companionship, too — a roommate who played a flute with more energy than skill, scholars who soon learned not to be in awe of his learning, cousins who welcomed him to their homes. And there was Miss Cabot. Lydia Cabot was the only daughter of John Cabot of Newton, well connected in Boston. She taught Sunday school at the Watertown Church, and boarded at Mrs. Broad's, a tall blue-eyed girl of nineteen, shy and demure, but with a citified air that came from long residence in the Hub of the Universe. Soon Theodore found himself teaching a class in the same Sunday school and escorting Miss Cabot home from church, or walking with her along the elm-shaded river road out to Prospect Hill, a grave young man having his first love affair.

They were opposites, Theodore later explained, in everything but "philanthropy," but it was sympathy and faith that he needed, not learning; he always had a curious distrust of strong-minded women. Lydia was like his mother, even in appearance; she was gentle and pious, and had all the domestic virtues. A lady, but not a great lady; she would make an ideal minister's wife. She sympathized with his ambitions and admired his talents, even if she did not understand them, and worried over his health and late hours. He read to her, passages from the long "History of the Jews" which he had written for the benefit of his Sunday school class, and she listened gravely and had nothing to say; when she went back to Boston for the winter, he sent her letters filled with an odd mixture of didactic criticism and protestations of devotion. "I am glad you advance so well in Homer," he wrote solemnly. "Somebody says 'Homer is the only royal road to poetry.' I think so." And then, "I love my books the more, my school the more, mankind the more, and even God the more, from loving you." So the affair progressed famously, and within little more than a year the two were engaged to be married.

"I walked to father's," Theodore wrote his betrothed. "He soon returned from church, and I caught him in the garden, and informed him of the 'fatal' affair, if you will call it so. The tear actually started to his aged eye. 'Indeed,' he said. 'Indeed,' I replied, and attempted to describe *some* of your good qualities. 'It is a good while to wait,' he observed. 'Yes, but we are young and I hope to have your approval.' 'Yes, yes, I should be pleased with any one you would select, but Theodore,' said he, and the words sank deep into my heart, 'you must be a *good* man and a *good* husband, which is a great undertaking.'

"I promised all good fidelity; and may Heaven see it kept."

3

But romance did not occupy all of Theodore's time, nor all of his thoughts either. Lydia's concern over his late hours was not without reason, and his roommate could tell her that the oil lamp burned much later than was good for Theodore's health or his own comfort. But it could not be helped. His passion for knowledge was as ardent as ever, and now he was in a great hurry to enter the Divinity School that he might the sooner settle down and marry and establish a home. The Reverend Convers Francis told him what he needed to know; he was mightily interested in this young man with the astonishing miscellany of learning and the appalling energy and the awkward but curiously winsome ways.

Few men exerted more influence on Theodore Parker than Francis, the genial, kindly scholar who presided so benignly over the Watertown church and, later, the Parkman Professorship at the Harvard Divinity School. His library was stored with the richest treasures of theological literature, and his mind crammed with encyclopædic learning. His erudition was both deep and broad, and he combined a genuine delight in antiquarian lore with an easy familiarity with the most recent volumes of German criticism or French philosophy. A thorough and precise scholar, discriminating and urbane, he had a sympathetic understanding of the history and traditions of the Church and an open-minded appreciation of the new currents of thought and of criticism. A conservative in everything concerning society and politics (democracy, he said, was the mother of all evils), he was a liberal in all that concerned theology and religion. The combination was ideal in the study, but paralyzing in the field of controversy: the orthodox regarded him as dangerous and the heterodox felt that he lacked courage. The students at the Divinity School found him "too all-sided," and even Parker, who owed him so much, wrote later, with cruel arrogance, "Poor old gentleman, he is dead, but thinks benevolently, as a corpse."

But it was the benevolence alone that Parker saw in those Watertown years. The handsome red brick parsonage on Mount Auburn Street, with its beautiful rose garden, was always open to him, and he was equally welcome at its hospitable table and its rich library. Doctor Francis was generous with his books; and when these were insufficient for Parker's voracious appetite, he brought others from the libraries in Cambridge. Even more valuable than the books was the friendly guidance and encouragement;

and Theodore carried home not only folios but ideas. Doctor Francis was a link, too, with literary Boston; he belonged to the Historical Society, and was intimate with that group of clergymen who were later to constitute the Transcendental Club, intimate with Mr. Emerson and Mr. Ripley, and Mr. Bronson Alcott, venerable even in his youth.

These men came occasionally to the parsonage on Mount Auburn Street, but even more interesting to Parker was Lydia Maria Child, sister to Doctor Francis, who brought with her an atmosphere of literary New York, and whose novels of New England life were so popular. She had all the courage, all the audacity, that her brother lacked; she seemed sometimes impatient of his moderation and his timidity. She was caught up, now, in this anti-slavery crusade, whose rumblings penetrated even to the peace of a country parish; she had just published the "Appeal in Favor of That Class of Americans Called Africans" that cost her her membership in the Athenæum; and her conversation was of Mr. Garrison and Mr. Tappan. It made the young teacher squirm to hear her, for he was already heartily ashamed that he had yielded to the insistence of parents and ejected a little colored girl from his school. He was fascinated by Lydia Child, a woman of the world, an author, and an abolitionist, and she did not fail to notice him and to remember him. Years later she was to write "Theodore Parker was the greatest man, morally and intellectually, that our country ever produced."

The greatness was not so clear, then; but these were years of growth, moral and intellectual. He studied with relentless perseverance, but not with discrimination. He read Herodotus and Thucydides, and the Greek dramatists as well, and translated Theocritus and Pindar. He even found time, somewhat guiltily, for fiction, and enjoyed the Waverley novels as thoroughly as did his Charleston kin, and he read the "misanthropic" Lord Byron with mingled feelings of delight in his art and disapproval of his morals.

Twice a week he walked in to Cambridge to study Hebrew with Mr. Thurston, and later he went to Charlestown to read Syriac with a Mr. Seixas. He wrestled with Hegel and Kant, and made the acquaintance of Cousin and Jouffroy, who failed to impress him (how much more thorough the Germans were than the French), and he dipped suspiciously into that new book that everyone was talking about — Coleridge's "Aids to Reflection." All this German and English idealism put a severe strain on his orthodoxy, and to reassure himself he carried on a long correspondence with a young friend, George Bigelow, in which he heaped ridicule upon those who questioned the inspiration of the Bible or the authenticity of miracles. But it was a sophomoric performance, and there was no conviction behind it.

Gradually the flood of learning which swept up all books, all subjects, with such eager impartiality, was becoming canalized; Doctor Francis saw to that. The studies now were in Greek and Hebrew and Mediæval Latin; the reading in dogmatics and hermeneutics and in the Church Fathers, whom Theodore found either wrongheaded or dull. Early in 1834 he wrote to Lydia: "Mr. Francis called here yesterday and lent me the necessary books, so I have commenced the great study, the criticism of the New Testament." And later in the same month, Theodore consulted with his minister about entering the Divinity School. Francis urged him to enter it that very spring, and gave him letters of introduction to the members of the faculty; it was Francis, too, who found for him a scholarship, which together with his own savings would carry him through his first year.

It was hard to leave Watertown, the kindly Mrs. Broad, the cousins, and the friendly townsfolk, the Whites and the Shannons and the Bigelows. Still, these he could come back to; but with the children it was different. He had come to love them, and the schoolroom that he had made over with his own hands; and when, on the last day of school, the children presented him with a loving-cup, he had to re-

tire so that they might not see his tears. He always came
back to Watertown as to home; here he preached his first
sermon, here he was understood and welcomed when other
churches were closed against him; and twenty-five years
later, when he was the greatest preacher in the whole land
and the busiest, with seven thousand names on his parish
list and a hundred lectures to give, he found time to come
out to Watertown and preach every Sunday for a year.

Now he was on the way to his career, and he set off for
Divinity School with high heart and high hopes. "Nothing
is too much for young ambition to hope, no eminence too
lofty for youth's vision," he wrote exultantly to Lydia.
"When we consider that sincere desires are never neglected,
we need not despair of making some *approaches* at least to
the eminence Mr. Palfrey now occupies. Would not this be
truly delightful? No situation can be more honorable, no
task more pleasant, no prospect more celestial, than that of
a virtuous, faithful clergyman."

4

With this celestial prospect in view, Parker entered the
junior class of the Harvard Divinity School and began his
formal preparation for the career which was to make him
the best-hated man in America. Years later he spoke of the
Divinity School with more severity than it deserved of
him — an "embalming institution," he called it — but while
he was there he found it good. The professors were learned,
open-minded, and generous, concerned less with the inculca-
tion of dogma than with the discovery of truth, and among
his classmates were many who were later to distinguish themselves in literature and the arts and bear witness to the
eclectic and liberal character of their training. The library
was small, but the College library was open to the students
of the Divinity School, as were the private libraries of the
professors. The teaching was practical rather than academic,
for the faculty knew that the Unitarian clergy was considered over-intellectual; there were few restraints on the

students, and every encouragement to individual explorations along the by-paths of learning.

Of the faculty, it was saintly Henry Ware, Junior, who exerted the greatest influence on the young Parker. He was the son of that Professor Ware whose appointment to the Hollis Professorship, back in 1805, had signalized Harvard's abandonment to Unitarianism. The old gentleman still preached in the chapel, and taught a course on the Evidences of Christianity, "grinding the toughest and mouldiest Hebrew grain," Parker remembered, "into homogeneous Unitarian meal which we were to knead, leaven, bake, and distribute as the Bread of Life." The younger Henry Ware was a man whose character was as distinguished as his presence, a scholar whose piety protected him against those shafts of criticism which would ordinarily have been directed against an editor of the writings of the infamous Doctor Priestley, and whose Life of Christ was one of the most widely read books in America. He was frail of health but never of spirit; he dared to belong to the Cambridge Anti-Slavery Society when abolitionism was regarded as very poor taste; and his hymn "Oppression Shall Not Always Reign" was one of the battle songs of the anti-slavery crusade. Professor Ware taught pulpit eloquence and practical theology, the first more naturally than the second; and he guided the activities of the Philanthropic Society, which sought to illustrate Christianity by good works. He taught Parker the art of preaching, polished his roughness, and tempered his enthusiasms. It was not an easy task, for young Mr. Parker was inclined to be both boisterous and flippant, his sense of humor bubbled up in the most unexpected and most indecorous of places, and he was the most ungraceful, the most rustic, of preachers. But Ware did what he could for this Lexington farm boy, and Parker tried to curb his high spirits and be a proper Unitarian; and years later he wrote of this teacher, "I loved him as I have seldom loved a man heretofore and perhaps shall never love another."

Professor Palfrey, whose lofty eminence Theodore had

admired from afar, taught Hebrew and the Literature of the Old Testament. A young man, he had already made a name for himself; his brilliance was matched by his versatility; he could turn out, with equal facility, a sermon on "The Duties of Private Life" or a ponderous contribution to the *North American,* and he was as learned in the history of early New England as in the antiquities of ancient Egypt. He thought well of Parker, and when he went off to New Orleans he had the young student take over his classes in Hebrew. But Parker thought better of his teacher's radical politics than of his conservative theology. No sooner was he out of school than he had the temerity to review Mr. Palfrey's "Lectures on the Jewish Scriptures," and critically ("my hair stands up when I think what I have written"), and it was only later that he came to appreciate the courage and magnanimity of the man whose abolitionism Lowell delighted to honor.

Besides these, there was the mighty Andrews Norton, no longer on the faculty of the school, but still a power in the church. He lived in the imposing mansion known as Shady Hill, not far from the Divinity Hall, and the rapt students could see his three lovely daughters strolling in the rose garden ("Norton's Evidences of Christianity," they were called), and sometimes they would have with them the curly-headed little Charles Eliot, who was later to add such distinction to the famous name. Norton was the aristocrat of the school, connected with all the first families, fastidious, aloof; the students pictured him, as he entered Heaven, looking down his fine Roman nose and murmuring, "This is a *very* miscellaneous crowd." He liked to think his home the literary center of Cambridge; he had edited the "Select Journal of Foreign Literature," introduced the poems of Mrs. Hemans to America (when he told her that the shore at Plymouth was neither stern nor rockbound, she wept), and even published a poem or two himself. But Professor Norton was no dilettante; he was even then working on that monumental "Evidences of the Genuineness of the

Gospels" which was to establish new standards of theological scholarship in America. Parker visited him in his fine library, where the walls were lined with richly bound books, the manuscripts piled neatly on his desk. The young student was bursting with enthusiasm for German scholarship, for De Wette and Schleiermacher and Bauer, but Professor Norton assured him coldly that all the Germans were "raw" and inaccurate, unfitted for the refinements of metaphysics. They made good dictionaries and grammars, he admitted, but even these were so large that no one could use them. Parker was considerably dashed, and that night he confided to his journal that Norton was a bigot. He never saw reason to change his opinion; years later he wrote to Doctor Francis, "Norton is a Pope, a *born* Pope."

Though Parker never attained with these men the intimacy and understanding that he had with good Doctor Francis, he did not lack for friendship. There were only some thirty students in the Divinity School, and he came to know them all. Among his classmates were many who appreciated him, and some whose appreciation he returned. Sam Andrews he loved, always; years later, when he was sick, he wrote: "I am not well enough to see you — it will make my heart beat too fast." No one understood him better than Samuel, and Parker confided in him his hopes and ambitions and even his love. "Sometimes, Samuel," he wrote, "I fear lest I have missed it capitally in becoming a minister; that as a lawyer I might have been more useful," or, when he was in a different mood, "There is a pulse in my heart that beats wildly for the stir and noise and tumult and dust of a literary course." For William Silsbee, too, he had a great affection, and he often visited in Silsbee's home in Salem, and they took long walks along the shore and settled the problems of philosophy. Then there was George Ellis, who introduced him to Ripley, and who was to be known as an historian and antiquarian, and John Dwight, later of Brook Farm fame, who abandoned the ministry for music and was admired by Emerson, and the irrepressible Christopher Cranch, who achieved some fame as a minor poet, but who was more skillful with crayon than with pen. There was John Parkman of anti-slavery fame, and Charles Brooks who translated Goethe and Schiller, and the amazing Henry Bellows who later organized the United States Sanitary Commission, so imperious that President Lincoln wanted to know if he was running the government, a genius and a mountebank.

His classmates remembered Parker for his inexhaustible industry, his cascading energy, for an exuberance of spirits that overflowed into mischief or coagulated into moodiness. "We all looked upon him," one of them recalled, somewhat equivocally, "as a prodigious athlete in his studies." They remembered him hurrying back from the college library, loaded down with books; he read as he walked and could not bother to keep to the path, and once he ran smack into a tree and fell unconscious, the books tumbling around him. Or they remembered him pacing back and forth in his room, memorizing a chart which, he assured them, contained *all* the dates in history, or declaiming some eloquent passage from the English State Trials, or sitting far into the night scribbling in that journal which reflected so accurately the hodge-podge of his mind, or writing those long letters to Miss Cabot. He was very busy indeed. He attended classes faithfully, prepared practice sermons (Professor Ware thought them pretty bad), studied, with a growing irritation, all the Church Fathers, joined eagerly in the discussions of the Philanthropic Society on "Intemperance" or "The Influence of Woman in Public Life," and taught a class at the state prison in Charlestown.

Nor was this all. He tutored two students in Hebrew and one in Greek and one in German. He translated, for Dr. Sparks, some papers of Lafayette, and undertook, just for his own satisfaction, a translation of Ammon's four volume *Fortbildung des Christenthums*. His zeal for the acquisition of new languages was as indiscriminate as ever; while at the Divinity School he learned the rudiments of Italian, Portuguese, Dutch, Swedish, Danish, Arabic, Persian, Coptic, and half a dozen others (so he claimed); he dabbled in some of the African dialects and had a fling at Russian, but found the difficulties of pronunciation insuperable. "The Swedish language is easy," he wrote in his journal, "and I expect to get much amusement and instruction from it. The Danish presents more difficulties than Swedish; and I shall not study it extensively, but soon make it give place to some other." Indeed, he studied few of them extensively; what interested him was the grammatical construction of a language, not the vocabulary. There were few languages which he could not read, after a fashion, and few which he could speak; he could dazzle any scholar with his knowledge of Coptic, but when he went to Europe he couldn't make himself understood in either German or French.

There was incessant reading: hundreds of heavy volumes, theology and philosophy and history, went down that voracious maw, all of them reviewed with an impudence that foreshadowed the acidity of later years. "Tertullian introduced more heresies and ridiculous doctrines into the Church than almost all the other Fathers. . . . Origen was not a good Hebrew scholar . . . Jerome loved glory rather than truth . . . St. Augustine introduced more errors into the Church than any other man . . . Chrysostom was better than most, but he was often absurd in his interpretations." It was no wonder that he concluded, "I am heart-weary and reason-weary of these same doting fathers." Already he had come to the conclusion that "the Scriptures have been interpreted in the interest of dogmatism, from Christ to the present."

Young Mr. Parker thought that he knew a thing or two about the interpretation of the Scriptures. With his classmates, Ellis and Silsbee, he was editing a little magazine designed not for scholars but for those hardheaded Yankees who loved nothing better than to unravel some doctrinal knot. This was the *Scriptural Interpreter*, and Parker wrote for it some forty articles — pretentious essays on the Messianic Prophecy or the Pentateuch or the Laws of Moses or the Traditions of the Elders. They were not such essays as Doctor Norton or Doctor Palfrey would have written; they reflected German scholarship, not brightly but with a diffused gentle light. The conclusions of De Wette and Eichorn swirled in the young editor's mind, but he clung hopefully to the anchors of conservative Unitarianism. He believed in the inspiration of the Bible, at least most of it; but he did not think the matter was of any importance. He believed in the miraculous birth of Christ, but he knew that other religions, too, had their virgin births. He had his doubts about the miracles, but Mr. Dewey, who gave the Dudleian Lecture, "removed the presumptions against them." So on the whole the *Interpreter* stayed within proper Unitarian bounds, and the editor undertook to explain away some of those difficulties which assailed the minds of the more skeptical. He put in a good word for Moses, and found extenuating circumstances for the annihilation of the Canaanites: "It must be remembered," he pointed out, "that all the nations to be extirpated were exceedingly vicious and corrupt." All this was comforting enough, yet there were some who were alarmed at the dangerous tendencies of the *Interpreter* since that sound scholar, Doctor Gannett, had surrendered it into immature hands. "I read," wrote one unhappy subscriber, "the article on the fifty-second chapter of Isaiah, with unmingled surprise and horror. What is the object of the theologians at Cambridge? Are they determined to break down the prophecies and make our blessed Saviour and his Apostles impostors and liars? Pause, I beseech you, before it is too late. Another such blow, and I must quit all I value."

But Parker did not pause, and soon the *Interpreter* came to an end. Fortunately it had not monopolized all his time or thought. Somewhere between Kant and the study of Swedish, he had managed to edge in some lighter fare. He read "Rienzi" with delight, revelled in "Tom Jones," and was transported by the "Pickwick Papers"; this was better than didactic moralizing over the sins of Byron. He scribbled little essays on Goethe and on Voltaire, and concluded that though Heine was a misanthrope, he was nevertheless a man of genius. He began to take pleasure in folk and fairy tales, and love made him susceptible to poetry. He even tried his hand at it himself: —

> I know not why, but heavy is my heart;
> The sun all day may shine, the birds may sing,
> And men and women blithely play their part;
> Yet still my heart is sad. . . .

This was nonsense, both form and substance, but he was much concerned about himself, his health, his character, his morals. He was unworthy, he wrote to Lydia, but how could she understand his unworthiness? "You have none of those stormy, violent passions that sweep, tornado-like, through my heart." He drew up canons of self-discipline: "Avoid excess in meat and drink" (for two weeks he tried living on bread); "Take exercise in the air at least three hours a day; always get six hours' sleep — more is better." Like Franklin he set himself Rules for Good Conduct: "Preserve devoutness by contemplation of nature, of the attributes of God, of my own dependence; preserve gratitude by reflection upon God's mercies to me in giving blessings unasked, in answering prayers. Restrain licentiousness of imagination, which comprehends many particulars that must not be committed to paper lest the paper blush." He was very selfconscious and very young.

5

"What an immense change," Parker confided to Lydia, "has taken place in my opinions and feelings upon all points of inquiry since I entered this place." He was ready to graduate now, and he found that the comforting assurances of the Lexington meetinghouse were no longer valid, and that even the radicalism of Harvard was really conservative enough. He had changed, no doubt about it, but he was not quite sure into what he had changed. He knew vaguely in which direction he was headed, but sentiment had not yet hardened into conviction, knowledge had not matured into philosophy. He was nothing yet, nothing formed or clear, just a learned young man, a vastly learned young man, who had begun to think about things, to ask questions, to feel his way, not too cautiously, toward some positive position. He knew his way smartly enough about the fields of theology, he had learned to avoid the bogs of dogma and the thickets of doctrine and the mirages of false faith, but he had not found a path that would carry him out of these fields and onto clear ground.

It was not only his opinions and his feelings that had changed; his character had changed, and for the better. He was outgrowing his youthful selfconsciousness and self-pity, outgrowing something of his vanity, his sensitiveness, his protective belligerence. He was becoming sure enough of himself so that he no longer needed to display his superiority, even to himself. That was partly Lydia's doing, for it was wonderfully inspiring to have some one in love with you. ("If love cures *one*," he wrote to Sam Andrews, "why may it not cure others, under like circumstances, of like disorders?") It was partly experience; he had edited the *Interpreter*, and a good job, too, he had lectured in Concord and talked with Mr. Emerson, he had visited in Boston and in Salem, he had met Dr. Dewey in New York and Dr. Furness in Philadelphia, he was not entirely unknown, not unsuccessful. He had his career now, all marked out for him, and then there would be marriage, and a home and a family; how sure of it he was. "Calamities may fall on that home; they come upon all men — but if it is built on the rock of holy affection, *it will stand*."

The ceremonies of graduation dragged out for a couple of months, but finally Visitation Day came, "a day of trembling," and young Mr. Parker, in his long dark blue gown borrowed for the occasion, read an essay on Gnosticism. And he was graduated, and could write "The Reverend" in front of his name. That July he preached for the first time to "a real *live* audience," and Lydia and her aunt came out from Boston to hear him, and by the end of the month he was back in Watertown, preaching from Mr. Francis' pulpit on "The Necessity of a Heavenly Life," looking down, not without nervousness, at all the familiar faces. Uncle Clarke was there, and Mrs. Broad, and old Deacon Bailey and the Robbinses and the Shannons, and Thomas Larned played for the choir. It was all very familiar and very moving, and afterwards they crowded around him to tell him how well he had done.

Finding a permanent place was a more serious business, and more difficult. Perhaps there was a feeling that young Mr. Parker was tainted with transcendentalism — a new word which embraced many sins — or perhaps the editor who had staggered the readers of the *Scriptural Interpreter* with his learning was considered overintellectual (they were afraid of that, the Unitarians), or perhaps he was too unprepossessing, this snub-nosed young man whom it was flattery to call plain, with an air of rusticity about him. Whatever the reason, it was almost a year before Parker got a "call" which he cared to accept. It was a little embarrassing; Andrews was settled, and Silsbee, and the rest of them, and all the while he was "candidating," looking over this church and that one, and being looked over.

August found him in Barnstable. It was good for him to be with these fishermen, who reminded him of the Disciples, and who looked upon him for what he was, not what he knew. He was on his mettle here; he remembered the biblical injunction, Now show what ye be, and he put aside his manuscript and spoke to them. A hard, taciturn people, unapproachable, not ready with soft words or flattery; the salt air had entered into their character. "How disqualified we are," Parker wrote to Silsbee, "for contact with the real world, I felt when first shown a real live man; and when brought to speak with him I was utterly at a stand, and scarcely knew what to say." But on the whole he was pleased with himself. "I have made some little advance since I came to Barnstable. Indeed, it seems to me I have *grown* in this regard, so that I can really talk to men as if I were also a man, and not a student merely." Soon the Barnstable folk came to know him, came to have affection and respect for the young preacher who stood so staunchly in the open pulpit and spoke to them directly, no cant, no doctrinal hair-splitting. The salt air seemed to invigorate him, to give him new energy and clarity of vision and purpose. "It seems as if the wire had touched the chaotic liquid," he said, "and crystallization had begun. It seems to me that Nature wears a new aspect and life has got a new meaning since I came hither." He tramped the sand dunes and the shore, and the grandeur of nature seemed to liberate his mind for bolder speculations. "How is Christ more of a Saviour than Socrates?" he asked himself. "What is the foundation of religion in man? What is the foundation of the idea of God? Why is man placed in life?"

But speculation did not absorb all his time. Parish duties were light, even with tea parties and sick calls and two funerals in one day, and there was time for excursions along the Cape, and a visit to Loring's great salt works at the Common Fields, and a trip out in the Bay on one of the fishing smacks. It was all a new world to a Lexington farmer; the talk here was of mackerel or cod or herring, or of the whaling that was no more, just a few blackfish flung up on the beach. There was time too for a visit to the famous Millennium Grove up at Eastham; the Methodists were holding another of their revivals, and all the Cape seemed to be there, sixteen tents full, a shouting, wild crowd (no room here for pale Unitarian doctrines — the Methodists had swept the Cape, from Provincetown to Falmouth). Parker thought poorly of the performance. "The women were always the most noisy," he noted disapprovingly. "Some of them were in *hysterics,* I should say, and should explain it on well-known physiological principles. They said it was the *Spirit.* How strangely men mistake the flesh for the Spirit. A twitching of nerves is often mistaken for inspiration."

Neither his studies nor his friends were neglected. He

read indefatigably, wrote three sermons a week, and filled the mail bag with letters to Andrews and Silsbee; to Lydia he wrote poetry.

> 'Tis sweet, my love, when day is o'er,
> And hushed each jarring sound,
> To turn and think of thee once more;
> It makes my heart rebound.

And in his Journal for August 11, 1836, he wrote: "Began to translate De Wette's 'Einleitung.' I cannot tell what will be the result of this. I shall leave that for another time to determine." But it did not take long; the translation was finished in a little less than a year, two imposing volumes, the first substantial product of Parker's scholarship.

Barnstable was anxious to have him stay there, but Parker decided that he would be happier in a less isolated place, and October found him out in western Massachusetts, supplying the pulpits of Greenfield and Northfield. Nature in all her aspects was lovely, the placid Connecticut and the bolder Deerfield, the hills all golden brown and russet red; this was better even than hearing Mr. Emerson lecture on Nature. But the people were less attractive — friendly enough, to be sure, but sectarian and narrow to an incredible degree. How insistent they were on the observance of the Sabbath, and what pleasure they found in a faithful record of the disasters that had come to ships sailing on a Sunday. Better the uncertainty of candidating than a parish here; besides, they were anxious to hear him in the East. He visited in Salem, preached from the pulpit of the old East Church, and talked gravely about Dante with the brilliant Susan Burley, and wrote, "I have been as happy as Adam was before he was turned out of Paradise." Soon he was back in Barnstable, and here he got word of his father's death, and he wrote a pious little letter to Lydia, filled with sentiment and moralizing. "I do not mourn for my father's sake, but for my own." He felt very much alone, and a little frightened, and anxious to be married.

Marriage had to wait on a permanent position. "Only to think," he wrote Lydia, "that after a little bit of courtship of some four years, we are on the brink of matrimony. Without a parish, too." But soon there were a flattering number of invitations: Greenfield and Leominster, Waltham and West Roxbury, all wanted him. He decided finally to accept the call to the Spring Street Church in West Roxbury. It was a small parish, and a small salary, but that was no matter. It was within walking distance of Mr. Francis at Watertown and his old teacher Caleb Stetson, now settled at Medford, and of the college libraries, and there would be abundant time for study and writing.

And so that April Theodore and Lydia were married, and the bridegroom wrote joyfully to his friend, "I know that two souls made one by love, can laugh at time and space, and live united forever." And to his journal he confided the solemn promise of the Codex Matrimonianus: "to promote her piety, to bear her burdens, to overlook her foibles, to love, cherish, and ever defend her, to remember her always most affectionately in my prayers; thus, God willing, we shall be blessed."

Ordination came two months later. It was a solemn occasion, a sacrament even among the Unitarians. He was surrounded by friends and he was happy. Doctor Francis preached the ordination sermon and Caleb Stetson delivered the charge, and young George Ripley gave the right hand of fellowship. There were delegates from the neighboring churches, among them old John Quincy Adams, up from Quincy. John Dwight and John Pierpont read poems, and Professor Ware, whom he loved, prayed "may no fondness for peculiar studies ever divert him from doing Thy work." Afterwards there was tea at the Tafts', and when Parker got there everything had been eaten up, and he wondered if that was an omen for the future.

CHAPTER III

WEST ROXBURY

"WE have always looked on the lot of a minister in a country town as our ideal of a happy and useful life," wrote Parker, many years later, and he recalled the West Roxbury years. Within walking distance of Boston, West Roxbury was nevertheless a country town, and life here was almost idyllic. The parsonage was about a mile from the Spring Street Church, a pleasant white house, shaded by large elm and maple trees and set back from the road behind a picket fence; it had formerly been occupied by "The Rain Water Doctor, I. Sylvan, Enemy of Human Diseases." From his study window Parker could look out through the branches of tulip trees over his own land and over the spacious grounds of his neighbors, the Russells and the Shaws.

He was a farmer, now, as well as a preacher; householding and husbandry kept him busy. He had a corn patch and a vegetable garden, a grape arbor and a few fruit trees; he kept a horse and a cow and even a pig, and when he talked over the crops with the hired man he could imagine that he was back in Lexington. There was a small flower garden, too, where he tried to raise some of his favorite lilies of the valley, and where he planted hibiscus and black-eyed Susans; and he saw to it that the hedge which separated the parsonage from the Russell estate was kept low, so that he could step across it whenever he wanted to.

The Russells were famous friends, and he had "many a long chaffer with the fine ladies" in the house, and sometimes there would be amateur theatricals in the barn, close with the smell of hay, or declamations by young Henry Lee, who was a distant cousin of Lydia; or Parker would read some of those sonnets of Shakespeare which he was always threatening to edit and never did. The Shaws, too, were always glad to see the new minister. Here Parker might find young James Russell Lowell, wavering between law and literature, and head over heels in love with Maria White of Watertown, or his friend Lydia Maria Child, more radical every time he saw her, or the famous Margaret Fuller, bursting with energy and learning and ready to tell you about her plans for the Conversations which she was to hold the next winter. And here was little Robert Gould, born the very year that Parker came to West Roxbury, and a few years later baby Josephine, who was to grow up and marry Charles Lowell; two children who were to give their lives to the things that Parker held dear and whose names were to be as famous as his own.

He could do some entertaining, now, too, and Lydia was a perfect housekeeper; everything was so well arranged, so orderly, so clean. Sometimes brother Isaac would come to see him; he had taken over the farm now, and he could tell Theodore all the news from Lexington, and how they were going to need a new minister there: perhaps Theodore would like to come back to the old church. More often it was some friend from the Divinity School who occupied the "prophet's chamber," Silsbee or Andrews or Cranch. Once when Cranch came, Theodore was ill. "I went out," wrote Cranch to their friend Dwight, "expecting to find him on his back, the nurse, doctor, and wife and aunt all in attendance, but no, the creature was up and alive, laughing and working and digging at Sanctus Bernardus like the very Theodore Parker he was. You might as well put a young steam engine to bed, cover it up and give it physic, as this young marvellous creature."

Plenty of time for Saint Bernard, and for all of the other saints in the calendar. Parish duties were light: services on Sunday, a Bible class for the women, and such visiting as was necessary in a parish of only seventy families. He took great pains with his sermons; most of his parishioners were plain people, farmers, milkmen, shopkeepers, and he was anxious to have them understand him. He resolved "to preach nothing as religion that I have not experienced inwardly and made my own," and he found that the life of the farmers and mechanics "of its own accord turned into a sort of poetry and reappeared in the sermons as the green woods not far off looked into the windows of the meeting house." And sure enough, one whole sermon was given over to a consideration of "The Duties of Milkmen."

There were better places, perhaps, than West Roxbury, more intelligent congregations; but where else could he find so much time for himself? "Ten hours a day," he exulted, "for duties not directly connected with the pulpit." Here he could carry through all of his ambitious projects, and all day long and far into the night he sat up in his study annotating the translation of De Wette, reviewing the latest work of German scholarship for the *Christian Examiner* or the *Boston Quarterly,* scribbling innumerable letters, all so illegible that they never failed to bring protests from recipients, reading insatiably, indiscriminately, the books tumbling into the study faster than he could stack them, spilling over the homemade shelves and onto the floor.

It was the annotation of De Wette's volumes on the Old Testament that took most of his time. The translation was easy enough — he had begun it back in Barnstable, and polished it off in less than a year. That was merely the mechanical part of the job, something to do while he was traveling or resting. The real work was still to come, the work of annotation and elaboration and interpretation; and for five years Parker labored to produce a piece of scholarship that should be worthy of the original. It meant a strenuous course of study in the whole range of theological literature — "often a weariness," he confessed. To the original text Parker added exhaustive references and long critical dissertations on ambiguous or controversial points. Finally the work was done and published, at his own expense, in two burly volumes: "A Critical and Historical Introduction to the Canonical Scriptures of the Old Testament." The critics treated it handsomely, and the *Examiner* admitted that the editor had fairly shared honors with the author, but no one bought the books, and few read them. "Nobody knows how much it cost me," Parker wrote later; "but if I were to live my life over again, I would do the same. I meant it for a labor of love."

2

But it took more than De Wette to exhaust Parker's torrential energy. He was reading everything he could lay his hands on, buying up German books by the hundred, and taking notes on them all in that curious Journal which was a catch-all of ideas, fancies, confessions, and facts. "I've got lots of new books," he would write to Silsbee. "Come and see." And to Francis, Cranch, and Dwight he would write of his latest forays into German scholarship, until his friends began to suspect him of an ambition for omniscience, and Dwight, who could not even remember to compose his sermons, chided him for "a mania for all printed things — as if books were more than the symbols of that truth to which the student aspires." But the criticism made no impression on Parker. After all, Dwight was a musician, a poet; what did he know of scholarship?

The results of Parker's studies were finding their way into the critical reviews. He was a regular contributor, now, to the *Christian Examiner;* here appeared that curious review of Strauss's "Life of Jesus," a mixture of learning and buffoonery that didn't quite come off, its skepticism blunt, its sarcasm heavy, its appreciation indiscriminate. Here, too, were reviews of Matter's "History of Gnosticism" (*there* was something he knew about), and Olhausen's "Genuineness of the New Testament," and Ackermann's "Christianity in Plato," and a dozen other learned books. But the *Examiner* was too specialized, too professional, to be an outlet for Parker's interests and enthusiasms.

There had been talk for some time of a magazine which might be a vehicle for the new faiths and hopes that were stirring the minds of men, for this new philosophy which was coming to be called "transcendentalism" and which was making headway throughout New England. ("Hearts beat so high, they must be full of something," wrote Margaret Fuller. "It is for dear New England that I want this Review.") Orestes Brownson thought his *Boston Quarterly* the fulfillment of these hopes, but Margaret Fuller did not agree with him, nor did Emerson. Parker admired Brownson immensely, admired his energy and his courage and his sympathy for the underdog. An able man, too; but not the man to edit a transcendentalist review. Finally Margaret herself took on the job, the wonderfully vital Margaret upon whom they all relied for inspiration and encouragement. Emerson and Ripley promised their aid, and Elizabeth Peabody agreed to act as publisher, and in 1840 the new journal was launched. Bronson Alcott named it the *Dial*.

Parker had been one of the sponsors of the *Dial*, and from the beginning he was a regular contributor. He was not always sure that he approved of the magazine: it lacked the forthrightness of the *Boston Quarterly*, he felt; it was ethereal, it was precious, and he suggested that it should take for its symbols "a baby, a pap-spoon and a cradle." He could not abide the poetry of Emerson's friend, Henry Thoreau, and Alcott's "Orphic Sayings" left him mystified, and he was not clever enough to see that that was what the sayings of a mystic should do. Yet no one, except Margaret Fuller, of course, and the conscientious Elizabeth Peabody, labored more loyally than Parker to keep life in the little quarterly. However dilatory the other contributors might be, Parker could always be relied on; every post brought a fresh contribution from his restless pen. There was nothing he couldn't write about: religion, society, labor, literature — it was all one to him; and every now and then there was even a poem, whose transparent anonymity it was easy to penetrate.

Real contributions, his essays, not windy, like most of
the essays in the *Dial,* but substantial and muscular, the
sort of thing you would expect to find in the *North American.*
The one on German literature, for example, what prodigious learning, what vaulting self-assurance, it displayed;
surely this young man knew everything. "To our apprehen-
sion," Mr. Parker wrote, "German literature is the fairest,
the richest, the most original, fresh, and religious literature
of all modern times." That was a beginning which gave him
lots of room, and he proceeded to support these generalizations with such an abundance of detail that the hardiest
reader would soon cry quits. "What scholarship," asked
Parker, "can compare with the German?" There was no
answer, so he pressed on to the attack. "Where are the
English classical scholars," he demanded, "who take rank
with Wolf, Heyne, Schweighauser, Wyttenbach, Boeckh,
Herrmann, Jacobs, Siebelis, Hoffman, Siebenkees, Müller,
Creutzer, Wellauer, and Ast? Nay, where shall we find the
rivals of Dindorf, Schäfer, Stallbaum, Spitzner, Bothe, and
Bekker, and a host more? For," Parker was careful to point
out, "we have written down only those which rushed into
our mind." It was a little disconcerting to find that all this
was merely preliminary to a review of a single book, Menzel's
"History of German Literature." It went hard with the hap-
less book. Parker attacked it like a pirate, struck it fore and
aft, boarded it, slashed its rigging and toppled its masts,
and made its master walk the plank. All very brilliant and
very impressive, but scarcely worth the trouble; the performance, one would say, of a very young man.

Quite different was the essay on labor (called, with characteristic casualness, "Thoughts on Labor,") that appeared
in the following issue of the *Dial:* a homely, forthright
piece, as radical as Brook Farm, and as provocative. Parker had long been troubled about problems of labor and of
property, and his worries had agitated many a page of his
Journal. "The present property scheme," he had written,
"entails awful evils upon society, rich no less than poor.

This question, first of inherited property, and next of all private property, is to be handled in the nineteenth century and made to give in its reason why the whole thing should not be abated as a nuisance. It makes me groan," he reminded himself, "to look into the evils of society. When will there be an end. I thank God I am not born to set the matter right."

But he had something to say on the matter, nevertheless; Brownson wasn't the only minister who could write on labor, or denounce the sins of capital and of industry. "Who," asked Parker, "shall apply for us Christianity to social life?" and he described the town of Humdrum (could it have been Boston?), ugly with crime and vice and want, boasting of its jails and its courthouses and its asylums. "The old Athenians," he wrote, "sent yearly seven beautiful youths and virgins, a tribute to the Minotaur. The wise men of Humdrum shut up in a jail a larger number, a sacrifice to the spirit of cupidity; unfortunate wretches, who were the victims, not the foes, of society. Is not the remedy for all the evils at Humdrum in the Christian idea of wealth and the Christian idea of work?"

But these were abstractions; just the sort of thing one might find on every page of the *Dial*. What, after all, was "the Christian idea of wealth, the Christian idea of work"? Everything passed for Christianity, now: the wealth of the merchant and of the slave owner, the work of children in the mills and of Negroes in the fields. Was Mr. Parker ready to distinguish between Christianity and the perversions of Christianity? He was, and he called his essay "A Lesson for the Day, or the Christianity of Christ, of the Church and of Society." It was a bold thing for a young man of thirty to write, a country clergyman at that, not calculated to command the approval of Doctor Norton or even of Professor Ware, who had deprecated the gentle heresies of Emerson's Divinity School Address. "Alas for us," cried Mr. Parker, "we see the Christianity of the Church is a very poor thing; a very little better than heathenism. It makes

Christianity a Belief, not a Life. It takes Religion out of the
world, and shuts it up in old books, whence, from time to
time, it seeks to evoke the divine spirit as the witch of En-
dor is fabled to have called up Samuel from the dead." The
Church was narrow, said Mr. Parker, it was formal, it was
polite, it was concerned with the letter and not with the
spirit, with means and not with ends; it was more anxious
that men should walk in the proper paths of dogma than
that they should reach the goal of salvation. Not only this,
but it was timid and stuffy and dull: it lacked not only
courage but honesty. Here was something for reverend
gentlemen to think about when next they looked at their
empty pews. "Anointed dulness, arrayed in canonicals, his
lesson duly conned, presses the consecrated cushions of the
pulpit and pours forth weekly his impotent drone, to be
blest with bland praises so long as he disturbs not respectable iniquity slumbering in his pew, nor touches the actual
sign of the time nor treads an inch beyond the beaten path
of the Church."

To Mr. Parker, all this was disheartening, but not fatal.
The Christianity of Christ, he was careful to point out, was
not dependent upon the institution of the Church. The truths
of religion could still be found in the lives and faith of men.
"Well is it," Parker concluded, "for the safety of the actual
Church that genius and talent forsake its rotten walls, to
build up elsewhere the Church of the first born and pray
largely and like men, Thy kingdom come."

3

These reflections, long in Parker's mind, had been crystal-
lized by his experience at the Groton Convention. It was in
midsummer of 1840 that this queer assortment of Millerites and Come-outers had gathered at the little town of
Groton, some thirty miles north of Boston, and Parker
determined to go and see for himself what it was all about.
Ripley wanted to go along; perhaps these unlettered men
and women, so simple and sincere, could teach him some-

thing about the problems of society and the church. So they started out from West Roxbury, and on their way they picked up the irrepressible young Cranch, whose interest was artistic rather than philosophical. Famous walkers, all of them, they gave themselves two days for the walk so that they might loiter on the way, know the feel of the earth, get in tune with nature and with natural man. The first day they stopped off in Concord and paid their respects to old Doctor Ripley, who warned the young men not to be "egomites," and they took tea with Emerson, who looked, said Parker, "as divine as usual." But Emerson was a disappointment, all the same; he could talk of nothing but the *Dial,* and to no one but Ripley, and even in the *Dial* he admired all the wrong things. The next morning along came Bronson Alcott, never too busy to attend a convention of reformers, and the little company proceeded on their way, their transcendental banners fluttering in the breeze, their high talk drifting in the dust across the open fields.

The town of Groton swarmed with reformers. How fine it seemed, how earnest and eager. The learned clergymen could not help feeling a little ashamed of themselves and of their learning, for these men and women had arrived at truth without benefit of stock or surplice. There were all sorts of reformers here, but best of all were the Come-outers from Cape Cod; how well Parker remembered them from his stay at Barnstable! A rough-looking lot, but "their countenances were full of the divine"; they reminded one of Christ's Disciples, or perhaps of Mr. Emerson, whose countenance, too, had been full of the divine. They disdained creeds and dogma, and found churches and ministers superfluous — just what Parker said, just what Ripley said. All nature was a church, so they held, and every house was God's temple, every man and woman was inspired. They rejected the Christian Sacraments — these, they said, are our daily work: "All our meals are the Lord's Supper, if we eat with a right heart." Could Emerson himself have put it better? The Bible, too, they held in light esteem: a good book, but merely the scriptures of the Word, not the Word itself, for the Word is written in the living heart. There was young Mr. Dyer, who explained that "Truth is Christ, and Christ Truth, and if we but knew all truth, this body would never die but be caught up and spiritualized." Alcott was delighted, but Parker thought it "rather weak." There was Joseph Palmer, guilty of wearing a beard because, as he said, God gave it to him for some good reason; he, too, was full of "divine thoughts." There was Captain Bearse, whose beaming countenance Parker remembered from Barnstable; a hard-headed man, he horrified Brother Hawley by insisting that the Come-outers were merely substituting one great Babel for the many little Babels of the Church; in a few years he was horrifying all Boston, filching slaves from their captors in Boston harbor and smuggling them into freedom. Then there were a group of Millerites, all aflame with zeal for the Second Coming; they could prove, by mathematical demonstrations, that 1843 was the year. This was rather tiresome, thought Parker, three years was too long to wait.

Mr. Parker spoke to the meeting, when would he not speak? With most of what he had heard he was in complete agreement. He, too, believed in inspiration — not the inspiration of the Scriptures, but the inspiration of all men who sought the truth; he, too, thought that it took the whole Church to preach the gospel. What was needed was to apply good sense to religion. What was needed was an escape from the slavery of the Church, for "where the spirit of the church is, there is slavery." Yet he had some criticisms to make: there was a good deal of illiberality here, a good deal of sectarianism, a good deal of sheer error. The convention thought well of Mr. Parker's sentiments, and one gentlemen, whom Parker dubbed Mr. Mantalini because he so resembled that dandy, congratulated him with "an air of the most intolerable patronage."

There was something infectious about these conventions.

Every morning when you picked up your paper you would read of some new scheme for saving the world. It was naïve, this faith that Utopia would crystallize out of the vapors of talk, but it was splendid too, and Parker did not want to stand aloof. Within a month of his return from Groton he had signed his name to a call for a convention to discuss Universal Reform, and soon all the zealots, all the Come-outers, all the transcendentalists of Boston gathered at the Chardon Street Chapel and harangued each other for three mortal days. They talked of non-resistance and Sabbath reform, of the Church and the Ministry, and they arrived at no conclusions. "It was the most singular collection of strange specimens of humanity that was ever assembled," wrote Edmund Quincy, and Emerson was even more specific: "Madmen, madwomen, men with beards, Dunkers, Muggletonians, Come-outers, Groaners, Agrarians, Seventh-day Baptists, Quakers, Abolitionists, Calvinists, Unitarians, and Philosophers, all came successively to the top and seized their moment, if not their hour, wherein to chide, or pray, or preach, or protest." Alcott was in his glory, and he was irresistible. Father Taylor ranted, Joseph Palmer flaunted his beard, and Abigail Folsom edified them all with passages from Saint Paul. Yet some who attended were not cranks, and Parker was not disposed at the time to apologize for his associates. Emerson was there, and Thoreau and Ripley; Doctor Channing provided dignity, and James Russell Lowell respectability, and Garrison, who was responsible for the whole thing, had the good taste to keep in the background.

Yet the Boston intellectuals made no such impression upon Parker as had the Come-outers at Groton. There was something artificial about the Chardon Street debates, there was a hothouse atmosphere in the Chapel. There was too much of suffering fools gladly, there was too much talk, too much display of learning and of wit, and there was, for all the talk of tolerance, an unchristian spirit. (Charles Torrey had called him an infidel, and so had Garrison.)

Better the earnestness, the unaffected enthusiasm, of Groton.
Better the goodness and sincerity of his own parishoners.
Better by far the dignity and honesty and beauty of Brook
Farm.

4

Nothing in all the country was more exciting than Brook
Farm. It was Plato's Academy flourishing here in the brave
new world; it was Paradise Regained. Ripley had planned it
and brought it into being, Ripley whose audacity was
rooted in courage, not, as with Alcott, in innocence. He had
resigned from his pulpit with a letter scoring the narrow-
ness and apathy of the Church, and he had come out here to
West Roxbury and bought from his friend Charles Ellis
this lovely Brook Farm, pledging his own and his wife's
fortune, selling even his library, the finest of its kind in
Boston. (I know now how a man would feel if he could
attend his own funeral, he said.) He had hoped much from
Emerson and from Parker; both were sympathetic, but
neither could see his way clear to joining this experiment,
as hopeful as first love, and as exciting. But Parker was
practically a member. Two or three times a week he would
walk over to the Farm, and every Sunday there would be a
delegation of the Farmers in his church; once they brought
their lunch and insisted on eating it in the pulpit, just to
prove that no mere wood was sacred. It was better to see
them in their own environment, then their oddities seemed
normal enough. And a wonderful group they were, oddities
and all. Parker had settled in West Roxbury because it was
near to Boston and to Harvard; now he found half of the
interesting men in the country in his own parish, and the
other half coming to see them. There was gentle Nathaniel
Hawthorne, weary from the stuffy routine of the Custom
House and from pot-boilers, in love with Nature and Sophia
Peabody, and wooing both with awkward self-consciousness;
he was in transports over the "transcendental heifer" with
"a reflective cast of countenance," and confessed senten-

tiously that "toil defiles the hands, indeed, but not the soul." The toil tired him, in time, and the visitors too, but he called Brook Farm the one romantic episode of his life, he who knew the beauty of Concord's Old Manse and the mystery of the Marble Faun. There was Charles Newcomb, beloved of Emerson, who "hated intellect with the ferocity of a Swedenborg," and elevated obscurity into an art. (When he first heard of Fanny Ellsler he called her a vile creature, but, having seen her dance, he hung her picture between those of Loyola and Xavier.) There was the cook, Isaac Hecker, whose bread was better baked than his ideas; he practised mysticism with volcanic energy, listened to Mr. Parker with disapproval, and as Father Hecker, found consolation in Catholicism. There were as many clergymen as you could find in a Berry Street Conference, and better company, too: John Allen, who had been driven from his pulpit because of his radicalism and abolitionism and who nevertheless could tell Parker that the Boston laborer worked a longer and a harder day than the Mississippi slave; George Bradford, so halting in the pulpit ("Your discourse," said Andrews Norton, "is marked by the absence of every qualification which a good sermon ought to have"), so inspiring in the schoolroom; John Sullivan Dwight, who had rebuked Parker for his intellectual gluttony, and who mistook, said Parker, "the indefinite for the Infinite."

But you could forgive Dwight all his vapors and vagaries when you heard him play. He was ecstatic with the crashing chords of Beethoven and the heavenly melodies of Mozart; and when Christopher Cranch was there too, and Signora Biscaccianti, and the Curtis boys, the musicales were not to be equaled in Boston itself. Not so their theatricals; they put on Sheridan's "Pizarro," and Parker, who could applaud the moral of the play but not the acting, stayed not to witness its sanguinary end.

Not all of them were intellectuals or mystics either. There was young Charles Dana, — "the Professor," they called him, — who had ruined his eyes reading "Oliver Twist" by

THE PARSONAGE

BROOK FARM BUILDINGS
After a contemporary drawing

CONVERS FRANCIS

SAMUEL J. MAY

candlelight, and had come out here for his health; afterwards the greatest and most cynical of editors, he never lost his homesickness for the pastoral innocence of Brook Farm. There were the Curtis boys, George William and James Burrill, out for adventure and adding much to the gaiety of life, remembered best for their good humor and good looks. There were plain farmers, men without pretensions but not without ideas — Minor Pratt, who named his son Theodore Parker Pratt, and Peter Baldwin, who wore a green jacket and looked like Andrew Jackson, and John Cheever, notorious for his dubious antecedents and his brogue.

Brook Farm was almost better than Boston; sooner or later everyone you wanted to see came there. Margaret Fuller was always in and out, seeking solitude but holding brilliant and interminable conversations. Bronson Alcott came and talked on "Insight" or "the Oversoul," and went off and founded at Fruitlands a community that made Brook Farm look like the most stiff-necked orthodoxy. Orestes Brownson came out to talk Catholicism with his friend Hecker. A queer fellow, Brownson, whom some thought a genius and some a charlatan, and who judged himself one of the three profoundest men in America. Wilful, mercurial, contrary-minded, he was as fanatical as Garrison, whom he resembled, but not as humane; in ten years he ran through more philosophies than anyone else could study in a lifetime, and he exhausted all of them, but he would never confess inconsistency or error. He thought well of Brook Farm, he wrote about it in his *Democratic Review*, and placed his son in the Farm school, and he was pleased that it preserved its independence of phalanxes and associations and all such dangerous things. But not so Albert Brisbane, who came often to lecture on Fourierism, or Horace Greeley, already cultivating his eccentricities. These men wanted to make something different of Brook Farm, they wanted to formalize it. Eventually they had their way, and Brook Farm went Fourierist.

That was the beginning of the end, and soon Parker had to share the melancholy duty of winding up the affairs of the Farm. For five years it had been a part of his life, and it made a lasting impression on him. He saw that for individuals it was a success but for the community a failure. To Dana and to Curtis, to Hawthorne and to Dwight, it was an excursion into Arcadia, to these, and to others, it had brought happiness, of a sort. But it advanced society not a whit: it did not solve problems, it ignored them; it did not reform institutions, it evaded them. It was an escape, a retreat, and it left social evils untouched. But what did Parker have to offer that was better? What could he say when Sophia Ripley rebuked him for losing his humanity in abstractions? He did not know, not yet, though he was beginning to put thought on it. He was ready to admit that society was in a bad way, but he didn't know what was to be done about it. That was one of the things he discussed with people when he went into Boston.

5

Boston drew him like a magnet, Boston with its churches and libraries and bookshops and its ferment of thought. He could hitch up his horse and buggy and, with Lydia at his side, be there in no time. Perhaps they went in to see Mr. Catlin's wonderful exhibition of Indian paintings and costumes, or Herr Driesbach's collection of lions and tigers and snakes, or, if they were in a more serious mood, they might go to hear one of Mr. Emerson's lectures on "The Times," or they might run out to the Perkins Institution to hear Sam Howe tell about his little deaf-mute, Laura Bridgman. Sometimes they would drive over to Doctor Peabody's bookstore on West Street, where Lydia would attend one of Margaret Fuller's Conversations, on Culture, or the Ideal, or What is Life, while Theodore stayed below to rummage among the books. A wonderful place, this bookshop, a godsend. Here you could get the latest French novel or the most ponderous German treatise on metaphysics or the best

of the English quarterlies. Better yet, here you could talk to
Elizabeth, whom Parker admired far more than the muscu-
lar-minded Margaret. There was nothing aggressive about
Elizabeth, nothing to startle and subdue you, as with Margaret, none of that disconcerting intellectualism. She was
graceful, womanly, she did not lecture to you as if you were
a group of young ladies, and it was easy to confide in her.
An extraordinary woman, Elizabeth; she had helped Bronson Alcott at the Temple School and she had written those
famous reports that excited so much attention everywhere;
she had been Doctor Channing's secretary, reading to him,
copying his sermons, listening to his soliloquies — it was like
listening to God. Now with her father she had opened up
this bookshop, the likeliest place in all Boston to find just
the book you wanted and to meet just the man or woman
you most wished to see. Here you might find that tempestu-
ous Mr. Horace Mann who had abandoned a brilliant
career in politics for the uncertainties of education, and who
was head over heels in love with Elizabeth's sister, Mary;
or perhaps Hawthorne, in from Brook Farm to see the other
sister, Sophia; or learned George Bancroft, with his Prus-
sian mannerisms, who had stopped writing history long
enough to help make it. Here you could talk to Bronson
Alcott, hear his objections to Brook Farm and his projects for something more nearly ideal. Or you might see
here the captivating Professor Follen, a great teacher and
a scholar, the man who had set all Boston afire with German
literature, now in disgrace with Harvard and with Beacon
Street, since he had taken up abolitionism, but bearing his
adversity with cheerful impudence. Sometimes Parker
would run into a fellow clergyman: Ezra Gannett, perhaps,
who regarded all transcendentalists with suspicion, or ardent
young James Freeman Clarke, fresh from the Blue Grass
of Kentucky and restoring his soul with the delights of
Boston, or bewhiskered Frederick Hedge down from Bangor
and brimming over with the latest philosophical ideas.

Whenever the Reverend Mr. Hedge came down there

would be a meeting of kindred souls. They called themselves the "Hedge Club," though they were better known by the more pompous name, "Transcendental Club." An informal group, this, meeting at the convenience of the philosopher from Bangor, and at the houses of members. Emerson was the central figure, Emerson whose "Nature" had sounded the transcendental note, no vulgar trumpet but a seraphic chord, and whose Divinity School Address was burning its way into Unitarian complacency like a social affront. Parker knew most of the others, capital men, all of them, men who concerned themselves with the problems of the day, sincere and idealistic, though their scholarship, he feared, left something to be desired. There was Ripley, of course, with his talk of Brook Farm ("a room in the Astor House, set aside for the transcendentalists," said Emerson cruelly). There was Convers Francis, more learned and timid than ever now he was at the Divinity School, and looking more like Martin Luther each year. There was the wit, Caleb Stetson, who had been Parker's teacher back at the Academy, and the elflike Cyrus Bartol, whose house on Chestnut Street was always open to the agitation of radical ideas. There were those young men of letters, Jones Very and Christopher Cranch, with their pale poetry and their twilight thoughts. Sometimes the club met at the home of Brownson, out in Chelsea, and then there was sure to be a clash of opinions. No respecter of persons, Brownson, or of institutions; on the slightest provocation he would harangue them on the wickedness of Boston or the decadence of politics or the sins of property. They agreed with most of this, of course, but eventually his manners became "unbearable," and they stopped asking him to their meetings. Sometimes they went out to Cambridge to sit with the aged Doctor Levi Hedge, who had reduced reason to a science, but it was not comfortable for them so close to the Divinity School. More often they met at Emerson's house, out in Concord; there Parker might see Henry Thoreau and his inseparable friend William Ellery Channing, that erratic genius who had recently married Margaret Fuller's sister and settled in Concord just to be near Emerson. Occasionally Margaret herself was there, or lovely dark-eyed Elizabeth Hoar, who had been engaged to Charles Emerson, and whose holiness, wrote Emerson, "was substantive, like the gravity of a stone."

They were great men, and deep, no doubt about it, though Parker was sometimes impatient with their attenuated minds, their excess of spirituality. They stimulated him, matched his learning with wit; they respected ideas, not facts, and challenged the value of learning that was encyclopædic rather than discriminating. They egged him on, too, in his criticism of religion and the Church; his article in the *Dial*, they thought, had gone true to the mark. Strange how many of them had left the Church — Emerson and Ripley and Dwight, and Brownson too, in his way, though with Brownson it was more like changing seats in a merry-go-round. Was there some irreconcilable difference between transcendentalism and Unitarianism? Was Parker going to end up like the rest of them, outside of the Church?

Yet he remembered old Doctor Ripley's admonition that he should not be an "egomite," one who claimed a divine mission for himself. It was for the Church that Parker claimed a divine mission; but what if the Church did not fulfill its mission? This question troubled him greatly; he had written of it, preached on it, lectured about it, but more to clear his own mind than to enlighten the minds of others. Emerson was little help here, or Ripley; they had settled the question by abandoning it, they had not exhausted its possibilities. Better go to Doctor Channing, that wise and good man whose faith transcended transcendentalism. He had managed to stay in the Church, nay, he even accepted the miracles, though not the Scriptures (an inconsistency, Parker thought); yet he had worked a revolution in the hearts and minds of men even as had Emerson. Many an afternoon Parker spent with Doctor Channing, discussing big words — "conscience," "miracles," "materialism," "inspiration"; no one could talk of these things more impressively than Channing, even his illogic was convincing. Sometimes they went together to the Tremont House, where the Friends aired these problems of religion and of society. Here Parker would find some of his associates from the Transcendental Club, Ripley and Alcott and Doctor Hedge, and here too were Horace Mann and Professor Follen and Channing's dearest friend, Mr. Jonathan Phillips, who had presided so nobly over the Faneuil Hall meeting to denounce the assassins of Elijah Lovejoy. Sometimes Mr. Phillips brought his cousin, Mr. Wendell Phillips, the young man who had startled them all with his eloquence on that tumultuous occasion. The Friends talked of religion and philosophy, of the Progress of Society and the Destiny of Man; they discussed Mr. Emerson's Address, and whether Emerson was a Christian or a Pantheist (a Christian, thought Parker, the charge of Pantheism was too vague). It was, said Phillips, a rare school of dialectics. But it was more than dialectics; you could not bring Channing and Follen and the Phillips cousins together without some discussion of the most urgent of all social problems, slavery. And this was too much for young Parker to take in. He was not yet ready for this question, or for any of the larger political and social questions. First he had to establish for himself a basis of life; time enough then for the specific problems. First he had to find out where he was, then perhaps he might begin to know where he was going and what was worthy of attention on the road. He had to learn values before he could apply them; he had to learn to distinguish between the transient and the permanent, the seeming and the real.

A sense of reality, that was what these Friends and Transcendentalists were groping for. Never was there a more realistic, a more practical group of men than these high-flying souls of Concord and Boston, for all their talk of the Over-Soul and the cult of mysticism. What they sought, with patience and courage, was the reality behind the façade of institutions, the kernel of truth within the husk of convention. They sought the reality of religion within the dogma of the Church, the reality of government within the artificialities of politics, the reality of economy within the chaos of business and industry. They distinguished between life and mere living, and audaciously put their distinctions to the test: Emerson in his study, Ripley at Brook Farm, Alcott in the Temple School, Howe at the Perkins Institution, Garrison in his printing office, Doctor Channing in his pulpit — all them trying to penetrate to reality, to truth, and confident that truth would make men free. No strutting and fretting, no empty declamations or perfervid harangues; these transcendental philosophers had poise and equanimity, they regarded the heavens and knew that the stars in their courses fought for them. How vain and insincere the public men of the time seemed in comparison with them: Everett with his nickel-plated eloquence, Rufus Choate who for a fee could plead so movingly, Winthrop whose name argued for freedom but whose voice spoke for slavery, even the great Webster, with his worship of property and his subserviency to State Street.

This is what they meant by their talk of the Divinity of Man: that man should come to know himself directly, not through the media of society or of the Church or of books; that he should walk upright, not bowed down by the weight of conventions or of learning; that he should feel his kinship with Nature and with God. Away, then, with the hypocrisies of institutions and the shams of property; away with the myriad tyrannies that exercised dominion over the minds of men — the tyrannies of dogma, of party, of material security, of manners and custom, of power and prestige and place. Men had forgotten their adventurous destiny and gave thought only to their safety. Men had lost themselves; things were in the saddle and rode mankind.

How stunted man was, how blind and infirm, with the blindness of the tradesman and the infirmity of the slave. How could man recover his vision so that he might see truth directly and spontaneously; how could he recover his integrity? Did the Church have the answer? Emerson thought not, Emerson, whose words were like the trumpets at Jericho. Ripley thought not, Ripley, who was so impatient for the Heavenly City that he had built it right here at Parker's back door. Was Communism the answer; could man find salvation in the gospel according to Saint Simon? Parker was sympathetic, but unconvinced, for he still felt the Kingdom of Heaven was within. That was the great, the elementary truth, toward which they were all struggling, he believed — the truth which defied proof and transcended experience: that the Kingdom and the Power and the Glory lay within.

CHAPTER IV

THE UNITARIAN CONTROVERSY

It was Emerson who had announced this truth, and his words went like morning over the land. Sadly, he had separated himself from the Church, because the Church required conformity, and he knew that authority must conform to the ideal, not the ideal to authority. He had left Boston, betaken himself not away from the paths of men and women, but away from the noise of the market place and the haste of commerce and the shallow contentions of the schools, and he had settled in Concord where he might discover himself, penetrate to the core of reality. He had no need of the machinery of society, he had his own faculties. One book, if read aright, was as good as the Bodleian Library, Concord was the world in miniature, his own household was mankind. Life was not activity, but thought and emotion, and the laboratory could never reveal truth, only discover evidence. So he sat in his quiet study and wrote in his journal, and beauty hung on his words like dew on a flower.

He had not renounced the world any more than he had renounced religion when he left the Church; he had preferred, merely, to question the vulgar interpretation of the world. He wished to look at nature as for the first time, to discover for himself its character and its meaning. He had returned from his adventure radiant with new truths, and announced them gently, reverently. "Every spirit," he said, concluding his lectures on Nature, "builds itself a house and beyond its house a world and beyond its world a heaven. Know then that the world exists for you. For you is the phenomenon perfect. What we are, that only can we see.

Build therefore your own world. As fast as you conform your life to the pure idea in your mind, that will unfold its great proportions. . . . The kingdom of man over nature, which cometh not with observation, — a dominion such as now is beyond his dream of God, he shall enter without more wonder than the blind man feels who is gradually restored to perfect sight."

But that was wonder enough, and it was such wonder as young men felt when they listened to Emerson's message, and turned with new confidence and new courage into this path which led to those mountain tops from which they might behold the Promised Land. Emerson was no leader, no pathbreaker, he knew that every man must find his own way to his own heaven. "The ruin or the blank that we see when we look at nature," he had said, "is in our own eye." He might teach men to use their eyes, he would not tell them what they should see, and woe to those who tried to cheapen him and to exploit him, who asked him for blueprints and a guidebook when he proffered a torch.

To Parker and his friends, Emerson's words came as a new revelation, and they came with such compelling, such irresistible force because men were prepared for them. It was not necessary to break new soil, not necessary to cut through the tough prairie grasses of orthodoxy or to girdle the great trees of false philosophy that cast a shade over the sunlit fields. This work had been done. The revolt from Trinitarianism, inaugurated by Freeman and Buckminster, had been successful all along the front, and Unitarianism was already tainted with respectability. No need to fight the great elementary battles; the principle of free inquiry in all matters of faith was accepted. Doctor Channing was the high priest of the new dispensation, and few were disposed to challenge his dictum: "The truth is that our ultimate reliance is and must be on our own reason. I am surer that my rational nature is from God than that any book is an expression of his will." Not only was this principle acknowledged, but fields of speculation had been thrown open, and the ground already broken, charted, and surveyed; this was the work of bold German and French and English thinkers. It remained only for Americans to rush in and take possession.

And how acquisitive they were. How buoyantly they strode across these broad fields of speculation, how confidently they set to work in the rich new soil, plowed it and furrowed it and made it their own. There was George Ripley, fascinated by the glittering idealisms of Cousin and Jouffroy, and translating them into the American idiom in fact as well as in letter; there was Dwight cultivating the Germans, Goethe and Schiller, while Doctor Hedge and Charles Brooks and Margaret Fuller cheered him on; there was Parker digging deep into Jacobi and Schleiermacher and De Wette and a host of others, burrowing down to the very subsoil of transcendentalism; there was Doctor Marsh wandering happily in the Elysian fields of Wordsworth and Coleridge, unperturbed by the chill blasts of orthodoxy from the Vermont hills.

It was Emerson himself who rebuked their excessive zeal and heat, who taught them, not by words but by precept, to look to their own resources, to plumb the depth of their own ideas. He knew Kant and Goethe, was not unacquainted with Cousin and Jouffroy, admired Coleridge, and introduced Carlyle to America. But none of these were his teachers, not even the lordly Immanuel; they could provoke thought, but they could not supply it. "What we are," he had said, "that only can we see. All that Adam had, all that Cæsar could, you have and can do. Line for line, and point for point, your dominion is as great as theirs. Build therefore your own world."

Parker had not heard the lectures on "Nature," but he read them, sitting on the bank of the Connecticut River, and was stirred by their beauty. "Blessed is the man who stoops and tastes of them," he wrote. "He erects himself in new vigor and freshness, and becomes a man divine." But there were others who felt differently, even this early,

who discerned in Emersonian idealism a threat to the
Church and to religion. Young Francis Bowen, who combined perspicacity with some learning and aspired to a professorship at Harvard, took it upon himself to rebuke Mr.
Emerson. Parker did not think much of the performance.
"Bowen has written a piece in the *Examiner*," he confided
to Andrews, "on what think you? Why, on Emerson's 'Nature.' Pelion on Ossa is bad, Jew upon Bacon, but Bowen
upon 'Nature' caps the climax. He has given transcendentalism 'sich a lick' that it is almost dead. Kant, Fichte, and
Schelling appeared to me in a vision in the night, and deplored their sad estate. 'Transcendentalism is clean gone,'
said Kant. 'Verdammt,' said Fichte. 'What shall we do?'
exclaimed Schelling. They could not be appeased."

But the protest was not to be so flippantly dismissed.
Soon staunch Unitarians, secure in their liberal respectability, began to realize the implications of the doctrine of
Free Inquiry and the philosophy of transcendentalism. If
men were to prove all things by the light of their own limited reason, what assurance was there that they would hold
fast to what was good? Transcendentalism, with its cele-
bration of intuitive faith, threw wide open the Pandora's
box of individualism. Soon Professor Walker of Harvard
was giving countenance to transcendental views, and Doctor Noyes was challenging the authenticity of the Messianic
prophecies; soon the Reverend Henry Walker was passing
around his copy of Strauss's *Leben Jesu,* and Doctor Follen
was lecturing on Pantheism, and impious old Abner Kneeland, pushing the principle of free inquiry to its extreme,
had to be indicted for blasphemy. When Ripley wrote fav-
orably of Martineau's "Rationale of Religious Inquiry,"
Professor Norton rebuked him sharply. "The last time I saw
Mr. Ripley," Parker wrote in his journal, "I suggested that
the first one who lifted a hand in this work would have to
suffer, and I wished to push some old veteran German to
the forefront, who would not care for a few blows; but
he thought there was no danger." But Parker was right;

the danger was immediate and pressing. Idealism, harmless enough when confined to the study of Kant, had become a menace, and it was clear that there would have to
be a showdown.

Once again it was Emerson who precipitated things, with
his Address to the Students of the Harvard Divinity School.
He had said, standing there with his fine head thrust forward in that characteristic manner, serene, immaculate,
that religion was, after all, a matter of intuition, not of evidence, an inner light, not an authenticated miracle. "Whilst
the doors of the temple stand open, night and day, before
every man, and the oracles of this truth cease never, it is
guarded by one stern condition; this namely; it is an intuition. It cannot be received at second hand . . . in the
soul, then, let redemption be sought." In the soul, not in
the church or the Scriptures or in miracles. "To aim to
convert a man by miracles," he observed, "is a profanation
of the soul. A true conversion is now, as always, to be made
by the reception of beautiful sentiments." Sentiment, indeed, is the essence of all religion, the sentiment of virtue,
of moral law. It lies at the foundation of society, at the
basis of worship. "If a man is at heart just, then in so far
is he God; the safety of God, the immortality of God, the
majesty of God, do enter into that man with justice." And
sentiment, Mr. Emerson pointed out, has nothing to do
with miracles, or with authority, or even with the person
of Christ. But the Church, he said, — and this was what
hurt, — the Church had ceased to concern itself with sentiment and had taken refuge in creeds and in ritual. "The
word Miracle, as pronounced by Christian churches, is
Monster. It is not one with the blowing clover and the falling rain."

The Church, Mr. Emerson charged, preaches miracles
and dogma; it does not preach the soul. "On this occasion,"
he said, "any complaisance would be criminal which told you
that the faith of Christ is preached." And because the
Church had acquiesced in a low view of religion, and the

pulpits had been usurped by formalists, "the church seems
to totter to its fall, almost all life is extinct."

The faculty, the alumni, of the Divinity School did not
think that all life was extinct, and it was annoying to be
told so, especially on an occasion which should have been
a festive one. It was distressing to be reminded that their
preaching was vain, their prayers futile, and their pews all
but empty. And it was almost intolerable that young Mr.
Emerson (he was barely thirty-five, think of it!), who had
stayed in the Church scarcely long enough to get acquainted
with it, should presume to take them to task. That charac-
terization of a preacher, now — "He had lived in vain. He
had no one word intimating that he had laughed or wept,
was married or in love, had been commended or cheated
or chagrined. If he had ever lived and acted, we were none
the wiser for it" — was that not a libel on the clergy of
Boston, of New England? And was it, after all, the business
of a preacher to lay bare his soul to his congregation? It
was in the worst possible taste, this turning of the pulpit
into a combination of confessional and forum. The Reverend Mr. Frothingham, who thought it improper to mention Beethoven's sonatas in a sermon, might well shudder
at the vulgarity of Mr. Emerson's transcendentalism.

But it was not enough for the few to shudder, there were
too many who went out of Divinity Hall that July evening
thinking they had heard the Holy Ghost. "It was the
noblest of all his performances," wrote Parker to his friend
George Ellis. "The noblest and most inspiring strain I ever
listened to." And in the pages of his Journal he added, "So
beautiful, so just, so true, and terribly sublime." It was the
spiritual declaration of independence for which they had
all been waiting; it loosened the floodgates of idealism, and
soon the waters were dotted with brave little transcendental
barks sailing boldly into Boston Harbor. There was a great
outcry, and the Unitarians rushed to their defenses, crying
"The Philistines are upon us." They sounded the alarm
from the belfries of their greatest churches, they piled high

their Bibles, and they prepared to stand siege against deism, pantheism, or atheism in whatever form.

The first protest came from the gentle Professor Ware (*"le bon Henri,"* Emerson called him, tenderly), who felt that Emerson's ideas would overthrow the authority of Christianity. Hurriedly he prepared a sermon on "The Personality of the Deity," designed, he confessed, to controvert transcendentalist views, and he sent it to Emerson, and provoked that memorable reply: "I delight in telling what I think; but if you ask me how I dare say so, or why it is so, I am the most helpless of mortal men. I do not even see that either of these questions admits of an answer. . . . I shall go on, just as before, seeing whatever I can and telling what I see; and I suppose, with the same fortune that has hitherto attended me; the joy of finding that my abler and better brothers, who work with the sympathy of society, loving and beloved, do now and then unexpectedly confirm my perceptions, and find my nonsense is only their own thought in motley." That, of course, was the trouble, that so many others might confirm Mr. Emerson's perceptions, and it was precisely this danger that must be averted.

It was Andrews Norton who undertook this task, who undertook to rebuke Emerson as he had already rebuked Ripley and Doctor Noyes. ("No clergy will be supported among us," he had told Doctor Noyes, "to teach transcendentalism, infidelity and pantheism.") Few theologians in the country had a greater reputation for exact scholarship; none was so confident of his abilities. Scarcely a month had passed before Norton's reply appeared in the *Daily Advertiser*. It had a sweep, a catholicity that no other disputant would have attempted or could have achieved. The indictment embraced not only Emerson's address but the whole transcendentalist school: Schleiermacher, Cousin, Carlyle — even Shelley — came under the general anathema of the Cambridge Parnassus; for their American disciples he had only contempt. There were replies, of course, blasts and counter-blasts, until Chandler Robbins called the whole thing a "vulgar clamor," and brought down upon his own head a new anathema. Parker followed it all with an interest not entirely impersonal, for he remembered those frigid silences in Doctor Norton's study. "It is thought," he wrote to Ellis, "that chaos is coming back; the world is coming to an end. Some seem to think the Christianity which has stood some storms will not be able to weather this gale; and that truth, after all my Lord Bacon has said, will have to give it up now. For my part, I see that the sun still shines, the rain rains, and the dogs bark, and I have great doubts whether Emerson will overthrow Christianity this time."

It was all very well for Parker to indulge his sense of humor, but to Doctor Norton, to the faculty and alumni of the Divinity School, it was no laughing matter. Everywhere people were asking, Were these the doctrines taught in Cambridge? Was this the destiny of Unitarianism? There had to be some formal repudiation of transcendentalism, and Norton was asked to undertake it. Within a year he addressed the Association of the Alumni of the Divinity School on "The Latest Form of Infidelity."

"The latest form of infidelity," he read from a manuscript as neat as a lady's album, "is distinguished by assuming the Christian name while it strikes directly at the root of faith in Christianity, and indirectly at all religion, by denying the miracles, the divine mission of Christ." Idealism was disposed of with a wave of the hand. "There can be," he said, "no intuition, no direct perception, of the truths of Christianity, no metaphysical certainty." Certainty must come from evidence, not from intuition. "We must use the same faculties, and adopt the same rules in judging concerning the facts of the world which we have not seen as concerning those of the world of which we have seen a very little." It was sheer sensationalism; it was science wedded to philosophy to bring forth the truth of revealed religion, and it was a logic that appealed strongly to the alumni of the Divinity School — men who loved peace and the quiet ways of scholarship, who distrusted the vagaries of transcendentalism ("A little beyond," said Miss Fuller, "a little beyond."), and who were justly alarmed at its social consequences. These Unitarians applauded Doctor Norton (mentally, of course) as he demonstrated the social and moral dangers implicit in the transcendentalist heresy and revealed the true foundations of progress. "But we may have a deeper sense of the value of our faith," he admonished them, "if we look abroad on the present state of the world and see, all around, the waves heaving and the tempests rising. Everywhere is instability and uncertainty. But from the blind conflict between men . . . from fierce collision of mere earthly passions and cravings, whatever changes may result no good is to be hoped." Much the same thing, they remembered, Judge Thacher had said when he sentenced Abner Kneeland for blasphemy.

But Doctor Norton was not one to do things halfway. It was not enough to denounce Mr. Emerson and his followers ("silly women and silly young men," he had called them); they were, after all, not the original offenders, their ideas came at second-hand. They were mere purveyors of romantic German emotionalism and undigested German pseudo-scholarship. It was time that Americans were warned against these impostors, who had gained such an ascendancy over the minds of students. And Doctor Norton turned from the analysis of Emerson's infidelity to arraign the foreign learning that was poisoning the pure stream of American Unitarianism, and he trained his guns particularly on gentle, inoffensive Friedrich Ernst Schleiermacher and learned, timid Wilhelm Martin De Wette.

It was a vigorous performance; its effect remained to be seen. "Some of the lay brethren," Parker wrote to his friend Silsbee, "think the matter fixed; that Mr. Norton has 'done transcendentalism up.'" Parker, of course, thought poorly of it. "Is it not the weakest thing you ever fancied?" he asked Elizabeth Peabody. "What a cumbersome matter he makes Christianity to be. . . . Did you notice the remarkable mistranslations of the German passages? They are such as no tyro could make, I should fancy." Emerson made no reply. He thought the whole thing a "storm in a wash-bowl." But soon the air was thick with pamphlets. James Freeman Clarke, whose *Western Messenger* had come in for gratuitous slurs, hastened to its defense; Richard Hildreth turned aside from his exposures of the miraculous character of paper money to expose the miracles of the Bible; Orestes Brownson thundered in the *Post*. But it was Ripley who entered the lists most formidably, Ripley who remembered Norton's slurs of an earlier year, and who had not forgotten Parker's warning. He took his friend into his confidence, and Parker observed judicially, "It will make a pamphlet of about one hundred pages octavo, and it is clear, strong and good. . . . But a long controversy will probably grow out of this; ink will be spilled on both sides and hard names called."

The forecast was, alas, all too accurate — all but the estimate of pages, which was much too modest. Ripley's first letter concerned the question of miracles and argued, with both skill and learning, the transcendentalist position. But Norton brushed this contemptuously aside; he had taught young Mr. Ripley all that he ought to know about religion. Nothing daunted, Ripley returned to the fray with two lengthy treatises devoted to the defense of Spinoza, Schleiermacher, and De Wette against the animadversions of his former teacher on these "devout, sweet, unselfish, truth-seeking men."

This was all very well, but it was somewhat distracting, thought Parker, to shift the discussion from pure idealistic grounds to the confused and littered battlefields of German scholarship. Men were losing sight of the original question which Emerson had raised, losing themselves in a futile quarrel over Schleiermacher and De Wette, forgetting, apparently, the central point of the transcendentalist thesis — that Christianity rested not on scholarship but on great universal moral truths. "There is a higher word to be said on this subject than Ripley is disposed to say just now," wrote Parker. And he decided to say it.

2

This was no sudden impulse, this decision to enter the controversy, to say what needed to be said. Even as a student Parker had looked irreverently at the pillars of the Church, had regarded the edifice itself as perhaps jerry-built and rickety. While still a candidate, he had preached on "The True and the False Religion," and he had scarcely settled at West Roxbury before he was writing sermons on the contradictions in the Scriptures. "I preach abundant heresies," he wrote cheerfully to his brother William, "and they all go down, for the listeners do not know how heretical they are. I preach the worst of all things, Transcendentalism, the grand heresy itself, none calling me to account therefor." Indeed, the heresies were abundant enough; to his old mentor, Doctor Francis, he was writing, "The Gospels are not without their myths — the miraculous conception, the temptation, etc. Do not all the miracles belong to the mythical part? The resurrection — is that not also a myth? I see not where to put up the bar between the true and the false. Christianity itself . . . will stand forever, but I have sometimes thought it would stand better without the New Testament than with it."

So the controversy between Mr. Emerson and Mr. Norton did not catch him unprepared. He had long known that there were two parties among the Unitarians; he had anticipated this conflict within the Church, he was not loath to enter it. And now that the revolution was under way, he wanted to make sure of first principles; he wanted to make sure these first principles were not confused by personalities and obscured by irrelevancies and superficialities.

So Parker spoke the higher word — and soon clergymen were reading "The Previous Question between Mr. Andrews Norton and his Alumni Moved and Handled in a Letter to All those Gentlemen, by Levi Blodgett." Mr. Blodgett thought it déplorable that the discussion between Mr. Norton and Mr. Ripley had drifted away from its philosophical moorings into the Sargasso Sea of literature; he wished to remind the gentlemen that the focal point of the discussion was that of the value — not the authenticity, but the value — of miracles. Do men believe in Christianity solely on the ground of performance of miracles? "How," Mr. Blodgett asked, "do men come to have any Religion, or on what evidences do they receive Religious Truths?" And the answer was obvious enough to anyone not blind to the teachings of his own nature. Religion was innate; the existence of God, the assurance of immortality, were given in human nature. The truths of Christianity were intuitive truths; they were not dependent for their authority upon the evidence of miracles or upon any other evidence. If religion is innate, it is superfluous to bolster it up with miraculous proofs; and if it is not innate, no miraculous proofs, if contrary to reason, would be accepted. All this, and much more, the perspicacious Mr. Blodgett pointed out to Mr. Norton and his Alumni, and he went on to add, quite gratuitously, some reflections on the Church, on Christianity, and on Christ. Christianity, he asserted, was merely one of many religions, and was subject to the same tests of its authority that we apply to the others. And Christ himself, the highest type of religious leader, was not infinitely perfect; he did not exhaust God's creative power, and Mr. Blodgett was not sure that God, who created Christ, could not create even greater Christs.

Soon everyone knew that Levi Blodgett was none other than Theodore Parker of West Roxbury. He had drifted far from the teachings of Professor Ware and Professor Palfrey; his dabbling in esoteric learning and in foreign literature was bearing its inevitable fruit; he had gone over, stock and surplice, to transcendentalism. Even Abner Kneeland had said nothing worse than this; how significant it was that Emerson and Ripley and Parker had all signed that petition for the pardon of the old atheist. And it was becoming painfully apparent that young Mr. Parker was a troublemaker. Emerson had long since abandoned the Church, and in any event, Emerson was not a man of words and of battle; Ripley too was leaving the Church; his resignation had already been accepted. But Parker was in the Church, and determined to remain. How meddlesome he was, and how energetic. He had dallied with the Come-outers and the Millerites in the Groton Convention; he had not failed to attend the Chardon Street Convention which met in Boston that same fall; no sooner was that adjourned than he had organized a meeting to reconsider the place of the Sabbath in the scheme of things. He was a busybody, an upstart; it was time he was put in his place.

Soon Parker began to be aware of hard looks and painful slights. When he spoke on "Inspiration" before the "Great and Thursday Lecture," one elderly divine denounced him as "impious," and Parker left him and went weeping through the wintry streets of Boston until he bethought him of his friend George Ellis, and dried his tears. When the Berry Street Conference met that spring, the members gravely discussed the proposition: "Ought differences of opinion on the value and authority of miracles to exclude men from Christian fellowship and sympathy from one another?" Hedge and Stetson spoke nobly for the negative, but Parker, who sat silent throughout it all, felt that the atmosphere was distinctly unfriendly, and when he came home he poured out his feelings in his journal: "This is the nineteenth century! This is Boston! This among the Unitarians!"

By the end of the year, Parker's position was uncomfortable. He began to find difficulty in arranging for exchanges, and a few of those he already had were canceled. Without the privilege of exchange — an inalienable privilege, he thought — he would be muzzled, tied down to his little parish church, forced to give all of his time to the composition of sermons. "I would laugh outright," he wrote bitterly, "to catch myself weeping because the Boston clergy would not exchange with me." But he did weep, all the same; wept and imagined himself in the heroic rôle of a martyr to religious liberty, and consoled himself with the thought (blasphemous, of course) that not ten churches in New England would admit Christ himself.

Elizabeth Peabody was worried, and counseled him to prudence, the good Elizabeth, whose contributions to the *Christian Examiner* Andrews Norton had stopped because they were too liberal. She had seen Doctor Channing survive so many crises, and she hoped that Parker might emulate his modesty and humility. But prudence is a vulgar virtue, said Parker, and besides, "You cannot fancy that I have any desire to set the world on fire by promulgating heresies!" Elizabeth would have been very obtuse indeed had she not so fancied, for that was precisely what Parker was about to do. Scarcely was the winter out before he perpetrated the next act of incendiarism. The occasion was the ordination of young Mr. Shackford, and Parker had been asked to preach the ordination sermon. It was a raw, cold day in May, and Parker roused himself from a sickbed to travel out to the Hawes Place Church in South Boston. He was not at all satisfied with the manuscript he carried with him; it was, he felt, tame and spiritless and cold, and Ripley had assured him it was one of the weakest things he had ever written. Not even the title was original; he had copied it from one of Strauss's essays: "The Transient and Permanent in Christianity."

"Heaven and earth shall pass away, but my word shall not pass away." This was the text Parker announced to the crowded Church, and it was the permanence of the great moral truths of Christianity that he celebrated. The creeds of the churches, he assured the young man who was being ordained into a creedless church, are ephemeral, but the truths of the Christian religion are eternal. And these truths derive their authority not from their origin with Christ but by virtue of their own character. "Almost every sect that has ever been," Parker pointed out, "makes

Christianity rest upon the personal authority of Jesus, not on the immutable truth of the doctrines themselves, or the authority of God who sent him into the world. Yet it seems difficult to conceive of any reason why moral and religious truths should rest for their support on the personal authority of their revealer any more than the truths of science on that of him who makes them known first or more clearly." Christianity rests neither on the Gospels nor on the teachings of the Church, nor does it derive added authority from the attestations of miracles; it rests on "great truths which spring up spontaneous in the holy heart."

Almost everything, it appeared, was transient, except intuitive moral truths. The Old Testament and the New, Christian rites and doctrines, even the personality of Christ, might go the way of other forgotten philosophies and creeds, and no harm done. "If it could be proved that Jesus never lived, still Christianity would stand firm and fear no evil." All these things were perishing; what was eternal was the moral element of religion, and to this Mr. Shackford must cling, and without fear. "Already," said Parker, with a glance toward the Reverend Mr. Lothrop and the Reverend Mr. Bartlett, who had refused to exchange with him, "already men of the same sect eye one another with suspicion and lowering brows that indicate a storm, and like children who have fallen out in play, call hard names." Mr. Shackford, if he would be true to the inner light, must inure himself to hard names.

Thus Parker deftly removed Christ, the Bible and the Church from Christianity, and called what was left "natural religion." The Unitarian Church was, to be sure, a creedless church, but gentlemen might well wonder whether it was to become an ethical culture society. Only one of Parker's auditors found it necessary to leave the church in the midst of the discourse, but the clergyman who offered the ordination prayer warned Mr. Shackford in the course of it against the heresies he had just heard. The sermon shocked not only the venerable; it left many of the younger clergy wondering. "What has Mr. Parker done for us?" wrote young John Weiss, who was later to be Parker's warmest admirer. "He has with justice annihilated the Transient, but where is the Permanent?"

Others, too, were asking this question; they were asking, moreover, whether the Unitarian church countenanced these peculiar doctrines. A Baptist, a Methodist, and an Episcopalian clergyman joined in a formal protest against this mockery of Christianity; and the Reverend Mr. Lothrop, of the Brattle Street Church, who loved authority, and print, took it upon himself to absolve the Unitarians from Parker's heresies. A layman with the noble name of Bradford wrote indignantly: "I would rather see every Unitarian congregation in our land dissolved and every one of our churches razed to the ground, than to assist in placing a man entertaining the sentiments of Theodore Parker in one of our pulpits." Others demanded that the heretic be punished for blasphemy, even as Abner Kneeland had been punished. Fortunately the Attorney General did not fancy a revival of the Kneeland incident, nor did the church see fit to follow barn-burner advice. There was, indeed, little that the clergy could do, for the Unitarian Church was congregational, and the West Roxbury congregation, all unaware that it nursed a viper in its bosom, continued to hear Parker gladly. This was just as well, for in any event Parker meant that he should be heard. "This is what I shall do when obliged to desert the pulpit," he confided to the reluctant Doctor Francis. "I will study seven or eight months of the year, and four or five months I will go about and preach and lecture in the city and the glen, by the roadside and the field-side, and wherever men and women can be found. I will go eastward and westward, northward and southward, and make the land *ring*."

There was little that the clergy could do, but that little they did. "A beautiful sermon," the Reverend Sam Jo May thought it, but he feared that as a Unitarian minister Parker had sealed his doom, and his fears were justified.

One by one the reverend brethren canceled their exchanges with him, and for the most transparent of excuses; and Parker wrote: "As far as the ministers are concerned I am *alone*, ALL ALONE." This was not quite accurate; Briggs still exchanged with him, and Pierpont and Sargent, and Shackford, too, the innocent victim of the great farrago. And young James Freeman Clarke, who had been out West imbibing notions of freedom and whose very name was eloquent of heresy, eventually offered to him the pulpit of the Church of the Disciples. Too bad, this, for it made dissension in that new church and all but broke it up.

Parker was not surprised by the ostracism from the pillars of the Church — from Frothingham (the "artful dodger of the Unitarians," Emerson called him) or Parkman or Gannett; but the derelictions of his friends pained him deeply. It was a shock to find Francis silent and evasive, Francis, so bold in his study, so timid in his pulpit. It was not so long since he himself had proposed to Parker the abandonment of the Bible and the substitution of a system of universal morality for the ethics of Christianity. But now he had been offered a professorship at the Divinity School, and he hesitated to engage in a controversy just then. So Parker wrote sadly in his Journal: "Francis fell back on acct. of his Professorship at Cambridge!" and advised his old friend that they had best not see each other. "I do not wish to stand in your way; I will not knowingly bring on you the censure of your brethren."

It was all very distressing, and that winter of 1842 was the darkest in Parker's life. Lydia was a faithful comforter, but even in his home there was sadness, for it was becoming apparent that he was to be childless, and above all things he wanted children. He had not the equanimity of Mr. Emerson in the face of criticism, Emerson who was writing in his Journal, "Steady, steady. I am convinced that if a man will be a true scholar, he shall have perfect freedom. The young people and the mature hint at odium, and aversion of faces to be presently encountered. I say, No; I fear it not. No

scholar need fear it. Society has no bribe for me, neither
in politics, nor church, nor college, nor city." Not so easy
for a young man barely thirty. Was he a stick or a stone
that he should not feel these slights? He thought himself
the most unfortunate of men, abandoned by all mankind.
What would it matter if he no longer preached? And when
he heard of Channing's death, he thought, Alas, why was
it not I? "Few would mourn my departure," he wrote. "Why
am I spared? Let me but finish the work now in my hands,
that my past life may have its fruits on earth. I will embrace death." He took down those sonnets of Shakespeare,
and read them again; he recited to Francis those lines of
Coleridge that were "graven on his memory":

> Now afflictions bow me down to earth:
> Nor heed I that they rob me of my mirth. . . .
> For not to think of what I needs must feel
> And to be still and patient, all I can,
> And, haply by abstruse research to steal
> From my own nature all the natural man
> This was (is) my sole resource, my only plan.

But even as he wrote, he was overcome with shame at his
weakness, his self-pity. It was not in his nature to be still
and patient, and he knew it — he, the grandson of Captain
John Parker. Nor did he stand alone. His parish stood by
him loyally; loving friends rallied around — Ripley and
Andrews and Silsbee, Elizabeth Peabody and Caroline Dall.
The editors of the *Dial* still welcomed his contributions, if
the *Examiner* did not. Many wished to hear him, for he
had become famous as well as notorious, and requests for
lectures poured in from all over New England. Even Boston, it appeared, was not utterly abandoned to orthodoxy.
Channing had written of it, "The yoke of opinion is a heavy
one, often crushing individuality of action and of judgment,"
but there were some whose independence of action had not
been crushed, and it was with special pleasure that Parker
received from a group of the leading citizens of that city

an invitation to deliver a course of lectures. At first he refused, but Charles Ellis urged him to reconsider; he permitted himself to be persuaded, and that winter he went in to Boston and read five lectures on Religion.

CHAPTER V

TEMPEST IN A BOSTON TEACUP

How rich a philosophic feast was spread before Boston that winter of 1841–42! Professor Walker came in from Cambridge and delivered a series of lectures on "Natural Religion," and the Odeon was crowded to suffocation as all Boston hurried to hear him. And Emerson lectured on "The Times," his face shining with faith though his heart was sore within him for the loss of little Waldo. Parker had no such fame as attended these giants, but the old Masonic Temple was filled nevertheless, those winter nights when he read his "Discourses of Religion." He meant them to be a vindication and a confession of faith. They were to recall men from the spiritual lethargy which had crept over them, to stir their hearts and gladden their spirits and set them on the road to salvation. This was to be a message not only for Boston, for Unitarians, but for all mankind.

So Parker reached out for a wider audience; and soon he was hard at work revising and expanding, developing that theme which he had but hinted at, qualifying this generalization which was, perhaps, too sweeping, adding a paragraph here, a section there, tying the whole together, fortifying it with notes and references that bristled on every page. Long into the night he sat up in the sturdy cane chair in his study, the wind rustling the leaves of the tulip trees by the window. A bronze Spartacus stood at one end of the roll-top desk, at the other a bust of Christ (Thorwaldsen's, it was — how wonderfully the Dane had caught the gentleness of Jesus), symbols, perhaps, of courage and humility. A labor of love, this "Discourse of Religion," of love and learning: a contribution to philosophy, not a tract in an argument. Careful, then, that it should not smack of controversy, that it should be free of personalities. Careful that it should take the highest ground, the most catholic view; that it should be deep as faith and broad as humanity and generous as truth itself. Careful that its scholarship should show nothing that even Doctor Norton or Doctor Palfrey might criticize. They little suspected, they who thought transcendentalism an easy refuge for fools, how deep his philosophic roots, how firm his scholarly basis, how formidable his academic bulwarks. All that he had heretofore announced as intuitive truths, he would substantiate with facts. The great transcendental religious doctrines implicit in the teachings of Emerson and Channing, and in his own preaching and writing, he would now, and for the first time, weld into a coherent philosophy, elaborate, clarify, justify, and prove.

The theme was that of the South Boston sermon. "It is the design of this work," Parker wrote, "to recall men from the transient shows of time to the permanent substance of Religion; from a worship of Creeds and Empty Belief to a worship in the spirit and in Life." The permanent substance of Religion — that was the point of departure. Religion, said Parker, was innate, instinctive; religious truths intuitive. Man is by nature a religious creature, and all men have made themselves some form of worship, have acknowledged some Diety. (Hadn't Voltaire said something like this, Voltaire whom Parker could not abide?) Religion is, has been, and ever will be; it is infinite and indestructible, it depends neither upon church nor creed nor clergy, neither upon Authority nor Tradition. "Has Religion only the bubble of Tradition to rest upon? no other sanction than Authority, no substance but Belief? They little know the matter who say it. Did Religion begin with what we call Christianity? Were there no saints before Peter?" Rhetorical questions, these, they answered themselves. "Religion is the first spiritual thing man learned; the last thing he will abandon. There is but one Religion, as one Ocean; though we call it Faith in our church and Infidelity out of our church."

All very well, but if the authority of the Church and the Scriptures was to be abandoned, what would the transcendentalist substitute in its place? What indeed, but the authority of instinct, conscience, emotion — and reason. Religion itself is transcendental, and infinite, and to attempt to demonstrate or authenticate the infinite by finite means is illogical. And is Christianity Religion? Not necessarily, said Parker, but only in so far as it is in harmony with Absolute Religion, only in so far as it contains spiritual truth. Christianity must be judged at the bar of truth (intuitive truth) just as any other system of morals must be judged; it can claim for itself no special dispensation, no unique immunity.

Thus Parker was fairly launched upon his examination of the Christian Church and the Christian Religion. He had established his premises, established them upon assumptions which defied challenge because they were transcendental, and he proceeded to strengthen them — a concession to the credulous and the weak — by argument and learning. And how powerful his argument, how eloquent and strong: that paragraph on Solid Piety, it pealed like a great organ. How impressive his learning, his pages crowded with works ancient and modern, famous and obscure. Here was something no American had done, and no Englishman; men like Emerson and Coleridge took their transcendentalism for granted. You would have to go to Germany for this sort of thing; alone the Germans were so learned that they couldn't keep their scholarship out of even a transcendental brew.

What then of Christianity, in Parker's argument, the Christianity of Christ, of the Bible, and of the Church? Let not men be imposed upon by these; they were valid only in so far as they recommended themselves to men's sovereign reason. Religion, Parker would admit, has gained immeasurably from the teachings of Christ, the morality of the Bible, and the philanthropy of the Church, but it depends upon none of these. The truths of Christianity have nothing to do with the personality of Jesus. If Jesus were divine, still his teaching might be erroneous; if Jesus were weak and misguided, still his teaching might be valid. The truths of Christianity stand on their own authority, not on the authority of Christ. "If Christianity be true at all," said Parker with what was thought to be execrable taste, "it would be just as true if Herod or Catiline had taught it." No wonder the Reverend Doctor Gray told Convers Francis, "A transcendentalist, Sir, is an enemy to the institution of Christianity."

With the Scriptures and the miracles, it fared even worse. Parker did not feel justified in giving extensive attention to the Scriptures: his edition of De Wette was ready for the press and he had in contemplation a no less exhaustive work on the New Testament. A rapid survey, then, slashing, severe, but reverent where reverence was due, and he penned a tribute to the beauty and the power of the Bible which satisfied even the most orthodox. But at all costs, hew to the line, be not misled by irrelevancies, beware seductive bypaths. The Bible, be it ever so true, added nothing to the authority of Absolute Religion. Its doctrines were to be judged by conscience, not conscience by the doctrines. "If all the Evangelists and Apostles were liars, if Jesus had never lived, but the New Testament were a sheer forgery from end to end, these doctrines are just the same, absolute truth." And as for miracles, Parker had only pity for those who sought in the aberrations of nature some divine revelation; nature itself was the supreme miracle. Doubtless miracles had occurred, and would continue to occur, but they proved nothing, and if the Church rested its authority upon this foundation, it built upon shifting sands. God did not need to fall back upon tricks in order to reveal his truth to men.

But it was the Church which, through the centuries, had

nourished these delusions which warped the minds of men, and it was on the Church that Parker trained his heaviest artillery, and Emerson jotted in his Journal: "T. P. has beautiful fangs, and the whole amphitheatre delights to see him worry and tear his victim." There was bitterness in this attack, though Parker would never admit it, bitterness which had its roots deep in the memories of childhood, and when he wrote that arraignment of Calvinism the fire spluttered from his pen: —

This system degrades Man . . . Man is subordinate to the apocryphal, ambiguous, imperfect, and often erroneous Scripture of the Word; the Word itself, as it comes straightway from the fountain of Truth, through Reason, Conscience, Affection, and the Soul, he must not have. It takes the Bible for God's statute-book; combines old Hebrew notions into a code of ethics; takes figures for fact; settles questions in Morals and Religion by texts of Scripture! It can justify anything out of the Bible. It wars to the knife against gaiety of heart; condemns amusement as sinful; sneers at Common Sense; spits upon Reason, appeals to low and selfish aims — to Fear, the most selfish and base of all passions. It does not know that goodness is its own recompense, and vice its own torture; that judgment takes place daily and God's laws execute themselves. . . . It makes Religion unnatural to men, and of course hostile; Christianity alien to the soul. It paves Hell with children's bones; has a personal Devil in the world, to harry the land, and lure or compel men to eternal woe. Its God is diabolical. . . . This system applies to God the language of King's courts, trial, sentence, judgment, pardon, satisfaction, allegiance, day of judgment. It dwells in professions of faith; watches for God's honour. It makes men stiff, unbending, cold, formal, austere, seldom lovely. They have the strength of the Law, not the beauty of the Gospel; the cunning of the Pharisee, not the simplicity of the Christian. You know its followers as soon as you see them; the rose is faded out of their cheeks; their mouths drooping and sad; their appearance says, Alas, my fellow-worm, there is no more sunshine, for the world is damned. It is a faith of stern, morose men, well befitting the descendants of Odin, and his iron peers; its Religion is a principle, not a sentiment; a foreign matter, imported into the soul, by forethought and resolution; not a native fountain of joy and gladness, playing in the sober autumn or the sunshine of spring. Its Christianity is frozen mercury in the bosom of the warm-hearted Christian, who by nature would go straight to God. The heaven of this system is a grand pay-day, where Humility is to have its coach and six, forsooth, because she has been humble; the Saints and Martyrs, who bore the trials of the world, are to take their vengeance by shouting "Hallelujah, Glory to God" when they see the anguish of their old persecutors, and the smoke of their torment ascending up for ever and ever.

Hard words, these, and Unitarians might comfort themselves that they were not as other Calvinists. But not so, said Parker; the Unitarians, too, were sunk in a sensational philosophy: they too sought refuge in miracles and authority. Indeed, Unitarianism had not even the dignity of consistency.

With a philosophy too rational to go the full length of the supernatural theory, too sensual to embrace the spiritual method, and ask no person to mediate between man and God, it oscillates between the two; humanizes the Bible, yet calls it miraculous; believes in man's greatness, freedom and spiritual nature, yet asks for a Mediator and Redeemer. It censures the traditionary sects, yet sits among the tombs and mourns over things past and gone; believes in the humanity of Jesus, yet his miraculous birth likewise and miraculous powers, and makes him an anomalous and impossible being. It blinds men's eyes with the letter, yet bids them look out for the spirit; stops their ears with the texts of the Old Testament, and then asks them to listen to the voice of God in their heart; it reverences Jesus manfully, yet denounces all such as preach Absolute Religion and Morality, as he did, on its own authority. Well might Jeremiah say of it, "Alas for thee, now thou hast forsaken the promise of thy youth."

Thus Parker disposed of the Unitarians, and it was not a polite performance. Yet he did not despair. There was a party within the Church, he pointed out, that professed absolute religion — "Its temple is all space; its shrine the good heart; its creed all truth; its ritual works of love and utility; its profession of faith a manly life." This party (Parker could speak of it with confidence) had broken with Protestantism even as Protestants had broken with Catholicism; it too had its Luther, though Parker was too modest to name him. It pointed the way to the one true religion; it held out promise for the regeneration of the Church and the recapture of Christianity; it discovered how Christ might once again become the Way and the Life. But of this party Parker did not deem it fit to speak at length. It had been Doctor Channing's party; it was to be Parker's.

2

But not without a struggle. The book made quite a stir abroad; the English scholars were "prodigiously struck with it," and James Martineau wanted to know more about this American preacher with "the excess of manly strength." But the Americans didn't think so well of it. Orestes Brownson, trembling on the verge of Catholicism, gave an entire number of his *Boston Quarterly* to pointing out its shortcomings. The Reverend Mr. Morison rebuked Parker in the columns of the *Examiner*, and when he tempered his criticism with words of praise, the editor cut them out. Young James Freeman Clarke went to all the trouble of publishing a pamphlet exposing the "shallow naturalism" of the book; there was a suspicion abroad that he was tarred with the stick of transcendentalism himself, and perhaps he wanted to prove his orthodoxy. Even Francis was critical: he wouldn't allow Parker to dedicate the book to him; Parker didn't mind what the others said, but this was too bad. Yet there was respect hiding behind all of this hostility and timidity. Some of the blows had struck home, and Doctor Gannett and Doctor Parkman had to admit that the Discourse was such a monument of learning as would not come from every young man of some thirty years.

Soon there was new provocation from the West Roxbury firebrand. Scarcely was the Discourse off the press of the courageous James Brown, than the Boston clergy were

affronted by an infamous article in the October number of
the *Dial*. It was called "The Hollis Street Council," and
was as offensive as its title was inoffensive, and concerned
the fate of the Reverend Mr. Pierpont of the Hollis Street
Church — Pierpont, whom Parker admired and who had
written a hymn for Parker's ordination. Mr. Pierpont, it
appeared, had an unfortunate manner of assuming the rôle
of John the Baptist and denouncing the sins of members of
his congregation. He preached on slavery, on vice and intemperance; his words were indelicate, and he castigated
brewers and winebibbers by name. Even Parker admitted
that "he allows himself an indignant eloquence which were
better let alone," Parker who could never let eloquence
alone. Dissatisfaction was inevitable, and the injured members of the church demanded an investigation. A council
of the Boston clergymen was called, an undignified body,
its membership fluctuating, its authority dubious; it
charged Mr. Pierpont with intemperance of speech and
manner, but exonerated him from graver errors. Finally Mr.
Pierpont resigned, but not before he had reached out to a
larger audience with his play "The Drunkard," and Parker
wrote to him: "Nothing has happened for years so reflecting
disgrace on the Boston clergy as your departure from the
city under the present circumstances."

The *Dial* article reviewed the report of the Hollis Street
Council, and called it "a piece of diplomacy worthy of a
college of Jesuits"; what was worse, everyone was soon
reading it and talking about it ("It sold the number," Miss
Fuller told Emerson). Now the Reverend Ezra Gannett had
been one of the mediators, Gannett who had succeeded
Channing at the Federal Street Church, but who would
never replace him, and Doctor Gannett did not like to be
called a Jesuit, nor charged with favoring the liquor and
slavery interests of Boston. He protested sharply, and he was
not alone.

All of these grievances and recriminations came to a
head in January, 1843, when the Boston Association of

Ministers invited Mr. Parker to tea at the Reverend Mr.
Waterston's, to thrash the matter out. Mr. Parker's case
had been the subject of discussion and correspondence for
some time, and the members of the Association felt that they
were forced to take some action in sheer self-defense. Not
only had this young Mr. Parker "introduced discord into
the Unitarian body," but his deism and pantheism were
bringing odium upon the whole Church. The Reverend Mr.
Frothingham put the matter plainly enough. "He that re-
jects the church," Mr. Frothingham pointed out, "must not
belong to it. If he wishes to throw stones at the windows, he
must go outside." Of course Parker might retort that sometimes it was necessary to throw stones through windows in
order to let in light and air, and that the thing could be done
from within just as well as from without. This might be good
logic, but it was not good taste, and Mr. Frothingham, who
was connected with all of the first families, with the
Brookses and the Adamses and the Everetts, thought he
knew something about good taste.

So Parker put away the proof-sheets of the translation of
De Wette, and the manuscript of the "Critical and Miscellaneous Writings," now all but ready for the printer, and
went dutifully out to Mr. Waterston's house to tea. And when
the amenities of tea had been observed, Mr. Frothingham
called the meeting to order, and, "with a considerable degree
of embarrassment," stated the business of the day. They were
not there to catechize Parker, Mr. Frothingham explained,
nor should he catechize them, but it was time that certain
things were discussed openly. Mr. Parker was making
trouble, so much trouble that he, for one, could not longer
have any ministerial intercourse with him. Mr. Parker had
written a book that was not only "vehemently deistical, in
the worst sense, but subversive of Christianity," and he contributed articles to that transcendental magazine, the *Dial*,
characterizing his fellow ministers as "Jesuits" and "Pharisees." Then Mr. Gannett chimed in: he had disliked the
Hollis Street article so much that he had not dared to read

it carefully. "I hope God Almighty will forgive him," he exclaimed, "but I can never grasp him by the hand again cordially." He did, of course, that very afternoon, for Doctor Gannett was as tender-hearted as he was hot-headed. There was much more of the same tenor: Mr. Parker was not a Christian, for he denied the miracles; Mr. Parker was not a Unitarian, for he denied Christ; the difference between Mr. Parker and the Association was the difference between no Christianity and Christianity. And, to return to more practical matters, since Mr. Parker compromised the Association, he would do well to withdraw.

Parker met this formidable assault with equanimity. He was quite able to take care of himself. If members did not wish to exchange with him, that was their affair, and he could not recall that he had complained of their refusal. As a matter of fact, he added, with some complacency, the closing of some churches had merely resulted in opening others; he had been deluged with invitations to lecture, he had lectured to thousands, all Boston, all Massachusetts, had heard him. As for his "vehemently deistical" book, he would be pleased to know just what Mr. Frothingham meant by the term; Mr. Frothingham would do him a great service in pointing out just wherein his book was contrary to Christianity, for a young man, like himself, not learned, had some difficulty in understanding this. And if gentlemen wished to draw inferences from his contributions to the *Dial*, that was their affair; he had not known that the Association maintained a censorship over the writings of its members. No, Mr. Parker hadn't the slightest intention of withdrawing from the Association. If the Association wished to expel him, that was their privilege. He remembered George Fox, he remembered Abelard and Saint Paul, who stood alone. Once again, great principles were at stake; and he proposed to vindicate them.

Three hours of this, and the meeting reached an impasse. Then Cyrus Bartol, who knew Parker from Cambridge days, rose and spoke warmly of Parker's sincerity and goodness.

It was somewhat confusing to have the meeting take this turn, and the much-badgered infidel was even more bewildered when Gannett seconded Bartol's remarks. But when Chandler Robbins, as conservative as Frothingham himself, began to speak of affection and sympathy, Parker hurried from the room in tears, only to be met in the anteroom by Mr. Frothingham, who took him by the hand and assured him of his esteem. And so the great heresy trial came to an end on a note of bathos.

But it had been a trying year, and Parker's health cracked under the strain. He had given these lectures on religion, and repeated them in six neighboring towns; he had delivered a series of lectures on "The Times" (just like Emerson) in no less than seven different places; he had seen the "Discourse" through the press, collected and edited the volume of "Critical and Miscellaneous Writings," put the finishing touches on the two great volumes of the De Wette, and spent twelve hours a day toiling over the proofs of these many books. There had been unhappiness and recrimination, affronts and ostracism; his fellow clergymen had forsaken him and his friends had failed him. He sought rest in a hurried trip to Nova Scotia; but the results were disappointing. He needed to get away from the press of affairs and the eager demands of the lyceums, from the clamor of controversy and the heat of battle. He needed distraction and perspective. His friend George Russell saw the need and provided the means, and in September, 1843, Theodore and Lydia sailed for a year in Europe.

3

To Europe, then, for the Grand Tour. To Europe to see at first hand what he knew so well at second, to confirm his principles and his prejudices, to absorb impressions and amass statistics and pay respects to the scholars and philosophers whose volumes he had read. No one more sturdily American, more deeply rooted, more provincial, with his love for his own countryside, for the homely customs, the native idiom; no one more catholic-minded, more deeply immersed in the literature and learning and intellectual atmosphere of the Old World.

There was everything to be seen and much to be remembered, and Parker invaded Europe with the ruthless thoroughness that ever characterized him: he carried the towns by storm, he harried the countryside, he swept through the galleries and museums, ransacked the libraries, plundered the churches, and despoiled the Universities of their treasures. Nothing escaped his voracious acquisitiveness; he levied tribute wherever he went, and few failed to pay.

The museums and galleries were a duty, and he performed it as faithfully as any Puritan and with as little æsthetic abandon. At scores of Madonnas and hundreds of Christs he gazed with rapt expectation, but he was never excited to ecstasy, only provoked to moralization. The Venus of Milo was "a glorious human creature, made for all the events of life," but the Venus de' Medici a toy woman, a plaything, a bauble. The incomparable frescoes of the Sistine Chapel brought to his mind the humility of Christ and filled him with compassion for the pride of men; the power and majesty of Michelangelo inspired him with awe. He was duly impressed by the leaning tower of Pisa, and could not forbear to note a vulgar copy which resembled the great tower only in its leaning. "This," he wrote, "is like all imitators; they get the prophet's halting step, but not his inspiration." He studied the art of Italy like a rite, but beggars swarmed over the cathedrals like maggots and the grandeur of the past only accentuated the misery of the present, and he concluded that "Italy is the land of artistic elegance and social deformity. She taught refinement to all Europe but kept treachery to herself." The Murillos and Raphaels of Vienna contrasted oddly with the frivolity of the city; he lingered lovingly in the galleries of Dresden; but in Berlin he had eyes only for the schools, and disposed of Sans Souci with a pun. Nothing impressed him more, anywhere, that the drawings of Holbein, and when, at Basle, he found the "Praise of Folly" with the great man's illustrations in every margin, he was ecstatic.

Far more interesting the daily life of the people, the husbandry of the farmer, the home of the laborer. Paintings were all very well, but potatoes were more important. He tramped the streets of Liverpool and Manchester and London until the iniquity of the cities and of industry sank into him; the houses of the common people held lessons not to be found in the palaces of kings, and the crooked streets of the Ghettoes were more fascinating by far than Place de la Concorde or Unter den Linden. It was the simple things he remembered best: the courtliness of the churchmen, the voices of the girls, the gestures of the beggars as they followed his carriage crying, *"Eccellenza, eccellenza, povero miserabile"* — the things that told the character of men and of nations. English servants looked like Methodist ministers; the women of Italy carried firewood on their heads, and walked barefoot to save their hobnailed shoes; in Genoa he saw a flower-girl who was the handsomest creature in the world. In Italy (brother Isaac would be interested in this) every inch of ground was cultivated with the nicety of a garden, but nowhere did he see a plow. Pressing the vintage from the grapes involved three processes: only the strongest pressure forced out the rich wine, and so it was with thought and learning. In the garden of the Villa Borghese, a few steps without the gates of Rome, he found a species of forget-me-not that he had never seen before. In Paris he saw a man kiss a horse. In Tuscany he fell in love with the asses: here they had *eyes* and *ears*, elsewhere only a bray. In Munich there was a sample of European despotism: the city in a state of siege, chains across the streets; that could never happen in America. The government of France spent almost half a million annually to support the theater — Massachusetts might try this. When they came to Naples, the Carnival was in full swing. Here they fell in with young Francis Parkman, whose father presided with such dignity over the New North

Church, and the three of them hired a carriage and joined
in the fun. There were masques and masquerades and fancy
dress, and everyone threw sugar plums; the King threw
real sugar plums, and the common folk plums of chalk
which hurt when they hit you — one of them struck Lydia
and another broke Parker's glasses. At Rome, too, they
found a Carnival, a much more pretentious affair: there
were Devils with horns and hoofs and tails, there were
Harlequins with wooden swords, and black-eyed girls who
concealed their beauty with fierce mustachios. No sugar-
plum foolery here: the girls threw flowers at you instead,
and it was both pleasanter and safer. No place so gay as
Italy, or so depressing, with its poverty and its superstition.
The pleasures of the North were less violent, but not less
satisfactory. The bear was the patron saint of Berne, and
Lydia fell in love with Bruin and was promptly christened
"Bearsie," and Parker began to make that collection of
bears which was eventually to crowd every mantelpiece in
his house.

Carnivals and churches were all very well, but it was
men that he went to see and that he remembered, and he
loved conversation no less than did Margaret Fuller. He
had heard much of the American scholar, now for the
European. No sooner in England than he hunted up Francis Newman, brother to the famous John, and a greater
man, thought Parker. He combined an acute and brilliant
mind with generous sympathies. No liberal cause but what
excited his support; he subscribed to Garrison's *Liberator,*
and had followed the Unitarian controversy with interest.
The Reverend James Tayler dined with them — Tayler
whose study of the Fourth Gospel had attracted so much
attention; and they talked about Plato's Republic. Parker
thought well of it, but Newman did not, nor did Tayler. In
London, too, he sought out Carlyle, — Carlyle with his
black blood and his berserker rages and his intemperate
enthusiasms, whom Emerson so incontinently admired, and
Carlyle wrote to his American friend that he had seen Par-

ker, "a most hardy, compact, clever little fellow, full of decisive utterance, with humor and good humor shining like a sun amid multitudes of watery comets and tenebrific constellations." He dined, too, with the starlike Sterling, beloved of Carlyle; in a few months Sterling was dead, and Carlyle remembered that it had been like "dining in a ruin, in the crypt of a mausoleum." In Liverpool Parker called on James Martineau, the patron saint of English transcendentalism. Martineau had read the "Discourse of Religion" and was preparing to review it; he rebuked the Boston Unitarians by asking Parker to preach in his pulpit, and five years later it was to him that Parker sent the fugitive slaves, Ellen and William Craft.

In Paris the Sorbonne was the center of interest, and Parker hurried from course to course like a gourmand. He heard Victor Cousin, the eclectic philosopher whom Ripley so admired, and who controlled public education in France: it was Bronson Alcott's dream come true, but it was not at all as Alcott would have had it. He heard brilliant, handsome Jules Simon lecture on Proclus, and that was something to tell Emerson about, Emerson who never tired of quoting the Alexandrine mystic. Damiron lectured on Gassendi, and De Portet on the Law of Nature, and Lenormant on the Unity of Humanity, which he demonstrated from the acknowledged fact that all men were descended from Adam and Eve. Stuff and nonsense, thought Parker, he could hear this sort of thing in Boston, and he rushed off to the Jardin des Plantes, where Geoffroy St. Hilaire was holding forth on Vultures.

But Germany was his spiritual home. England frightened him (was it to be the destiny of America, too, to pay so great a price for wealth and power?), France amused him, Italy saddened him. But in Germany the scholar was the first citizen, philosophy was supreme. Behind every hill, around every corner, was a university, and the streets were thick with great men — it was almost a disguise to be a great man. And what scholars they were: they sat eighteen hours a day in their studies, and lo, the great tomes tumbled forth in a remorseless confusion. But he had read them all. He would go up to one of these scholars and say, "I am an American, I have read your books." These were his credentials, and they were always acceptable. No need to tell what *he* had written or done, no one read an American book. It was surprising enough to find an American who read a German book, but this young man carried the whole of the *Theologische Jahrbücher* in his head.

First, then, to Berlin, where George Bancroft had learned Hegelianism, and Motley had escaped philosophy. "Do you know what sort of a place Berlin is?" Parker wrote to Francis, "Imagine 1000 hackney coaches, the drivers with cows'-tails on top of their caps, 100 private carriages, 400 drags for beer, 150 carts and wagons for other business, 30,000 soldiers, 1600 students, 180 professors (it will take you a day to imagine them all), a King, Baron von Humboldt, and 270,000 others. Imagine the King with a belly like Uncle Tom Clarke, the students with mustachios, the professors lecturing on *Dagesh lene*, Baron von Humboldt sleeping on his laurels, and the 270,000 smoking, walking, weaving, making pipes, and getting dinner, and you have an idea of the *personale* of Berlin."

It was the 180 professors that interested Parker, for the young University had already taken from Göttingen the intellectual leadership of Germany, and the Motleys, the Everetts, and the Ticknors no longer went to the lovely town on the Leine. Parker heard the aged Schelling lecture on Revelation: he had been brought to Berlin, cosmetics, hair dye, and all, to put down Hegelianism, but Hegelianism, for all its obscurity, would not down. Parker went to hear Professor Werder expound Hegelian logic. "He made a great fuss about *Bestimmheit* and was, I thought, in a remarkable fix himself, trying to discover the *Ur-bestimmung*. He said, in *Bestimmung* there was *Daseyn* and *Realité*. Hereupon a fat chubby student, evidently his Ma's darling, tried hard to conceive the difference, but after numerous ineffectual attempts, gave up in despair." So, too, did Parker, and went off to see if the other Professors had something better to offer. He heard Hengstenberg and Twesten and Vatke and Boeckh; whom did he not hear?

There were a hundred universities, and a pity to miss a one, so, breathless, Parker hurried from Berlin to Halle, to Heidelberg, to Bonn, to Leipzig, to Stuttgart, to Freiburg, to Tübingen, and then to the Swiss schools: Zurich, Geneva, Basle. Heidelberg was a grand place: here was old Schlosser, bringing his World History up to date, and young Gervinus, thrown out of Göttingen for his liberalism, and the venerable Paulus whose rationalism was notorious and whose attack on Schelling was a scandal. Parker saw them all, and with Gervinus he struck up a lasting friendship. More interesting even than Heidelberg were those citadels of theological learning, Tübingen and Basle. At Tübingen Parker found Ewald and Baur, great men whose fame he had helped to spread. Parker spoke learnedly of Ewald's "History of the Hebrews," but Ewald did not know his visitor's "Discourse of Religion" nor his translation of De Wette. A man of genius, Ewald: a scholar, a democrat, a transcendentalist, one of the hardest heads in all Germany, but "of course" a little wrong. Baur was a great man too, burly and savage, a veritable thunderbolt of Hegelianism. He had penetrated to the mystery of the Trinity, analyzed it, and dissected it; he wrote those terrible articles for the *Theologische Jahrbücher*, which would have jailed him for blasphemy in Massachusetts, but he stood all undisturbed in his Lutheran pulpit.

At Basle Parker found De Wette himself, "A compact little man, with a rather dry face." Parker visited him, dined with him and heard him lecture. "He cut right and left and made no bones of saying that such a passage was probably spurious, that John knew nothing of it, etc. Carpenter's *Harmony* would set the Professor right on this point!" He was an irritable old man, soured by misfortune and exile, growing more conservative every year: when the students at

Jena came out to greet him, he told them to study their
books, get their lessons, and keep quiet. He and Parker
talked of a thousand things, but, alas, De Wette had not received Parker's translation of the "Introduction to the Old
Testament"; he was already preparing a new edition of the
work, could Parker make any suggestions? They parted
affectionately, tenderly; but it was a sad anticlimax.

4

By September Parker was back in West Roxbury, freshly
charged with the electricity of German scholarship, and
ready to administer new shocks to the Boston clergy. He
had known that he was right before; Europe confirmed
him in his knowledge and demonstrated the strength of his
position. He had looked carefully into the religious institutions of the Old World; he had seen Catholicism at first-
hand, he had talked with Father Glover and with Bishop
Baggs and even with Pope Gregory XVI. He was convinced that Catholicism was the logical consequence of a
supernatural, a sensational philosophy, and that the Protestant compromise was untenable. "Absolute Religion" —
transcendentalism — offered the only alternative; how right
he had been, all the time! Nor was it to no purpose that
he had looked upon the bones of martyrs, wandered through
the Catacombs, studied the Inquisition, and stood in Luther's study in Wittenberg. He was humbled at the thought
that his own martyrdom was so easy.

How delightful it was to be back in West Roxbury,
back with his own people. The parsonage on Cottage
Street welcomed him, the garden was colorful with mignon-
ette and marigold and phlox, the roses still lingered on
the bushes, and the hedge that bordered the Russell estate
was as low as ever, and all the little Russells and the little
Shaws were there to be caressed. How good to stand once
more in the familiar pulpit: the congregation had listened
gratefully to Francis and Ripley during his absence, but
they were glad to have him back. This was where he be-

longed. Now he could settle down to work — now for the "History of the Reformation" and the "History of Religious Thought" and all the other books that he planned. Now to study, like Baur, eighteen hours a day.

But it was not to be. There was an interlude of peace. Parker was busy with parish duties, and with lectures — to Fall River, to Bedford, to Salem; forty times that winter he lectured from lyceum platforms. Then the problem of exchange bobbed up again. First there was the unfortunate affair of Mr. Sargent. The Reverend John Turner Sargent, distinguished for good works and philanthropy, was minister to the Suffolk Street Chapel, and under the authority of the Benevolent Fraternity of Unitarian Churches. He invited Parker to exchange with him, and was summarily dismissed from his church. Then Clarke asked Parker to preach at the Church of the Disciples. Fifteen parishioners protested, and there was a great to-do, but Clarke stuck by his guns, writing in his Journal: "Black Sunday. T. P. preached morning and evening. I went to West Roxbury to preach." The pious fifteen withdrew to Mr. Waterston's chapel, but Clarke's church weathered the crisis after all.

Soon a new difficulty arose. The "Great and Thursday Lecture" was an ancient institution, more honored in fame than in attendance; for a century and a half it had been given in turn by the Congregational and Unitarian clergymen of Boston. Lately it had fallen on evil days; a score of elderly spinsters glided cheerlessly into the First Church on the inevitable Thursday mornings, a substitute choir sang listlessly to the efforts of an amateur organist, and young Octavius Frothingham, who pumped the organ bellows, remembered that "the sacrifice lasted a painful hour. None came but the saints, and these came not with jubilant feet." Parker's turn to give the lecture came the day after Christmas of 1844, and what a change to the astonished eyes of the organ boy! The pews were filled, the galleries crowded, and men stood in the aisles to hear the West Roxbury heresiarch. He spoke of "The Relation of Jesus to His Age

and to the Ages." It was a noble sermon, charged with faith
and piety, but Parker did not deny that the God who had
inspired Christ might have other and greater Christs in
store for his people. To the minister of the First Church,
the sermon was a rejection of Christianity itself. Mr. Frothingham hurriedly withdrew all outstanding invitations to
deliver the Great and Thursday Lecture, and returned control of the lectureship to the First Church, where it was
originally lodged; thus the possibility of a recurrence of
the painful episode was quietly eliminated. "The device,"
his son, the young Octavius, later remarked, "was ingenious
but not handsome. The ungodly called it a trick." Trick or
no trick, it was effective. It removed not only Mr. Parker,
but the Lecture itself. For attendance soon fell off, and the
institution died of inanition. It was, Mr. Frothingham felt,
justifiable suicide.

Parker asked for an explanation, but none was
vouchsafed. The whole thing had become petty and child-
ish; better bring it to an end with what dignity he could.
So he prepared a parting shot, and fired it into the heart
of the Unitarian camp. It was an open "Letter to the Boston
Association of Congregational Ministers Touching Certain
Matters of their Religion."

Gentlemen [he wrote], it is not altogether plain why you put
yourselves in your peculiar attitude toward me. As you have
not as yet made a public statement of your theological beliefs,
I must beg you to inform me what is Orthodoxy according to the
Boston Association. The Orthodoxy of the Boston Association is
not an easy thing to come at. As I try to comprehend it, I feel
I am looking at something dim and undefined. You will do me
a great service if you will publish your Symbolical Books, and
let the world know what is the true doctrine according to the
Boston Association. Gentlemen, you are theologians; men of
leisure and learning; mighty in the Scriptures. It is therefore to
be supposed that you have examined things at large, and been
curious in particulars; have searched into the mysteries of things,
deciding what is true, what is false, what Christian and what not.
Some of you can sling stones at a hair's breadth in the arena of

theology. Of course I shall take it for granted that you have each and all, thoroughly, carefully and profoundly examined the matters at issue between us; that you have made up your minds thereon, and are all entirely agreed on your conclusions, and that on all points; for surely it were not charitable to suppose that a body of Christian ministers would censure and virtually condemn one of their number for heresy, unless they had made personal investigation of the whole matter, had themselves agreed on their standard of orthodoxy, and were quite ready to place that standard before the eyes of the whole people.

Would the gentlemen be good enough to let him know just what they meant by certain terms which they had used — by "salvation," "miracle," "inspiration," "revelation," and would they be good enough to answer twenty-four other questions relating to certain problems of theology. "Gentlemen," Parker concluded, "I shall pause impatiently for your reply."

His impatience was not to be rewarded, but events soon sharpened the chagrin of his critics. For in January, 1845, a group of Boston gentlemen met and resolved, "That the Rev. Theodore Parker shall have a chance to be heard in Boston." It was the summons for which he had been waiting, and he was prepared.

"I feel that I have a great work to do," he wrote. "I think I shall not fail."

CHAPTER VI

THE HUB OF THE UNIVERSE

THIS was where he belonged, and he knew it. How he loved the city; he had seen Rome and Florence, Vienna and Prague, and many a neat German town, but not one of them could compare with Boston as he looked down upon it from the State House, its harbor studded with island jewels and the masts of the sailboats rising like lances to the sky. It was the city of Hunkerism: the Custom House was its Temple and Webster was its God; but it was not unregenerate. The winds of doctrine blew noisily down its crooked streets and rattled many a windowpane, and not all of the windows were closed. Surely a city that listened, however reluctantly, to a Garrison, a Phillips, a Mann, would find room for a Parker.

His friends had organized the Twenty-Eighth Congregational Society, and rented the old Melodeon on Washington Street: from his study windows Parker could see the great ugly building. He had taken a house on Exeter Place — Number 1, it was, an unpretentious dwelling of four stories located in the heart of fashionable Boston: at the end of the little lane was a huge trellis covered with ivy, and before it stood a plaster Flora as if to apologize for this sorry attempt to simulate a rural atmosphere. To the north was Summer Street, the loveliest street in all Boston, lined with magnificent chestnut trees; to the south Essex Street, with its great English elms. Near by were Otis Place and Winthrop Place and Franklin Square with its sixteen mansions built by Bulfinch himself. This was the citadel of the Boston merchants; here in the stately houses behind the elms and chestnut trees lived the Cushings and the Lodges, the Perkinses and the Lees. Here any morning on his walk Parker might meet black Daniel Webster, back from Washington, or the terrible Rufus Choate hurrying down the Franklin Street alley, gilded Edward Everett, the new President of Harvard, or eccentric John Perkins Cushing who had built a wall of Chinese porcelain entirely around his house on Summer Street. Here, too, he might meet men more to his liking, Wendell Phillips, or Ellis Gray Loring, or Doctor Jackson, or the angular William Lloyd Garrison, looking more like a parson every day.

How exciting Boston was, pulsating with life, growing so fast that not even the census could keep up with it, yet keeping its character, its individuality, its beauty. It was all so familiar, for he had lived here as a young man and he had come in so often from West Roxbury, but now it belonged to him, and he trod its streets with a different air, the streets and lanes whose very names he loved: Joy Street and Blossom Street, Snow Hill Street and Charter Street, Love Lane and Bumsted Place and White Bird Alley. The harbor, too, was his, and the wharves, the Cornhill bookshops and the Common. It was just two blocks from Exeter Place to the Common, with its elms and its maples and its mottled sycamores, and even some tulip trees to remind him of West Roxbury days. On summer afternoons the air was filled with the noise of baseball games, and in the winter the boys and girls skated on the Frog Pond and coasted daringly down the Big Hill. North of the Common on Beacon Hill and Mount Vernon were rising the spacious brick mansions of the first families, for the exodus from Pearl Street and Summer Street had already begun. Elsewhere too there was activity, but of another sort: tenements could not be built fast enough to house the thousands of Irish paddies who poured into South Boston and North Boston and Noddle's Island. Boston was turning into another Dublin and every newsboy had a brogue. When the famine hit Ireland in 1847 it was the Boston merchants who rallied to her support, for they paid their debts, these men, and all New England rejoiced when Black Ben Forbes brought the sloop *Jamestown* into Dublin harbor in record time, its hold bursting with flour and potatoes.

Best of all were the wharves, and ten minutes' walk brought Parker from the respectability of Exeter Place to the water front. Even the names of the wharves told of Boston's far-flung empire: here was Russia Wharf and Wales Wharf and India Wharf with its granite warehouses. The West Indiamen loaded at Arch Wharf and the southern packets at Rowe's Wharf and at Lewis Wharf you could find clipper ships bound for California gold fields. At the Central Wharf you could see the new Semaphore Telegraph; T Wharf was sacred to the mackerel and the cod; and of a Sunday the Long Wharf was crowded with eager excursionists bound for Cohasset or Nahant.

Here was commercial Boston, here and in the new Merchant's Exchange and the Coffee Houses, Revere House and Adams House and Tremont House, where the New York and Philadelphia bankers stayed, and the planters up from the South. But it was not the China traders or the State Street bankers who had earned for Boston the name of the Athens of America. There was another Boston whose empire was wider than that of State Street. This was the Boston of the Athenæum and the Cornhill bookshops and the literary clubs and the churches, of Doctor Holmes and Doctor Frothingham, of Prescott and Ticknor, Lowell and Dana, and its citizens ranked with the Cushings and the Crowninshields. Parker was not sure that he belonged to this Boston any more than to the other; he was not even sure that he wanted to belong to it. He was always a sort of poor relation, he felt, respected, but not welcomed. He was not a member of the Athenæum, though as a clergyman he had access to its shelves; if he did not loiter at the fashionable Old Corner Book Store it was because he found better company at Doctor Peabody's house on West Street. He was a member of the short-lived Town and Country Club which young Higginson had organized; but who was not? (Not Elizabeth Peabody, not Mary Lowell Putnam. When these were proposed Emerson serenely drew a line through the names.) The Town and Country crumbled gaily into bankruptcy and when the exclusive Saturday Club came into being, Parker was not asked to join. Nor was he to be found in the drawing-rooms on Beacon Hill. They did not think well of him there. "We will make Boston too hot for you," said Thomas Appleton to Mrs. Apthorp when he met her on the street, and Julia Ward Howe's friends could scarcely forgive her perverse habit of attending Mr. Parker's church. "I am as much an outcast from society," Parker said, "as if I were a convicted pirate." Thackeray when he came to Boston regretted that he had not moved in the best circles, for no one took him to see Theodore Parker. Yet he managed to hear Parker preach, and he met him, too, at Ellis Loring's house; and Parker wrote of him: "A great monstrous man, six feet and a half high, a large *stumpf* nose and a long *old* chin. He seemed a little shy." Parker was not often asked to meet distinguished visitors, but he dined with Clough at the Tremont House, and of course Howe asked him to the dinner which he gave for Kossuth — Kossuth, whom Phillips refused to greet. And if his walks did not often take him to Mount Vernon Street, one house stood always open: that of Sampson Reed, the Swedenborgian. His windows fronted on lovely Louisburg Square, and Parker could watch the play of the fountain in the sun and wonder about that curious statue of Aristides the Just, while he listened to this mystic in whom Emerson delighted.

No, he was not without friends; he had, indeed, his own salon. The whole of the second floor of the Exeter Place house was a parlor, and here, on Sunday evenings, Parker received a varied company. Here you might find Wendell Phillips, the Boston Demosthenes, whose house was just around the corner and whose garden Parker enjoyed from his study windows. He had been converted by Lyman

Beecher, and he had no use for Parker's theology, but he loved Parker all the same. Here, too, came Charles Sumner, his handsome features already heavy with affairs of state. He had scandalized all Boston with his oration on "The True Grandeur of Nations," but Parker thought it a great speech, and he hurried to make Sumner's acquaintance; and Sumner was glad to know a man with whom he could talk about the classics or law or reform. Samuel Gridley Howe and his lovely wife, Julia Ward, were frequent visitors, and Parker all but fell in love with Julia, she was the most poetic woman in the world. One evening Mrs. Howe found herself singing side by side with William Lloyd Garrison, and was astonished at the gentleness and good humor of that saturnine man. Young Frank Sanborn might be here, tall and handsome and eager, brimming over with transcendental enthusiasm, chock-full of anecdotes from Concord. Ellis Gray Loring came, too: a frail little man, but Phillips and Garrison both drew strength from his dauntless spirit and Channing loved him. Sometimes Elizabeth Peabody would bring Horace Mann, who had married her sister, Mary, and Parker came to count him one of the great men of his generation. For the most part the Unitarian clergy steered clear of Exeter Place, but occasionally some of the younger ministers would find their way to Parker's house: Starr King, bright and elfish, whom Parker thought a genius, or Thomas Wentworth Higginson, who was always in and out with some mad scheme, or young Frothingham, down from Salem, and scarcely on speaking terms with his venerable father of the First Church, or Henry Spaulding, in from the Divinity School, who would play Mozart sonatas if you asked for them, or better still "Dundee" or "Brattle Street," or some of Parker's favorite hymns. More often on these Sunday evenings there would be members of the parish: Mrs. Apthorp and her sister Sarah Hunt, or Caroline Dall, who was always bringing presents, Seth Cheney, the artist who had painted the reluctant Lydia, and the indomitable Ednah Cheney, John Manley and John Haynes and Deacon

May, pillars of the Church, Eliza Follen, busy with her books and her philanthropies, and Maria Chapman who helped Garrison edit the *Liberator* and ran the Anti-Slavery Fairs.

Parker's hospitality was warm and generous and a little careless, but Lydia was always there to help him, Lydia so cool and so calm. Parker charged upon his guests, swept them away in a torrent of speech, but Lydia insinuated herself into their hearts. She kept herself in the background, had little to say, but the parlor spoke for her, so clean, so orderly, the flowers on the table, and the mantelpiece crowded with bears, big and little bears, black bears, brown bears, polar bears. She was a little startled, perhaps, by all this hurly-burly of talk, by these great names and great men. She did not pretend to understand these men of the world, these philosophers and scholars, but she saw that they admired Theodore and that was enough. And how he depended on her for sympathy and approval; when she was away he was only half a man, distracted by a thousand trifles, impatient for her return.

His own household was growing, too. There weren't any children, — that was a real sorrow, and he never got over it, — but they had adopted a little boy, George Cabot, a distant cousin of Lydia. Then, just after they moved to Boston, Hannah Stevenson came to live with them. An elderly spinster, depressingly plain, she was, said Parker, "one of the noblest and most intellectual women I have ever met." She was a tart old lady, and some of Parker's friends were afraid of her, but she got along famously with Lydia and was devoted to Theodore, a little jealous of some of the other ladies who fluttered around him, of the Hunt sisters and Caroline Thayer and Matilda Goddard. She helped him with his work, copied his sermons and some of his letters; she was secretary, companion, and housekeeper, all in one, she was indispensable. When Parker was out of town he would write her long letters, on Wordsworth, or Goethe ("she was interested in all the literatures and humanities"), or gossip about people that they knew, or nonsense about his fanciful society, "The Sirti"; and when she was away on one of her frequent vacations, he would write her, "Poor Dear Old Ladye, You don't know how sad all things are here without you. Nothing goes well without you. The birds have forgot half their singing." And he would sign himself "Boo."

He was happy in Boston, but sometimes the city was too much for him, for he was a country boy and a country man. He missed the long walks across the fields and the cattle grazing in the pastures, the familiar trees and the flowers whose appearance he could foretell almost to the day. Then he would hurry out to West Roxbury, to the house on Cottage Street, where he had planted lilies and phlox and marigolds, and where his successor planted only Hunkerism. The house and the church looked different, now, but the countryside was the same and the friendly farmers welcomed him back, and he could go and sit in his favorite seat under the willow trees or gather lady-slippers and forget-me-not in the woods or lie in the long grass until he was drowsy with the fragrance of clover. Every spring he would come out here to see the apple trees in blossom, and he would look to see how it was with those he had grafted. In the summer, when the heat of the city was stifling and even the breezes from the harbor brought no relief, he and Lydia would go out to West Newton, to Lydia's home, and he would gather strength from the soil and learn patience from the cattle and the growing things, and pick cherries in the orchard and remember Lexington.

2

But there was little time for these excursions, and Parker came to begrudge himself his vacations. Boston was not the scholar's paradise West Roxbury had been, and the demands on him were incessant. He had a great parish now, the largest in all Boston, the largest, so it was said, in all America, and his time was not his own. So when he had break-

fasted and said grace, he climbed the three flights of stairs
to his study, and then to work. This was his refuge, his
acropolis. There were letters to read and letters to write,
sermons, lectures, articles and reviews, new books that
clamored for instant attention, old books that had not yet
been read. He had built the bookshelves himself and put
each volume carefully in its proper place; they stretched
from wall to wall, from floor to ceiling, and tumbled out
onto the chairs, the desk, the floor. Over by a window
wreathed in ivy stood his roll-top desk; he liked to sit there
on his cane chair, surrounded by his books and papers and
by tributes of affection: the Parian Christ and the bronze
Spartacus, the leather portfolio, the wicker letter-basket,
the bear-shaped paperweight and the bear-shaped seal, the
delicate porcelain vase, ever bright with flowers, the very
lamp by which he read — all of them gifts from friends.

The basket was always full: letters, letters, letters, they
poured in on him like an avalanche, it was the penalty of
fame, or of notoriety. Here was a letter from a physician
out in Utica, New York, who had just read Parker's essay
on John Quincy Adams and wanted to tell him how well
he liked it; here a letter from Thomas Barnard of Norway,
Maine, who had come across the "Discourse" and had been
converted from Methodism to Natural Religion. Little
Patience Ford of Dorchester was writing him again: this
time it was an unhappy love affair, he must give her what
advice he could. This formal-looking letter was a request
from the lyceum committee of a small town in upstate New
York: would he give them a lecture on some noncontro-
versial subject — "English Literature," or "Plato," or "The
Times"? This envelope with a Charleston postmark would
be abusive, of course; he was used to that. Here was a
young man who wanted to go to college: they must think
that he was as rich as Crœsus, these people; he would do
what he could. A Peter Robertson from Aberdeen, Scotland,
wanted to tell him of his influence there; he had read the
"Discourse," and it opened up a new world of thought —

more valuable than "all the gold of California." It was something to know that he was read in England: his publishers told him that they had disposed of thousands of copies of the "Discourse" in that country.

Some letters he put aside for more careful consideration. Charles Sumner wanted to know his opinion on European law journals: what should he say? Of course Sumner knew about the "Revue de Legislation et de Jurisprudence" which they had at the Athenæum; was he acquainted with the "Kritische Zeitschrift für Rechtswissenschaft und Gesetzgebung"? It was undoubtedly the best of the continental reviews; the Germans always did these things better than the French. Here was a note from young Francis Parkman, whom he remembered from Italy; he had written a book on the "Conspiracy of Pontiac" and was anxious to have Parker's opinion of it. It was a capital book, but it might have been better, much better — a little more critical, more specific, more muscular in style. But this young man would bear watching. And here was a letter from Doctor Francis. A joy to read, these letters from Francis; it was like having the good Doctor here in his study and talking with him about the things that really mattered. Francis wanted to know about the "Evangelium Æternum." Surely he must know Mosheim's account and the references in Fleury, but perhaps he hadn't seen the notes in Gieseler's "Church History" or that monograph by Englehardt, or Grätze's remarks in his "Lehrbuch Allgemeine Litteraturgeschichte" — they could be found in Band II, Abth. 2, 1e. Hälfte. How those Germans wrote! And here was the Honorable John Appleton of the Maine Supreme Court, asking about the Roman law of manumission and the rights of freedmen: had he seen the essay by Pitiscus in the "Lexicon Antiquitatum Romanorum"? It was really much more valuable than the older book by Rosini. Jacobus Cujacius' commentaries on Justinian weren't to be neglected, either, for all that they were published back in 1577.

Many of the letters bore foreign postmarks (George

would like the stamps), for Parker was almost as well known in England and in Germany as in America. How excited he was, that Christmas morning of 1847, when he opened a package and found the German edition of his "Discourse," which Archdeacon Wolff of Kiel had translated. "Is it possible," he asked himself, "that I am henceforth to be a power in the world, to move men, a name which shall kindle men to goodness and piety?" Francis Newman wrote him from England, words of appreciation, but of warning, too. Controversial articles, he said, were all very well, but the pulpit should not be turned into a debating forum, for there is no opportunity for the opposition to hit back. He heard from the Reverend James Martineau, too, who remembered his brief visit, and from a young woman, Frances Cobbe, whose mind was as metaphysical as Margaret Fuller's, and better balanced.

It was a joy when a letter arrived from Neuchâtel, for Desor always had something to say. How he missed the genial Desor, who had come over to help Agassiz in his Lake Superior explorations and had settled down in East Boston. It was George Cabot who had discovered him; he took Uncle Theodore over to see the crabs and echinoderms, and soon Parker and Desor were the dearest of friends. A much greater scientist than the touted Agassiz, Parker thought, and a greater man, too. Agassiz was charming, no doubt, but superficial, no philosopher; his science was written in the spirit of the Bridgewater Treatises. But happy was Desor, for he knew the causes of things. No one better for good talk, his mind stocked with varied and abstruse information, his imagination soaring on splendid flights; no one better as a walking companion — to the White Mountains or the Berkshires. All too soon he had gone back to Combe-Varin, and Parker missed him sorely. They had planned so much together, these two — a trip to Sweden to worship at the shrine of Linnæus, a trip to the tropics where Desor might study his precious sea-urchins and Parker might season his academic interest in anthropology with some first-hand experience. Desor kept his friend informed of all the latest scientific developments on the Continent, and he looked to Parker for the latest information from America, for accounts of the meetings of the Natural History societies, of the progress of science at the universities (very slow, Parker would say), of the work of the state geological surveys, of a hundred and one things that only Parker could be trusted to note.

Parker always fancied himself as a scientist, and Desor indulged him in this conceit and listened to him cheerfully. Parker read Vogt's "Zoologische Briefe" and his "Thierleben," but, he told Desor, he did not think well of them; Vogt's "view of the universe," wrote Parker, "seems to me utterly unscientific." Nor did he think better of Louis Vertisch's "Jüngste Katastrophe des Erdball," or of Dr. Whewell's "Plurality of Worlds." Few scientific works, indeed, met his approval. But had Desor seen the new edition of Carpenter's "Physiology" — "a grand work," which accepted Owen's distinction between the *lover* and the *loved?* And surely he would be interested in Mathieu's "Études cliniques sur les Maladies des Femmes," with its fascinating chapters on hysteria, exaltation, clairvoyance, and all manner of psychological aberrations. He must tell Desor, too, about that last trip to Plymouth, where they noted the curious formations on the sand: what could they be? And his friend Agassiz was attacking spiritualism, in "insolent and boastful language," but there was more in spiritualism, said Parker, than these people knew. The intellectual arrogance of the Cambridge professors was appalling.

Many of the letters were from German scholars, especially after the fiasco of '48. They all wanted to come to America, and they looked to him for aid, but what could he do? There wasn't a university in the whole of America that would have him on its faculty, and his recommendation would be a disfavor to any man. Here was Doctor Fock, a professor of philosophy at the University of Kiel. "If you come," wrote Parker, "we will do all that we can for you, but I am a very unpopular man, and must therefore work for you in secret." Doctor Lobeck of Königsberg, a distinguished classicist, hoped to find a position in this country. Parker had read his book on the "Ionic Question," and thought well of it, and he wrote to Professor Felton of Harvard: "Can you help a poor man to any place where he can get bread for himself, his *liebliche Frau* and *drei Kinder?* It is a hard case, and one that touches my heart most tenderly." Felton had treated him shamefully, and Parker hated to approach him this way, but this was no time to remember personal differences. Perhaps Bancroft would be more sympathetic: here was a Doctor Günther from Leipzig, a philologist and an historian, who had been eking out a living in Boston by giving lessons in Icelandic and Gothic. He had helped Parker polish up his Danish and Icelandic, but he needed something more substantial than the little that Parker could give him — couldn't Bancroft help, Bancroft whose word went so far? There were others, too. Doctor Edouard Pelz, a refugee of '48, wanted literary work, and was finally taken care of in New York — Ripley was helpful there. The Reverend Friedrich Munch was looking for an American publisher for a capital volume on religion — could Parker help, Parker who had difficulty in finding a publisher for his own volumes on religion? And something must be done for old Doctor Füster, a rare scholar and a rare friend, as fat as a beer barrel, his heart bursting with kindliness. He gave hours in German, in Russian, in Polish, in anything that one wanted, for he was a manifold linguist; in his spare time he translated Parker's sermons.

Often these men would come to his study, for they found Parker a congenial companion, astonishingly familiar with just the things that interested them most, and he was generous with his library. Then they would sit late and talk of the Homeric question (Parker had his own theories about that), or of the new German dictionary that the Grimm brothers were preparing, or of poor Delia Bacon and her mania about the authorship of Shakespeare's plays, or of the project for a public library in Boston which the Frenchman M. Vattemare had launched and which was already commanding such support.

It was not only scholars, however, who came to the crowded study in Exeter Place; everyone made free of it, and of his time. Students from Harvard or from the Divinity School came to get advice, and sometimes more substantial aid; friends from the West, who had read his sermons, wished to see him in person, to lay their doubts before him and catch something of his own conviction. Methodist and Baptist clergymen came to pray for him that he might see the error of his ways; the poor and the halt and the blind came for help — a laborer out of work, a newly arrived immigrant who found Boston too crowded and wanted to go West, an abandoned wife looking for her husband, fugitive slaves who wanted a hiding place, friends from West Roxbury, their arms full of lilacs or daisies from the meadows, to tell him how they missed him out there. Sometimes he jotted down in his Journal: —

Adventures of a Day — After attending to numerous little matters, I sat down to complete my sermon; and there came, 1. A black man — a quite worthy one — for some pecuniary aid. 2. An Orthodox minister from Ohio, seeking aid to erect a free church in his State. He wants five thousand dollars . . . 3. Came a clergyman to talk about the Zoroastrian doctrine of the immortality of the soul, and to get Oporin's *De Immortalitate Mortalium*, which I had imported for him. 4. Silas Lamson, with his full beard and white garments. He has two machines which he wished me to look at. They are to facilitate spading, ploughing, etc. He wants to get them before the Exhibition in New York. 5. Mrs. M.—— relative to Ned and the medicine we sent him yesterday. 6. Greeley Curtis, just from Rome, and now for California . . . a brave good fellow. 7. Dear Mrs. Russell came at five, and staid till nine. She consecrated the first introduction of gas into the house; so the light of the house and the light of the heart burns at the same time.

How good Sally Russell was, coming all the way in from West Roxbury, with news of George and of the children, her arms full of flowers and preserves; she was his closest link with West Roxbury now that the Shaws had moved on to New York. He was singularly blessed in his friends, especially in his women friends. There was Sarah Hunt, and her sister, Mrs. Apthorp; Sarah was in for tea almost every day (Hannah didn't like it at all), and when the sisters went off to Europe for three years, Parker was desolate. There was Caroline Thayer, one of that "glorious phalanx of old maids," who was always busy with parish work; she had no use for girls, but any boy was divine. There was Matilda Goddard and her sister Rebecca, — saints, both of them, — and Caroline Dall, who had the courage to rebuke him when he was bitter or cantankerous, and Ednah Cheney and wonderful Julia Howe, and a score of others. How was it that his dearest friends were women? Much as he loved Ripley and Desor and Francis and Andrews and Silsbee and Lyman, he never achieved with them the intimacy, the intuitive understanding, that he had with these women. It was not that they gave him intellectual stimulus; he was not overly fond of strong-minded women like Margaret Fuller, or Sarah Ripley. No, it was not easy to understand. "I wonder at this," he confessed to his Journal, "I never willed it so. I have always been intimate with eminent women, and I number few eminent men among my acquaintances. Yet in literature I am no great admirer of women. Is it their affection or their beauty of mind that attracts me to them? I love to look at a handsome woman. I love the subtlety of woman's mind. I like not this dazzling subtlety in men."

How fortunate he was, in Lydia, in his friends, in his work. Sometimes, self-consciously, he would remember that he was ostracized by his fellow-clergyman and snubbed by Boston society, but even that gave him a sort of satisfaction — smug, unworthy, but there it was. Perhaps Howe was right, after all, in warning him against this tendency to be supersensitive, to exaggerate slights and imagine affronts and dwell on his sad lot. He was becoming ingrown, introspective, vain. Sometimes he would write, "I am the best hated man in the land"; sometimes he would write, "My life is a singularly happy one." Better put aside this adolescent concern with his own state, with the opinion of men and of society. What had he to do with the opinion of men? Better to go about his business. He had work to do.

3

Sunday after Sunday the great hall of the Melodeon was crowded as Parker preached the cardinal tenets of his faith: Natural Religion, the Infinite Perfection of God, the Adequacy of Man for all his functions. From all parts of the city, from the outlying towns, men and women thronged to the forbidding building on Washington Street; there were seven thousand names on the parish register, but the hall could not house one third of that number, and eventually they had to move to larger quarters. A gloomy place, the Melodeon, unkempt and stuffy, hot in the summer and cold in the winter, the feeble light filtering through the narrow windows, but Parker always loved it and the very stains on the walls came to be dear to him. Here he had come that first dark Sunday in February, 1845, when every other hall in Boston was closed to him; the rain and the sleet had beat down on the roof and turned the snow to slush while he preached on "The Indispensableness of True Religion for Man's Welfare." It was a queer congregation that met to hear him each Sunday morning: men and women from all classes, but mostly the humblest, men and women who had never gone to church before, or who had drifted away from their orthodox moorings and hoped to find refuge here, reformers, zealots, and fanatics, strangers curious to hear the notorious heretic, critics solicitous for new blasphemies, here and there a reporter from the newspapers, in the galleries a liberal sprinkling of Negroes, and on the platform the friends whose generous support kept the whole thing going — Deacon May and Deacon Goddard and Deacon Haynes, the Lymans, the Dalls, the Apthorps, the Jacksons, and a dozen more. How different it all was from West Roxbury, where he had known every man and women and child in his parish, worried over their problems and shared in their plans. How different this vast Music Hall from the trim white meetinghouse on Spring Street with its slender white steeple pointing so confidently to heaven; here the atmosphere was painfully secular, and often, as he came on the platform, he would see on the floor beside him the spangles of the dancers who had performed on the stage during the week. He had hated to give up his Spring Street church, and for a year he had carried the double burden of the city and the country parish, but it was too much for him. Here in Boston he had tried to keep as many of the customs of the New England church as he could: he had inaugurated a Sunday school, but it was not a success; he had organized Sunday afternoon meetings for free discussion, but these were spoiled by outsiders who loved argument overmuch; he had taught a class in Biblical criticism, but his teaching was too learned, and the class petered out.

It was his preaching that men wanted to hear, and into his sermons went all that was best of his learning, his philosophy and his wit. There was nothing haphazard about them; they were blocked out months, sometimes years, in advance, with a view to canvassing the whole moral and intellectual character of man; they constituted a course of lectures on philosophy that was coherent and logical, and their continuity was broken only by the most pressing of interruptions. Into their preparation went an immense labor, but he wrote them swiftly, his pen racing over the pages in a hopeless effort to keep pace with the thoughts, resorting to desperate expedients of shorthand and hieroglyphics which only he could read. Strong, muscular sermons, crammed with facts and figures, closely reasoned, they made few concessions to mental indolence, and they took

THEODORE PARKER

LYDIA PARKER

MARGARET FULLER OSSOLI
From a daguerreotype

ELIZABETH PEABODY

From a portrait in the possession of the Elizabeth
Peabody House, Boston

OLD BOSTON MUSIC HALL, WHERE PARKER PREACHED

VIEW OF SUMMER STREET

Showing the Meeting-house of the New South Society, designed by
Bulfinch on Church Green

THEODORE PARKER'S STUDY

GEORGE RIPLEY

WILLIAM ELLERY CHANNING

WILLIAM LLOYD GARRISON AND
WENDELL PHILLIPS

T. W. HIGGINSON, AET. 20

From a crayon drawing by Eastman Johnson

CAUTION!!
COLORED PEOPLE
OF BOSTON, ONE & ALL,

You are hereby respectfully CAUTIONED and advised, to avoid conversing with the

Watchmen and Police Officers of Boston,

For since the recent ORDER OF THE MAYOR & ALDERMEN, they are empowered to act as

KIDNAPPERS
AND
Slave Catchers,

And they have already been actually employed in KIDNAPPING, CATCHING, AND KEEPING SLAVES. Therefore, if you value your LIBERTY, and the *Welfare of the Fugitives* among you, *Shun* them in every possible manner, as so many *HOUNDS* on the track of the most unfortunate of your race.

Keep a Sharp Look Out for KIDNAPPERS, and have TOP EYE open.

APRIL 24, 1851.

THEODORE PARKER PLACARD

Placard written by Parker and printed and posted by the Vigilance Committee after Thomas Sims had been returned to slavery

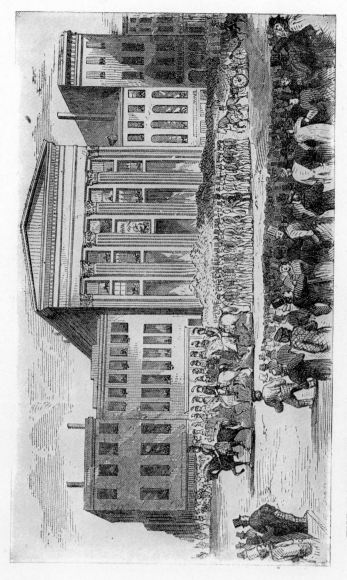

THE MARSHAL'S HORSE, WITH ANTHONY BURNS, MOVING DOWN STATE STREET

SAMUEL G. HOWE

CHARLES SUMNER

From a Cameo, Rome, 1859

THEODORE PARKER, 1859

sometimes an hour in the reading, sometimes more. They dealt with the present, not the past, with concrete problems, not with abstractions of dogma, with the sins of Boston, not of Babylon. Learned and logical, yet they were meant for the ear rather than for the eye; the language was that of the farm and the home and the street, the figures of speech homely and idiomatic, the illustrations drawn from things intimate and familiar. He spoke not of the Ægean but of Cape Cod, the Charles River was better than the Jordan, and while men could see Monadnock why tell of Lebanon? How much simpler to remind men of the whippoorwill than of the nightingale, the apple tree than the olive, and the lilacs of New England were as fragrant as the roses of Sharon. This was what Parker admired in Emerson, this sturdy Americanism; the Concord philosopher had his roots in his own soil. This was what he admired in Luther, that he did not disdain the speech of the common man, but made it a mighty vehicle for religious truth. And was he not the Emerson of the new religion, the Luther of the new Reformation, his walk, too, with the humble?

And how becoming the speech to the man! He stood there on the platform, simple, unaffected, a stocky, ungainly figure in black broadcloth, a little awkward, but never ill at ease, his great Socrates-like head almost bald, his features plain, yet with a certain beauty, and when he folded his hands in prayer you could see that they had guided a plow. He had dignity, and strength, but none of the grace of an Everett or the magnificence of a Sumner; he was no orator, he put no pebbles in his mouth, it was the message that counted, and he read his sermons slowly and earnestly. Lowell heard him, and drew him with sure pen: —

There he stands looking more like a ploughman than priest,
If not dreadfully awkward, not graceful at least,
His gestures all downright and same, if you will,
As of brown-fisted Hobnail in hoeing a drill;
But his periods fall on you, stroke after stroke,

Like the blows of a lumberer felling an oak,
You forget the man wholly, you're thankful to meet
With a preacher who smacks of the field and the street.

There was a ruggedness, a rusticity, about him, but no
diffidence, no servility. In his sermons he took high ground;
not the successor of Saint Peter spoke with more authority,
for he felt that his was the ultimate authority of truth.
His conception of the function of a minister was an exalted
one: the minister was to elevate by his character, instruct
by his wisdom, inspire by his piety. He must command
the respect of all men and their confidence; in all good
works, in all reforms, he must lead the way. Neither Church
nor State, neither laws nor opinion, could impose on him;
he was no apologist, but a judge, and he passed in review
all merely human institutions. He was to see to it that the
science of society kept pace with the advance of mechanical and physical sciences; he was to supply the leadership, he was to assume the authority. It was a staggering
responsibility, but it was not to be evaded. Not as an individual, but as a spokesman, he was to be the conscience of
his generation.

But this position was not to be reached by mere learning
and argument, and there was more than that to Parker's
sermons. It was not his learning that attracted Julia Ward
Howe and Louisa Alcott and Ednah Cheney; they had
learning of their own. Religion, after all, was not an intellectual exercise; that was the trouble with the Unitarians,
they had formalized their faith, intellectualized their religion, made it a bundle of pale negations. Unitarianism
had dignity and austerity, but no passion. But religion was
an emotion, an affair of the heart as well as of the head, it
was an inspiration, a magnificent affirmation. It proclaimed
the divinity of man and the surpassing beauty of nature;
it taught the delights of piety, and gave transcendental
assurance of immortality. These were not dogmas to be

insinuated with subtlety and learning; they were great intuitive truths that burned their way into the consciousness
of men. And Parker preached sermons reminiscent, in their
power, their piety, their imagery, of Taylor and Edwards;
even the titles suggested a richer, a more abundant philosophy than was to be found among the Unitarians: "Of Piety
and the Relation thereof to Manly Life," "Of Conscious
Religion as a Source of Strength," "Of the Grandeur and
the Beauty of Man," "Of Beauty in the World of Matter
Considered as a Revelation of God." How he rejoiced in the
consciousness of the infinite perfection of God, of his infinite mercy and compassion and understanding; how he
delighted in the promise of the divinity of Man, a promise
fulfilled in the person of Christ and to be fulfilled for all
mankind; with what rapture he told of the beauty of Nature
in all her forms. He found beauty everywhere, beauty and
joy and order: in the voiceless fish, white-fleshed and bloodless, moving with the flapping of the sea; in the snake, symbol of evil, basking delighted in the sun, and the frog
croaking happily in the pond; in the new-born calf opening its eyes to the world, and in the matronly cow ruminat-
ing beside her playful calves.

Even animals we think austere and sad, the lonely hawk, the
solitary jay, who loves New England winters, and the innumerable shellfish, have their personal and domestic joy. The toad
whom we vilify as ugly and even call venomous, malicious, and
spiteful, is a kind neighbour and seems as contented as the day
is long. So it is with the spider who is not the malignant kidnapper that he is thought, but has a little, harmless world of
joy . . . Go into the fields, at morning, noon, or night, and all
creation is a-hum with happiness, the young and old, the rep-
tile, insect, beast, and fowls of heaven rejoice in their brave
delight. All about us is full of joy, fuller than we notice. Take
a handful of water from the rotting timbers of a wharf; little
polyps are therein, medusae and the like, with few senses, few
faculties; but they all swim in a tide of joy, and it seems as
if the world was made for them alone.

So, too, in the vegetable kingdom: the water-lilies lie on the surface of the pond, white and gold and green, and along its edge blossom the arrowhead and the cardinal and the pickerel-weed and the honeysuckle, sprouting bravely out of the swamp. And the commonest things have loveliness and grace, the grass springing up even in the cracks of cobblestones, the golden wheat and the bearded oats and the tall corn with its silken tassels, the potatoes lying in heaps in the fields, wet earth still sticking to their sides, the reds and yellows and russet browns of apples, and the varicolored grape.

These things he preached, for he rejoiced in Nature and gloried in Man, and for these things he gave thanks in prayer. Simple and devout, his prayers had a warmth, a passionate sincerity, that was singularly moving. Not even the gorgeous Easter service at St. Peter's in Rome, wrote Julia Howe, impressed her as did Parker's prayers; and to little Louisa Alcott, setting out on her career, they came as a consecration. Years later, she remembered the slow folding of the hands and the reverent bowing of the gray head, and the voice veiled in tears as he prayed to Our Father and Our Mother God, and gave thanks for the beauty of the physical world and the goodness of man. "Like spring rains on new ploughed fields," she wrote, "came mercy after justice."

CHAPTER VII

THE INTELLECTUAL GOURMAND

HE was still determined to be a scholar. He knew that he could not be a power for good unless he had both knowledge and wisdom, and when he wrote that tribute to Doctor Channing he described the ideal minister as master of the greatest subjects of human thought, familiar with history and philosophy and poetry, understanding the nature of man and of society. He remembered well that his teachers in the Divinity School had prophesied for him a career of scholarship, and he had already done something to justify that prophecy. But so many of the young theologians from Cambridge had embarked hopefully upon the seas of learning only to founder: some chose the softer ways and were becalmed in the Sargasso Sea; some went adrift on the rocks of controversy; some were driven far off their course by trade winds. How few there were who held steadily to their chosen ways: you could count on the fingers of one hand the real scholars among the Unitarians; and they had always been so proud of their scholarship, too, looking down their noses at the plebeian denominations. There was Doctor Francis, of course; and Noyes, and Lamson, and Furness down in Philadelphia, and Hedge in Providence. But who else was there? Andrews Norton had shot his bolt, such as it was, and nothing more could be expected of him; Palfrey had abandoned his Jewish Antiquities for the more glittering rewards of politics; Frothingham and Gannett, trained to exact scholarship, were hedged in by their theological preconceptions, lacked boldness of thought and of inquiry; Bellows, who had great gifts, was really but a showman, young Higginson was a popularizer, a dilettante in religion as in letters, and so too James Freeman Clarke.

Who else was there, indeed, but Parker himself? In breadth of intellect, in range of information, in catholicity of interests, he stood alone. His training was thorough, his equipment complete, his standards high, and to these qualities he added acuteness of understanding, boldness of thought and incisiveness of speech, indefatigable industry and inexhaustible energy. He had these talents, and he knew that they carried with them responsibilities. Never was religion more in need of scholarship, the Church of learning. Unitarianism could not find refuge in authority, as other Churches could; transcendentalism had abandoned dogma and creed, and the truths of that Natural Religion which Parker preached were to be authenticated by science and demonstrated by history. There was none more zealous to hold fast to what was true, but he could not forget the injunction first to prove all things.

To his books, then; he had so little time, and every minute was important; it was no wonder that Phillips, when he came home late from some lecture, would see the light burning in the study of Number 1 Exeter Place. There was everything to do, and he was not dismayed; his ambition was colossal, his appetite omnivorous, he wasn't happy unless he was buried in work. He was going to write an "Introduction to the New Testament," a continuation of the book by De Wette; he was going to write a "History of the Development of Religion"; he was going to write a "History of the Reformation"; he was going to write a "History of Religious Thought since the Reformation." What was he not going to write? Enthusiastic Thomas Wentworth Higginson came up from Worcester with a proposal for a series of volumes on religious history and philosophy; no subject was mentioned but what Parker had already accumulated material for just such a volume himself, and the project fell through.

There was everything to be done, but he was no dilettante, he had no use for the superficial tracts and homilies that passed for scholarship among those who knew no better, no use for those adventitious essays and critiques, inspired by an anxiety to get into print, that sprouted in every review. Scholarship, he felt, was nothing to be trifled with. Its basis should be broad, its roots should be deep, it must embody painstaking research, it must represent a reasoned philosophy. The Germans knew these things, and that was why every book worth reading was written by a German. None so learned as these Germans, so thorough, so patient, so subtle, so profound; they were the teachers of all the world, they set the standards, furnished the examples. Whatever it was you wanted to know, the Germans had the answer; they stalked their prey remorselessly, and when they got it, they embalmed it in four or five big volumes, and there was no more hunting in that wood.

He knew. He had all their books, row after row of them, from floor to ceiling of his study, decorously bound in black and brown, the gilt-lettered *Band* and *Abtheilung* and *Hälfte* certifying to the thoroughness of the job. Back in Brook Farm days Parker had bought Ripley's library of German literature; he had not neglected the bookstalls of Paris and Frankfurt and Leipzig, and every mail, now, brought new accessions to swell the richest and most varied private library in the whole of New England. There were handsomer libraries, to be sure, — Ticknor's or Everett's or Crowninshield's, — but his was the real thing, a library made for work. The books sprawled over on to the floor, crowded on to the great oaken table (great-grandfather Parker hadn't meant it for that, when he made it), flooded out of the study and down the stairs, swarmed up into the attic, filled the closets, the bedrooms and the parlor. There were thousands and thousands of them, stately folios and fat substantial quartos and plebeian octavos, but he knew them all, and he would write, when he was away: "Go to the case next the fireplace, the third shelf from the bottom, it is a small brown book" — and there it would be, sure enough.

There was everything here, standard works and obscure volumes, sets and monographs, fiction and poetry, sermons and tracts, and the serried volumes of the learned societies, but they all had their place, they all earned their keep. This library was no vanity, no showroom; he had no hankering for first editions, no money for fine bindings. It was the library of a worker, not of an antiquarian or a bibliophile. It filled his needs, it revealed his hopes and confessed his fancies, it told the biography of his mind.

Parker remembered always that trip to Boston when he had bought his first book out of the proceeds of berry-picking. He was eleven, then, and many years had passed, and he had many rare books, but Ainsworth's "Latin Dictionary" was still the most cherished of them all. The choice, too, came to seem prophetic of his later interests: his library was rich in dictionaries and glossaries. He could never resist the challenge of a new language, the fascination of a strange vocabulary; and the well-thumbed volumes bore witness that his linguistic achievements were prodigious; even the African dialects were represented. Nor had he been unfaithful to his youthful love for the literatures of Greece and Rome: here were the sets of Suetonius and Polybius, Pindar and Juvenal and Pliny and Livy, as well as the more obvious Plutarch and Plato, Herodotus and Thucydides, Aristotle, and Æschylus, Euripides, and Aristophanes, Horace and Tacitus, Vergil and Cicero, and all the rest of them — well used, annotated. He seldom embellished his writing with quotations from the classics, but his Journal attested his study of the Homeric question, his unabated interest in Plato and Neo-Platonism, his priggish dislike for the licentiousness of Aristophanes, his enthusiasm for the ethics of Pindar or of Æschylus, and John King of Salem remembered that Parker was the one man with whom it was possible to argue intelligently a disputed reading in a Greek play.

When it came to theology, he had almost as many books as Doctor Francis himself; it was here that he expected to do his own work, and he wanted his materials at hand. There were over a hundred editions of the Bible, innumerable commentaries and glossaries, hundreds of learned German monographs and dissertations, cheek by jowl with the pious volumes of the Church Fathers. Here were the two hundred volumes of the "Patrologia Latina," the "Maxima Bibliotheca Veterum patrum," the "Annales Ecclesiastici," Mabillon's "Annales ordinis S. Benedicti," and here, too, the sources of Protestant history, the writings of Luther and Calvin and of the English churchmen. It was in Parker's study that young Octavius Frothingham made the acquaintance of the Tübingen School of theology; it was here that he found the *Theologische Jahrbücher* and read them clean through; the result was well-nigh fatal to his orthodoxy.

Comparative religion was not neglected, and a sizeable collection of volumes on heresies and persecutions and martyrdom, on witchcraft and magic and the occult, showed his interest in the dangerous subject of religious psychology. Here was the "Dictionnaire Infernale," the "Directorium Inquisitorium," Bodin's "De la Demonomanie des Sorcères," Johannis Nideri's "De visionibus ac revelationibus," the "Geschichte der Deutschen Geistlichkeit im Mittelalter," and the inevitable Fox, illustrated with those dreadful woodcuts that had terrified generations of children. Here was ammunition for those sermons on the popular theology, on superstition, on the errors of the Church; here was vindication of his own heresies and the heresies and vagaries of his friends. No wonder he was inclined to sympathize with mysticism and pantheism and thought that spiritualism might well become the religion of the future.

He had a passion for the universal; his critics charged him with an affectation of omniscience, and his shelves were loaded with monumental encyclopædias and the publications of learned societies; he could get along without the Athenæum if he wanted to. There were a hundred and fifty volumes of the "Allgemeine Encyclopædie" and sets of the "Biographie

Universelle" and the "Allgemeine Deutsche Bibliothek" and the "Encyclopædie der Wissenschaft und Kunst" were almost as imposing. Literature was represented by the "Bibliothek des Literarischen Vereins in Stuttgart," and the "Heidelberger Jahrbücher der Literatur"; history by the gigantic "Monumenta Germanica Historica," and the "Corpus Scriptorum Historiæ Byzantiæ," and LeBeau's many-volumed "Historie des Bas-Empire," and even a few American sets were allowed to joggle their way in between the French and the German. The collections of the American Antiquarian Society were there, and the volumes of the Massachusetts Historical Society — of which he was not a member.

But these were merely the general works of reference, such things as everyone would have to have. It was not on these that Parker relied for that astonishing fund of information with which he weighted his sermons and his lectures and his letters. Scarcely an historian, ancient or modern, eminent or obscure, but found lodgement on those shelves. Here they all were, the great Greeks and the lesser Romans, the mediæval chroniclers and the Renaissance scholars, the ponderous Germans, the polished but partisan French, the English from Camden to Carlyle, the Americans from Bradford to Bancroft, their narratives big with the moral of liberty: it was upon these that Parker drew for those essays on Prescott and Macaulay and Buckle and Hildreth that looked so learned. The writings of the Fathers were here too — annotated and digested: Sparks' "Washington" and "Franklin," and the new editions of John Adams and of Jefferson; every page of those essays on "Historic Americans" showed how carefully he had read these sources.

No one believed more devoutly in the Higher Law; no one knew more thoroughly what was the law. He had thought to be a lawyer (how long ago that was!), but he had felt even then that there was too great a gap between law and morals and that all too often the study of law quickened the wits at the expense of the heart; when lawyers pled the fugitive slave law and judges sent Negroes back to slavery he knew that his misgivings had been right. But he still fancied himself as a lawyer. He read all the law journals, and told Sumner which ones were the best; he studied the law of freedom and of bondage and could tell you offhand just what the provisions were in the Roman law or the Salic law; and when he was put on trial for violation of the Fugitive Slave Bill, he undertook his own defense. Here in the library were his juristic credentials: the "English State Trials" (he gave them to Hale, but Hale gave them back), Campbell's "Lives of the Chief Justices," — there was the whole story of judicial tyranny — , the immense "Parliamentary History of England," a file of Savigny's "Zeitschrift," the "Collectanea Juridicæ," a shelf of the "Jurisprudence Musselmane" and another of the "Corpus Juris Germanici Publici ac Privati." He used them, too; in a single reference in his "Defence" he noted "the well-known" works of Grimm, Rogge, Biener, Michelsen, Möser, Phillips, Eichhorn, and Maurer — and most of them were on his shelves.

Desor's influence was here, too; Parker liked to show him his latest acquisitions in science. It was vanity, perhaps; what other clergyman read the reports of the scientific expeditions or the transactions of European scientific societies; who else was familiar with Humboldt and Lyell and Vogt; who but he dared to be critical of Agassiz? His library embraced all the sciences: zoölogy, geology, botany (that was his favorite), mineralogy, paleontology, anthropology, even a little chemistry and physics. He used these books, too; it was a satisfaction to be able to sustain his philosophical theory of evolution with evidence from the exact sciences, and when he preached those sermons on "The Testimony of Matter to the Existence of God," he put on such a show as Agassiz might have envied. And what fun it was, when he visited Desor at Combe-Varin, to be able to meet all of those distinguished scientists on their own ground!

But the library was not all heavy going; there were grace notes too. He read poetry, though he rarely quoted it, and in his letters he liked to try his hand at criticism, or, better yet, to dash off some poetry of his own, or translations from Heine or from Paul Gerhardt. He had thought, once, to edit Shakespeare's sonnets, and the poems of George Herbert, but these plans he put aside, and it was just as well. His taste was changing, now; he missed the ethical element in Shakespeare and found much to underline in Wordsworth and Browning and Keats. He wrote charmingly of ballad literature and built up an extensive collection of folksongs and popular tales. There was little time for novels, but Richardson and Fielding and Smollett described for him the society of the eighteenth century as Dickens did the nineteenth, and his set of the Waverley Novels might have told him more about the mind of the South than did the well-read stories of Mrs. Stowe or the travel books of Olmstead. He found little time for the theater, but he owned Bell's "British Theatre" and the works of most of the English and French dramatists; the last year of his life he was busy catching up on Molière, whom he had somehow missed. He could ornament his lyceum lectures with stories culled from Walpole's "Royal and Noble Authors" or from the "Anecdotes of English Painters." He had visited faithfully the museums of the Old World, and he would listen hopefully to music, but he made no effort to pretend to an interest that he did not feel, and the library was richer in everything else, even in science, than it was in the arts.

What a collection it was, and how he loved it. It was not for himself alone that he was building up this library; it was for the men and women of Boston, for he had already decided that it was to go, after his death, not to Harvard College but to the new public library. Many of the volumes had been acquired only after years of search. In the flyleaf of Alexander Murray's "History of the European Languages" he wrote, "I had long been looking for a copy of this curious book, which I borrowed years ago and studied, when I found it advertised in a newspaper published in Charleston, S. C., and sent to me that I might profit by a violent and abusive article against me. *Fas est et ab hoste doceri.*" In his copy of the 1535 edition of "Claudii Ptolemaei Alexandrini Geographicae Enarrationis" he had written: "I received this long-sought volume on the seventy-ninth anniversary of the Battle of Lexington. It is the edition of Michael Servetus." And one long-sought volume by a Dutchman, Nieuwendt on "The Existence of God," he found only a few months before his death: he needed it for a book of sermons that he was going to get out soon.

But he couldn't buy everything he wanted, and he passed up many of the choicest items in the auction catalogues because they were too costly. The money earned in lecturing he set aside for books, but there were many unforeseen inroads upon this capital — the needs of fugitive slaves or of young men eager to go to college were far more compelling than the needs of his library. It was just as well. He had too many books rather than too few. They tempted him and distracted him, they dissipated his energies and his thought. "I think your love of learning is a passion," John Dwight had written him years before, "that it injures your mind by converting insensibly what is originally a pure thirst for truth into a greedy, avaricious, jealous striving, not merely to know but to get all there is to be known," and the prophecy was fulfilled. Parker had heard Emerson lecture on "The American Scholar," but he did not remember Emerson's warning that "Man thinking must not be subdued by his instruments." He was in danger of forgetting that he was a transcendentalist, for what need did a transcendentalist have for this mountain of facts? He did not concentrate, he did not discriminate; he was becoming an intellectual gourmand, and he was threatened with the consequences of gluttony.

Yet it was a virtue, too, this massive accumulation, this ambition for omniscience, and in keeping with his character. He was not niggardly of himself, he would not bury his

talents nor even invest them, and there was something attractive about his extravagance. He could not concentrate,
life would not let him concentrate; not for him the serene
aloofness of the Seer of Concord. His study was no ivory
tower, sacred to philosophy, but a workshop, the atmosphere
electric with emotion and passion, its windows fronting on
the hurrying town, its doors open to every democratic idea.

2

"I hope," Parker wrote, shortly after he had settled at
Exeter Place, "for the next five or six years to have less to do
with social, civil, and political duties, and attend to my
function as scholar, philosopher, theologian, and writer."
Soon the slave power was to invade New England and slaves
were to be hunted in the streets of Boston town, but there
were a few years of relative calm, and Parker attended to his
function as scholar, philosopher, theologian, and writer. But
he felt keenly the want of a vehicle for his scholarship, an
organ for his opinions. The *Dial* was gone; it had been too
esoteric, too ethereal, wanting in masculine vigor, but for all
its limitations it had welcomed his contributions, and he realized now that there was nothing to take its place. There was
the *North American,* of course; Francis Bowen was editor,
now, the same who had put Mr. Emerson in his place on the
occasion of the Divinity School Address, and the magazine
was more conservative than ever: it made you feel like an
old man just to look at it. Brownson's *Quarterly* had once
competed with the *Dial,* but the acrobatic Brownson had
gone over to Rome and taken his journal with him. New
York had its *Knickerbocker* and Philadelphia *Graham's* —
but what transcendentalist cared to contribute to them?

"We need a new periodical," Parker wrote. "We want a
tremendous journal, with ability in its arms and piety in
its heart." It was to be literary, philosophical, poetical, theological, religious, what was it not to be? It was to have all
of the literary quality of the *Dial,* and something more; the
Dial with a beard, Parker said, and when he wrote Mar-

tineau about it, that wise man agreed with him. "May it last longer than the *Dial*," said Martineau, "and be a little more acceptable to plebeian apprehensions like mine." Soon Parker broached the subject to Sam Howe, to Sumner, to Phillips, and Emerson came to see him about it. How to find the right man to edit the new journal, that was the problem. Parker would not thrust himself forward, he did not wish to be conspicuous, to blight the magazine with his own theological odium. Would Emerson take over the editorial duties? No, Emerson would not; he shuddered to think of the trouble the *Dial* had given him. They agreed that Charles Sumner was the man for the job, and forthwith Sumner was sounded, but he too refused. Parker was getting impatient. A council was held at Emerson's house; Parker was there, and Howe, and Emerson's friend J. E. Cabot, and Margaret Fuller of course, and young Henry Thoreau, who looked disdainful. All were agreed on the necessity of a new journal, all but Thoreau, who was so impolite as to ask whether anyone present had ever found difficulty in publishing in the existing journals whatever he had to say.

But this objection was brushed aside, and in the summer of 1847 the new journal was launched, and it was named *The Massachusetts Quarterly Review*. Parker and Cabot assumed the editorial duties, and Emerson, too, though his sole contribution was an editorial address. It was an excellent address, it struck just the right note, typically Emersonian, yet as vigorous as anything that Parker himself could have written. "Where is the great breath of the New World," he asked, "the voice of aboriginal nations opening new eras with hymns of lofty cheer? Our books and fine arts are imitations; there is a fatal incuriosity and disinclination in our educated men to new studies and the interrogation of Nature. We have taste, critical talent, good professors, good commentators, but a lack of male energy. . . . The moral influence of the intellect is wanting. We hearken in vain for any profound voice speaking to the American heart, cheering timid good men, animating the youth, consoling the defeated, and intelligently announcing duties which clothe life with joy and endear the face of land and sea to men."

Emerson wrote the editorial address, and he was through; Cabot did nothing; so the whole of the editorial duties fell upon Parker, and he was ready enough to assume them, though in the end he confessed, a little sadly, "I was never a fit person to edit the *Quarterly*." Yet he went about the task systematically enough. He drew up lists of potential contributors: "Certain and valuable: Emerson, Weiss, Cabot, W. H. Channing, Shedd. Valuable but not certain: Giddings, Palfrey, S. C. Phillips, Ripley, Hawthorne, J. P. Hale." And a third list — "Certain but not valuable: William Ellery Channing, Thoreau, *et. id. genus omne*, Margaret."

Some of these failed him. Emerson, for example, wrote nothing but a brief notice of Clough's poems. Yet the list of contributors was impressive enough: Henry James, Wendell Phillips, Samuel Gridley Howe and Julia Ward Howe, Richard Hildreth, James Russell Lowell, and T. W. Higginson, and a half-dozen Englishmen and Germans besides. A heterogeneous group: they were not all transcendentalists, not by far; they represented a much more varied opinion than had the contributors to the *Dial*.

The *Quarterly* ranged over a wide variety of subjects, but its interests were mostly social. It grappled with the problems of the day, its concern was more largely with politics and economics than with literature or criticism. "Can it front this matter of Socialism?" Emerson had asked, in his address. "Will it cope with the allied questions of Government, Nonresistance, and all that belongs under that category? Will it measure itself with the chapter on Slavery? . . . Here is the great problem of Natural Science, and the merits of her great interpreters to be determined. Will it venture into the thin and difficult air of that school where the secrets of structure are discussed under the topics of mesmerism and the twilights of demonology?" Difficult questions for Emerson to ask, especially when he left the answering to others, but Parker answered them all in the affirmative. Almost every number of the *Quarterly* contained an article on some phase of the slavery question, and so pressing were political issues that the editor left untouched many of those philosophical and literary themes which he had hoped to present. Articles on Swedenborg and on Mesmerism were sympathetic enough, even for Emerson, and more space was found for contributions to science than for theology. Literature was by no means neglected: there were appreciations of Landor and of Keats, of Browning and of Clough, critical essays on Emerson and Thoreau and Hawthorne, and the heavy pages were decorated with a smattering of poetry.

Many of the articles were Parker's, for despite the coöperation of friends in America and Europe, from first to last it was Parker's magazine. It was Parker who found the authors, edited the articles, and filled the empty spaces with his own writing. He prepared an article for each of the twelve numbers, and made himself responsible besides for a good many of the brief notices and reviews. He had the usual trials of an editor: Lowell was right when he warned him, "Your experience as an editor will bring you nearer orthodoxy by convincing you of the total depravity of contributors." There were procrastinating authors, authors who failed him, authors who couldn't write. Lowell himself was bad enough, and Parker had to hammer away at him to get his article, but Lowell was unperturbed. "Your note," he wrote, impudently enough, "was so illegible that I was unable to make out that part of it in which you reproached me for my remissness. I shall choose rather to treasure it as containing I know not what commendations of my promptitude and punctuality. I will have it framed and glazed and exhibit it to editors inquiring my qualifications, as the enthusiastic testimony of the Rev. Theo. Parker, and fearlessly defy all detection."

He had to face questions of good taste as well as of politics or society: it was not every editor of the forties who would have printed Doctor Loring's review of "The Scarlet Letter" (a book, said Orestes Brownson, which should never have been written). "We forget," wrote the versatile Doctor Loring, "that what society calls chastity is often far the reverse, and that a violation of this perverted virtue may be a sad, sorrowful, and tearful beauty, which we would silently and reverently contemplate." It was a little awkward, too, when he had to write about his friends, or review their books. His own essay on Emerson presented some animadversions that might have been misunderstood by a less generous soul, and the review of Thoreau's "Week on the Concord and Merrimack" contained some rude remarks that a more circumspect editor (Doctor Sparks, for instance) might well have deleted.

In 1850 the publishers failed, and the *Quarterly* came to an end. It had not been unsuccessful, even financially, — though it cost Parker some three or four hundred dollars, — but Parker wrote its obituary notice without any ostensible regret, remarking that "the Journal has never become what its projectors designed that it should be." Despite the radicalism of its editor, the *Quarterly* was conventional in character and in form, closer to the *North American* or the earlier *Southern Review* than to the *Dial*. No aura of transcendentalism enveloped the *Quarterly;* its editor had been engaged with matters of pressing and public concern, not with those things which pass understanding, and it lacked entirely the charm, the incoherence, the mysticism of the *Dial*. It was, as Thomas Higginson remarked, not the *Dial* with a beard, but the beard without the *Dial*. Perhaps its chief value was as a vehicle for Parker's writing.

3

Nowhere did Parker reveal more clearly the virtues and the defects of his scholarship, the resources and the limitations of his thinking, than in these contributions to the *Quarterly*. They ranged over a wide variety of subjects, but catholicity was his boast; they embraced a diversity of forms, but versatility was his pride. Yet all of them were characteristic, all displayed wide learning, critical acumen, immense self-assurance, vigorous partisanship, and an incisive style. They confessed his enthusiasms and discovered his aversions and betrayed his prejudices, and mere anonymity could not conceal their authorship.

He was as autobiographical as a novelist. When he described the "Position and Duties of the American Scholar," he told what he had done and what he wished to do, and his analysis of the dangers that beset the scholar in America was realistic because he had experienced them. When he praised Emerson he praised transcendentalism, and he knew that Emerson had penetrated somehow to the quintessence of that philosophy while he himself had only traversed it and surveyed it and bounded it, and he knew that he had missed something. When he drew the saintly Channing he portrayed the ideal minister, who turned out to be not so much Channing as a curious amalgam of Channing and Parker. When he prophesied the "Political Destination of America" it was his own New England that he described, idealized, but authentic and provincial. The reviews of Prescott's books gave him an opportunity to announce his own philosophy of history; the critique of Hildreth (what could you say about Hildreth, it was like criticizing the Almanac) turned into an essay on liberty and democracy; the essay on Buckle, which appeared years later, gave him a chance to display his own erudition and to formulate his own laws of civilization. What he read was provocative merely; he had so much to say that he forgot to notice what others had to say. He was readier to teach than to learn. His criticism was subjective, as became an intuitionalist; he interpreted himself rather than his material; he was as bad as Bronson Alcott, who had, so it was said, but one topic of conversation — Bronson Alcott on the Universe.

His criticism was didactic. He was above all anxious to establish moral truths, and he had the immense advantage of a philosophy and the inescapable habit of a preacher. He thought it was the business of the scholar to stand in judgment upon the past and to assume responsibility for the future. He was neither tolerant nor subtle, and was impatient with those historians who were able to see both sides of every question and who carefully restrained their indignation for wickedness and their enthusiasm for nobility. No such bloodless history for him, he knew right and wrong; a transcendentalist, he judged mankind by an infallible standard. He knew what he was about, it was not rashness that led him to tackle every problem with confidence, how could he be other than confident when intuition was his guide? He advanced boldly into an array of facts and emerged with magnificent generalizations and universal laws.

Nothing lent itself better to Parker's talents for generalization than the interpretation of national character, and in nothing did he display these talents to better advantage than in the essay on "The Political Destination of the American People." It was a grand theme, none grander, for if he could discover the true genius of the people, he would have a standard by which to test all social and political action. "Every nation," he announced, "has a peculiar character in which it differs from all others," and he proceeded to dispose of the Hebrews, the Greeks, the Romans, in three breathtaking sentences. The Anglo-Saxons he treated less cavalierly, but no less incisively, and the centuries reeled under the strokes of his pen: —

They are yet the same bold, handy, practical people as when their bark first touched the savage shores of Britain; not over religious, less pious than moral; not so much upright before God as downright before men; servants of the understanding more than children of reason; not following the guidance of an intuition and the light of an idea, but rather trusting to experiment, facts, precedents, and usages; not philosophical, but commercial; warlike through strength and courage, not from love of war or its glory; material, obstinate, and grasping, with the same admiration of horses, dogs, oxen and strong drink; the same willingness to tread down any obstacle which stands in their way; the same impatient lust of wealth and power; the same disposition to colonize and reannex other lands; the same love of liberty and love of law; the same readiness in forming political confederations.

There it all was, no qualifications, no subtle refinements. The genius of the Hebrews was for religion, of the Greeks for beauty, of the Romans for law, of the English for commerce; the Americans were the heirs of all the ages and of all peoples, and for them was reserved the highest destiny. The genius of America was for liberty. "This is so plain," said Parker, "that the point requires no arguing," so he proceeded to argue it at length. Of course it wasn't plain at all, it was far from plain, what with slavery and Hunkerism in control. But this difficulty was superficial rather than real; it was the same difficulty that the transcendentalist encountered when he proclaimed the perfection of man and was reminded of the existence of sin and of evil. When Parker wrote that the American genius for liberty was plain, he meant that it was plain to the intuitive, not to the historical, understanding. Just so it had been plain to Jefferson that all men were created equal and endowed with certain unalienable rights. "It is true," Parker acknowledged sadly, "that much of the national conduct seems exceptional when measured by that standard, and the nation's course as crooked as the Rio Grande; it is true that America sometimes seems to spurn liberty, and sells the freedom of three million men for less than three million annual bales of cotton; true she often tramples on the most unquestionable and sacred rights." No one more painfully aware of these things than Parker, but it was the duty of the scholar to penetrate through the husk of circumstances to the inner truth. If slavery was a fact, so too was the idea of liberty, and the history of America was the history of the actualization of ideas. If Americans had not lived up to their great heritage, if they had not fulfilled their destiny, it was a pity; they would yet be true to themselves and to nature.

How well he understood this restless, impetuous, materialistic America, impatient of the past and greedy for the future, questioning tradition and fearing authority, never satisfied, eager for new things, living fiercely and superficially, racing against time and against life itself, the most gullible, the most tolerant, the most careless of people, but breasting life with incomparable courage.

All that we do we overdo. It appears in our hopefulness; we are the most aspiring of nations. Not content with half the continent we wish the other half. We have this characteristic of genius, we are dissatisfied with all that we have done. The American soul passes from its work as soon as it is finished. We are more spontaneous than logical; we have ideas rather than facts or precedents. We are not so reflective as forecasting. We lack the phlegmatic patience of older nations. We are impatient of the process but greedy of the result; so that we make short experiments but long reports, we talk much though we say little. Quickness is the great desideratum with us. It is said that an American ship is known far off at sea by the quantity of canvas that she carries. We are so intent upon our purpose that we have no time for amusement. We are the most restless of people. How we crowd into cars and steamboats; a locomotive would well typify our fuming fizzing spirit. In our large towns life seems to be only a scamper. Not satisfied with bustling about all day, when night comes we cannot sit still but alone of all nations have added rockers to our chairs.

Worse yet was our materialism: an old charge, but always pertinent. We mistake size for greatness, love ostentation, and worship wealth. We give lip-service to labor, but with all our democracy labor is thought less honorable in Boston than in Berlin; we think work is for Irishmen, and no American wants his son to be a cobbler. Our society is vulgar, our culture meretricious, our literature imitative. We want integrity of mind and of character, we mistrust ourselves and every day deny our genius.

All this Parker saw, but he did not despair. This American nation was not like other nations. It had inexhaustible springs of strength, infinite potentialities for idealism. He had laid bare its sins but he remembered that these were the indiscretions of youth; he had rebuked its vices but he resolved that these were fortuitous and ephemeral. He had applied his great idea of liberty and tested it by the facts, and he discovered that more often than not it was contemned and disgraced. But he was not to be disconcerted or dissuaded by irrelevant facts. Just so the individual might sin against the Holy Ghost, yet every transcendentalist knew that he was a child of God and partook of divinity. So, confounded by his facts, Parker fell back upon intuitive truth, and looked to the future for vindication.

Nor did he doubt his ability to read the future, or his duty to announce it. That was the business of the scholar in the Republic (the transcendental scholar) — to realize, to embrace the future. He had given much thought to this matter of the position of the scholar in the Republic, and he felt that he spoke with some authority, and his essay on the subject was reminiscent and personal. He knew the scholars of the Old World and the New, and he felt that there was a difference between them. The scholars of the Old World depended upon patronage, upon an aristocracy or a government; they served the few rather than the many, they wrote for each other, not for society, they worked and lived in an artificial world. Not so in America. Here the greatest scholar was the most democratic, here the man of learning spoke to the whole of the people, not to an exclusive segment.

To large and mainly unlearned audiences Agassiz and Walker set forth the highest teachings of physics and metaphysics, not sparing difficult things, but putting them into plain speech. Emerson takes his majestic intuitions of truth and justice, and expounds them to the mechanics' apprentices, to the factory girls at Lowell and Chicopee, and to the merchants' clerks at Boston. The more original the speaker, and the more profound, the better is he relished.

But this democratic patronage carried with it new responsibilities. In America the scholar was a teacher rather than a savant; his duties were moral, not scientific — "He is to represent the higher facts of human consciousness to the people, and express them in the speech of the people; to think with the sage and saint, but talk with the common man." He must speak in the vernacular, be familiar with common things. He must use the most popular of agencies, the newspaper, the schoolroom, the platform, the pulpit. Not only his speech but his science must be instinct with nationalism, with provincialism. Every book, every speech, every sermon, must bear a national or a local trade mark, and be instantly recognizable. The School, the Government, the Press, the Church, all must reflect the countenances of free men.

And in America the scholar must rest his conclusions upon the facts of human nature rather than the facts of history, for here of all places the science of society is not experimental but ideal, here of all places history is to be made, not observed. The scholar in the Republic is more interested in natural law than in precedent (the doctrine of the Declaration, this), more concerned with the character of institutions than with their origins, more sympathetic to the expression of ideas than to the display of art, more reverent toward the religion of Man than toward the religion of the Church. He is not a slave to the past but master of the present and prophet of the future; he is to play his part in the making of a new world.

Here was the American scholar, and his features, as Parker delineated them, were curiously familiar. The ideal scholar was neither an abstraction nor a prophecy, and there were few who would not have recognized in this portrait the minister of the Twenty-eighth Congregational Society. Yet Parker was not without modesty. He did not consciously regard himself as the original from which the picture was copied; rather, he had imagined the ideal, and he was trying to conform to it. Emerson had been equally autobiographical — he had projected his ideal scholar along intimate and familiar lines — , and none would suspect him of conceit.

It was hard, indeed, to improve upon Emerson. There was little in Parker's essay that was new, and it created no sensation comparable to the stir which greeted the famous Phi Beta Kappa Oration of 1837. But Parker could give the prose of Emerson's poetry, the proof of his conclusions, the mathematics of his philosophy. Emerson had spoken as a transcendentalist, relying upon the self-evident truth of his assertions. Parker, too, was a transcendentalist, but his was another way. He was not bold enough to disdain evidence, nor clever enough to conceal it. He lacked, after all, the lordly assurance, the divine authority, of his Concord friend. He subscribed to the same philosophy, but his method was different, and the method was everything. Where Emerson confounded doubters with a flash of lightning, Parker laid siege to them with batteries of heavy artillery. Where Emerson converted by a spiritual miracle, Parker convinced by argument. Where Emerson gave the law, Parker submitted an attorney's brief. The batteries were formidable, the argument persuasive, the brief learned, but what had these things to do with intuitive truth?

Because he thought it the function of the American scholar to represent democracy and to vindicate morals, Parker disapproved of those scholars who failed to perform this duty, and of none more heartily than of Mr. Prescott. Indeed, his disapproval of Mr. Prescott was so profound that it could not be contained in a single essay, but spilled over into two: the one a sweeping indictment, the other a bill of particulars. The stately volumes of the "Ferdinand and Isabella," the "Conquest of Mexico," and the "Conquest of Peru," had been greeted in two hemispheres with a chorus of praise, and it was a bold thing to file a dissenting opinion. But Parker did not lack courage; he had given much thought to the philosophy of history and some time to the study of Spain and the Spanish conquests in America, and he felt sure of his ground. His objections were characteristic and logical. Mr. Prescott's concept of history was narrow and aristocratic, Mr. Prescott's interests were superficial and frivolous, Mr. Prescott's moral judgment was warped. In short, Mr. Prescott was no philosopher. And just for good measure, Parker threw in so many gratuitous slurs on Mr. Prescott's scholarship as to arouse a suspicion that Mr. Prescott was no historian.

Now Parker knew how these books should have been written. They should have been written in the interest of mankind, in the spirit of the nineteenth century, in the style of an American. They should have denounced the intolerance of the Church, the vices of the Court, the arrogance of the aristocracy, the brutality of war, and the iniquity of slavery. They should have revealed the growth of institutions, analyzed the details of administration, set forth the achievements of trade and commerce and agriculture, described the daily life of the people. Nothing but pageantry here, nothing but the pomp of the court and the alarums of the battlefield, nothing but the monotonous and distressing details of conquest. That was no way to write history. Better to have adopted Parker's plan: —

The historian is to tell of the origin of the people, of their rise, their decline, their fall and end. The causes which advanced or retarded the nation are to be sought, and their actions explained. He is to enquire what sentiments and ideas prevailed in the nation; whence they came; how they organized, and with what results. Hence not merely the civil and military transactions are to be looked after but the philosophy which prevails in the nation is to be ascertained; the literature, laws, and religion. The historian is to describe the industrial condition of the people, the state of agriculture, commerce, and the arts, both the useful and the beautiful. He must tell us of the social state of the people, the relation of the cultivator to the soil, the relation of class to class. It is well to know what songs the peasant sung;

what prayers he prayed; what food he ate; what tools he wrought with; what tax he paid; how he stood connected with the soil; how he was brought to war; and what weapons armed him for the fight.

Nor was this enough. "In telling what has been," said Parker, "the historian is also to tell what ought to be, for he is to pass judgment on events, and try counsels by their causes first and their consequences not less. When all these things are told, history ceases to be a mere panorama of events; it becomes philosophy teaching by experience, and has a profound meaning and awakens a deep interest, while it tells the lessons of the past for the warning of the present and the edification of the future."

But if history is to teach by experience, what becomes of *a priori* truths? If consequences are to be the test of actions, what becomes of first principles? If the enslavement of the Indians by the Spaniards was wrong, it was absolutely and eternally wrong, and consequences had nothing to do with the matter. If religious liberty was right and just, its validity was not to be put to the test of experience. In these instances Parker's appeal to history would seem safe enough. But suppose it could be demonstrated that the enslavement of the Indians was, in the long run, beneficial — or that the work of the Inquisition purified society? Would Parker be forced from his high ground? If intuitive truth transcends experience, what is the value of an appeal to experience? If *a priori* principles are not susceptible to scientific proof, what is to be gained by an appeal to history? Parker professed scorn for the application of the scientific method to history, but it was that method he himself adopted. He elaborated the absolute and submitted first principles to laboratory tests. He was naïve enough to believe that if only he stated his conclusions first instead of last, he would be true to transcendentalism. He never abandoned his intuitional philosophy, but every new accumulation of proof represented a vote of no confidence.

4

Writing learned essays for the *Quarterly* was all very well, but Parker could not persuade himself that this fulfilled the whole duty of the scholar. He had developed a talent for the popularization of learning, and he rationalized it into a duty, but how small his audience was, after all. A few hundred people read the *Quarterly,* a few thousand listened to him at the Melodeon and the Music Hall. So far, he had made scarcely a dent in Boston Hunkerism, and he knew now that his ostracism was to be permanent; aside from his own church, there was not in the whole city a pulpit from which he could preach or a platform from which he could speak, and they would scarcely let him inside the Divinity School. Was his influence, then, to be confined to his own congregation; was he to acquiesce meekly in this isolation? He had faced this same problem back in West Roxbury when they had threatened to drive him out of his pulpit, and he had written, "I will go about and preach and lecture in the city and the glen, by the road-side and field-side, and wherever men and women can be found. I will go eastward and westward, northward and southward, and make the land *ring.*" No danger now that he would have to abandon that church; he had as large a congregation as Mr. Beecher himself. But had he made the land *ring?*

It was not hard to answer this question. Ever since the Unitarians had so ostentatiously closed the doors of their churches on him, he had been deluged with requests for lectures. "This business of lecturing," he wrote, "is an original American contrivance for educating the people. The world has nothing like it. In it are combined the best things of the Church, and of the College, with some of the fun of the theatre." There were three thousand Lyceums in the East alone; their members were eager and enthusiastic, and insatiable in their demands; it was a wonder how men wanted to be talked at. So everyone lectured:

men of letters, journalists, clergymen, reformers, even scientists, all brought their wares to the common counter. Some, like Beecher and Starr King and the eloquent Phillips, reveled in the opportunity; Emerson came with reluctance, Thoreau with positive disdain. Parker took to the platform like a sailor to the deck. Year after year he filled up the winter months with lyceum engagements — ten, twelve, fourteen of them a month. He canvassed New England, he invaded New York, he stormed Pennsylvania, he reached out into the great Northwest, to Illinois and Wisconsin, and everywhere he went men and women hurried to hear him as he poured forth his prodigious learning or passed in review the great moral questions of the day.

This was better than waiting for exchanges or editing the *Quarterly*. Soon the infidel who had been barred from a score of pulpits had spoken in a hundred towns; denied admission to the sacred columns of the *Examiner,* he was reported in the New York *Tribune* and the *Post*. (Catch Greeley napping, or Parke Godwin!) He was a public figure now, an educator, a missionary, a crusader, his face familiar in every Northern town. "I think scarcely any American, not holding public office, has touched the minds of so many men," he wrote, and his pride was not unwarranted, for every mail brought testimony to his influence. That influence was secular rather than religious, for he tried to keep clear of theology on the lyceum platform (it would creep in, though) and spoke on popular themes: "Transcendentalism," "The Anglo-Saxons," "The Harmony of Nature and Man," "The Education of the People," or, if a subject failed, "The Signs of the Times." His lectures were like his sermons, packed with information, long, hard, and unadorned, but Thomas Wentworth Higginson thought that in the art of popularization Parker had no equal in the country, and he remembered that one audience listened to a two-hour lecture on the Anglo-Saxons "as if an angel sang to them." There was something exhilarating about lecturing when you could hold your audience that way, or better yet, when you could break through their prejudices and dissipate their fears, persuade them into tolerance, startle them into enthusiasm.

It was wonderfully educational, too, this business of stumping the country. Lexington, Cambridge, Boston — his American experience had been limited. Now he came to know more of the country, came to know this America whose character he was always trying to penetrate. He visited the towns of New Hampshire and Vermont, and found that they were by no means abandoned to orthodoxy. He spoke in Fall River and Providence, and the mill workers came to hear him and applauded him. He lectured in New Haven and met Noah Porter there, fresh from a year in Berlin, and young Andrew Dickson White who could talk with him about the ethnology of Russia. He traveled through Connecticut and concluded that the whole State was one vast Barnum County, and he proposed to a fellow traveler that the prayers of all the churches be concentrated upon Phineas Barnum who could then engineer the salvation of the rest of the country. He spoke at Union College, where the venerable Eliphalet Nott had presided for so long that the memory of man ran not to the contrary, and where, he observed, they trained "politicians, not scholars." He lectured in Syracuse, and his dear Sam Jo May took him out to the Onondaga Reservation, where he seized the opportunity to brush up on his languages. He visited Oberlin College, which Finney had made a laboratory of democracy, boys and girls studying together and learning to use their hands as well as their heads, and he heard thrilling narratives of fugitive slaves and of the Underground Railroad. He saw for himself how great a work Horace Mann was doing at Antioch College, but he felt sorry for Mann, out there in Yellow Springs, in the barbarous West; and when he got back he wrote him: "I fancy you now and then feel a little longing after the well-cultured men and women whom you left behind at the East and find none to supply in Ohio." He was in Ohio when Chase led the fight on the Nebraska Bill; he was in Illinois when Douglas stumped the state for Buchanan.

The West was a new experience, so different from his compact, neat, intimate New England, so vast and raw and tough, changing so rapidly he could never keep track of it from one visit to the next. Most of all he was impressed by the sheer immensity of this West — the endless prairies, the vast forests, the broad rivers; even the apples and pumpkins grew larger out there, the nuts were big, the apples were coarse, even the fishes were uncouth monsters, catfish and suckers. The West had quantity, but not quality. This was true, he feared, of the people too. The men were rangy and rough and jaundiced; the women bony, thin-faced, flat-breasted creatures, not a rosy cheek among them. Out here men were toughened and coarsened, they lacked the refinement, they lacked even the energy of New Englanders. "I fear," he said, "the West deteriorates Americans."

He wasn't happy until he got back East. Chester county, Pennsylvania, was an earthly paradise, so fat and succulent; New York City was the most thoroughly American place in the country; upstate New York was almost as trim and clean as New England. But it was New England that he loved, for all it had treated him badly; and when he travelled through it he wrote, "The superiority of New England civilization over all the rest of America is quite clear."

But it was a hardship, too, this lecturing, a nomadic, unchristian life, and he planned to give it up when he was fifty. Sometimes he would be in the trains every night for a week; sometimes the discomforts of the train were preferable to the discomforts of a mean country tavern. The trains always ran at the wrong hours: how many mornings he had been routed out of a damp bed at five o'clock, and then a long ride in an open sleigh through the wintry countryside to some cold station. How many times he had gone without food, or, what was worse, experimented with cold coffee and greasy steak. Well now that he had been a farm boy, well that he had been inured to hardship, to cold and wet and privation. But sometimes it was too much, even for him. He wrote to Sarah Hunt: —

Monday last at seven, I walked down to the Lowell Depot and at eight started for Rouse's Point, two hundred and eighty-seven miles off, sick and fit only to lie on a sofa. A dreadful hard ride ends at nine P.M. and I find myself in the worst tavern in the Northern States. Bread which defies eating, crockery which sticks to your hands, fried fish as cold as when drawn from the lake. Rise at half-past four, breakfast at five, off in the cars at half-past five, lecture at Malone that night, lie all day on the sofa, ditto at Potsdam the next day. The third day leave Potsdam at nine, reach Champlain (if I get there) at half-past eight, spending ten and a half hours in travelling by railroad ninety-three miles. Thence, after lecture, to Rouse's Point, and at half-past five to-morrow morning return to the cars which are to take me home. Next week three days in the "East Counties" and the next four days in Central New York.

"The task was always disagreeable and contrary to my natural disposition," Parker concluded later; but it was not so. For all of the hardships, he would not give it up, even when he could. It was exciting to be known every-where, his name on every tongue and in every newspaper, the farm boy from Lexington who was a power in the land. It was pleasant to meet old friends — Lydia Maria Child in New York, who remembered him as a snub-nosed school teacher, Octavius Frothingham in Jersey City, who had learned his theology in Parker's study, James and Lucretia Mott in Philadelphia, the Quaker Saints, Sam Jo May, the Syracuse Archimedes who could tell him all about break-ing down jails and assaulting officers of the law. Pleasant to meet old friends and fun to make new ones — men like Charles Loring Brace, who had discovered the perishing classes of New York and was interested in Scandinavian antiquities, or great bearded Henry James who was more Swedenborgian than Sampson Reed himself and whose house on Washington Square was open to all the reformers of

New York, or young George Frisbie Hoar, in Worcester, who had organized a lyceum society just for him and Phillips and Emerson, or William Herndon, out in Springfield, who hated slavery and loved his law partner, Abraham Lincoln.

Every Sunday would find Parker back in the Music Hall, weary but with a sense of duty well done; only his long trips to the West were permitted to interfere with preaching, and then his absences so weighed on his conscience that he could scarcely be persuaded to take his regular vacations. In some ways he did not really approve of all this gallivanting about the country; he was uprooted, dissipated, his life was not his own. "I sign myself," he wrote ruefully, "Theodore Parker of everywhere, and no place in particular. I live in taverns, move in railroad cars, and have my being in the Music Hall and other places of public speaking." He knew that a minister should serve his parish as well as his pulpit, and he longed to find time for the intimate, kindly things that were the privilege of the minister: visiting the sick, relieving the poor, consoling the bereaved. But he remembered that his parish was not Boston but the whole North. He was a circuit rider, and his circuit stretched from the Penobscot to the Mississippi.

More serious were the inroads of this itinerant life upon his studies. He was anxious to get back to his books, to the manuscript of his "History of the Development of Religion," to the hundred and one scholarly projects that haunted him. But he could not believe that he discharged his duties as a scholar by writing for the few. "It is easy to discourse with scholars," he had said, "and in the old academic carriage drive through the broad gateway of the cultivated class, but here the man of genius is to take the new thought on his shoulders and climb up the stiff, steep hill, and find his way where the wild asses quench their thirst, and the untamed eagle builds his nest. Our American scholar must cultivate the dialectics of speech as well as of thought." Since he had set these standards, he could not fail to live up to them. Yet he was loath to abandon his studies. Trains and hotel rooms were miserable substitutes for the library in Exeter Place, but he accepted them with good grace, and a heavy sack of books was part of his regular traveling equipment. "The motion of the railroad cars gave a pleasing and not a harmful stimulus to thought," he insisted, with pathetic cheerfulness, "and so helped me to work out my difficult problems. While traveling I could read and write all day long, but I would not advise others to do much of either."

With each passing year, Parker's conception of the function of the scholar and of the minister had broadened, and it became increasingly difficult for him to confine himself to the study, the pulpit, the lecture platform. His responsibilities mounted with his influence. He had hoped to announce great moral truths, to elaborate and vindicate them with learning, to proclaim them wherever men would listen to him. All this he was doing, now, but it was not enough. He had won a hearing for his principles, but their application was still to be assured.

Action, then, Parker. Not for you the aloofness of Emerson, Emerson who knew his singular talent for inspiration and provocation and who would not dissipate himself. ("Are they *my* poor," he said.) Yours is not a message for the future, but a work for the day. There are sins to denounce, there are evils to expose, there are reforms to achieve. There is a new society to be built, a new world to create.

CHAPTER VIII

THE UNIVERSAL REFORMER

WHAT is a man born for, but to be a reformer. So Emerson had said, and was startled when they took him at his word. Every institution was called before the bar of reason, and of sentiment — the Church, the State, labor, slavery, law and punishment, war, the school, the press, the family. Nothing was taken for granted, nothing but the right of inquiry and the authority of conscience. It was downright uncomfortable to live in Boston in the forties and the fifties; it was not enough that you paid for your pew and stood well in State Street and sent your boys to Harvard College; someone was sure to tell you that the Church was rotten and State Street wicked and that Harvard College taught nothing that a good man need know. Wherever you went the reformers demanded your credentials and your passport, and challenged every signature but their own. Even your private life was not immune; you could not eat or drink in peace but someone would bob up to warn you that to touch meat was a vice and to sip wine a sin.

For the reformers, at least, Boston was the Hub of the Universe. Every town in New England sent its delegate there; they filled the halls with their conventions and the air with their clamor. There was an Aristides at every court, a Diogenes in every countinghouse. Here in this city of the Appletons and the Lees there were as many reformers as there were merchants. Call the roll of the radicals and their names crack out like a volley of musketry: Phillips, Sumner, Garrison, Mann, Quincy, Parker, Pierpont, Channing, Emerson, Alcott, Ripley, Loring, Lowell, Rantoul,

Higginson, Howe. No mere fanatics these, no half-baked bedlamites; you could not dismiss a Quincy or a Channing or a Higginson, they were connected with half the families of the State. They could preach pantheism in the pulpit, transcendentalism in the schoolroom, socialism in the market place, abolitionism in Faneuil Hall; they could agitate the most inflammatory of issues, announce the most outlandish ideas, champion the most extravagant causes, and you would have to listen to them. And they consorted with the worst of men, and of women too. Wherever they went they trailed behind them clouds of high-flying enthusiasts — spiritualists, phrenologists, Swedenborgians, Millerites, vegetarians, Grahamites, prohibitionists, feminists, non-resistants, Thomsonians, Come-outers of every shape and every hue.

What had they in common, these reformers, men and women, rich and poor, educated and illiterate? What was it that persuaded Edmund Quincy to preside over the Chardon Street Convention and gave Channing patience to listen to the rantings of Abby Folsom and Sylvanus Brown? What was it that sent Parker and Ripley hot-footing it out to Groton to participate in the wrangling of the Millerites and the Come-outers? What was the magic of Brook Farm that it stirred the hearts of the sanest of men and made them tolerant even of Fruitlands and of Hopedale? Bronson Alcott had made a failure of everything but life, but no matter how fantastic his notions everyone loved him, for he had proved the Dignity of Man. Margaret Fuller was as dangerous as Fanny Wright, but all the women of Boston flocked to her Conversations, and Emerson was glad to contribute to her biography. Horace Mann succumbed to phrenology and Thomas Appleton flirted with spiritualism; Parker was fascinated by mesmerism and Emerson avowed himself a Swedenborgian and took lessons from Sampson Reed. Josiah Quincy thought well of the Mormons and admired Joseph Smith, and Ellis Gray Loring circulated petitions on behalf of Abner Kneeland, who was

a convicted atheist and a Thomsonian too. Francis Jackson
gave refuge to female abolitionists, Higginson hobnobbed
with Lucy Stone and Amelia Bloomer, and Phillips championed the Woman's Movement as the greatest reform in
history. Orestes Brownson founded a Society for Christian
Progress, Robert Rantoul labored with Seth Parker for the
ten-hour day, and John Allen of Brook Farm organized
a New England Workingmen's Association, while Channing
preached socialism from the pulpit and Parker congratulated the Shakers that they alone had solved the problem
of industrialism. Charles Sumner enlisted with Garrison and
Elihu Burritt in the war against war, and William Ladd projected a plan for a World Congress of Nations. Pierpont
worked for temperance and Neal Dow for prohibition;
wealthy Reverend John Sargent and poor John Augustus
tried to stamp out prostitution; Dorothea Dix forced legislatures to ameliorate the lot of the insane, and Samuel
Gridley Howe gave light to the blind. Phillips spoke for
penal reform and Parker described the criminal as the
victim, not the foe, of society, and James Russell Lowell
rebuked the aged Wordsworth for his defense of capital
punishment: —

> And always 'tis the saddest sight to see
> An old man faithless in Humanity.

What had they in common — what but a belief in the
perfectibility of man and in the doctrine of progress? Emerson had put it well, Emerson who spoke for them, however reluctantly: — "The power which is at once spring
and regulator in all efforts of reform is the conclusion that
there is an infinite worthiness in man, which will appear
at the call of worth, and that all particular reforms are the
removing of some impediment." They were all transcendentalists, though they read not Coleridge and knew not
Kant. They were all idealists, howsoever they rationalized
their emotions or tested them by experience. The ability
of man to attain divinity, that was the point of departure.

It was assumption, as Rousseau's "Man is born free and is everywhere in chains" was an assumption — as magnificent, as revolutionary in its logical consequences. For if Man is a God, how is it we find him a brute? If man was born free, how is it we find him in spiritual chains? The Calvinists met this issue squarely enough: they rejected the assumptions. But transcendentalists took no stock in Original Sin or the Downfall of Man. They knew that men were born not only free but to the pursuit of happiness, and no matter how sharply Mr. Garrison and Mr. Phillips might take issue with Mr. Parker's theology, they too were transcendentalists at heart.

No need to go to Saint Augustine for the City of God — nor to Fourier, either. No need to escape from reality into the past, or to disown the present and go off by yourself to some Brook Farm or Walden Pond. What better place to build the Heavenly City than here in Boston? And what if the spirit of Hunkerism ruled the town? What if dogma was preached from the pulpits and servility taught in the schools, and one third of the people were from County Cork and went to Mass? What if the merchants built their proud houses on Beacon Hill while the slums grew apace in South Boston and the salt tide flooded the cellars of the ramshackle tenements, bringing disease and death? What if there was a grog shop on every corner and Deer Island was crowded with wretched harlots; what if the law made criminals and then killed them, and Negroes were hunted in the streets of Boston and sent back to the cotton fields of the South? These things did not prove the depravity of Man, for you could not prove an untruth. You could not invalidate a Natural Law by refusing to obey it.

That law was the Law of Progress. Nature and Philosophy united to prove the progress of mankind. Science (not Professor Agassiz's) lent its support, and even history — if you but read it aright — even history demonstrated the sure advance of civilization and the triumph of right over wrong. Theirs was no easy optimism, not the optimism that

shaded dangerously into a smug assurance that whatever
was, was right, nor yet an optimism so supremely confident
of the wisdom of Providence that it faltered into fatalism.
But they read with approval those lines from Locksley
Hall —

Yet I doubt not through the ages one increasing purpose runs,
And the thoughts of men are widened with the process of the suns.

and felt themselves in tune with the Infinite.

This is what gave them fortitude, the conviction that
they were on the side of the angels, that they were fulfilling
Nature and Nature's laws, and that the stars in their
courses fought for them. This is what gave dignity to their
zeal and strength to their numbers. It made them courageous in the face of opposition, resolute in the face of
discouragement, eloquent in the face of apathy. It armored
them against attack and fortified them against contumely.
It gave them a militant, an unconquerable faith, that was
at last triumphantly proclaimed by one who knew them
all: —

He has sounded forth the trumpet that shall never call retreat;
He is sifting out the hearts of men before His judgment-seat;
O, be swift, my soul, to answer Him! be jubilant, my feet!
Our God is marching on.

2

God was marching on, but the Church lagged behind. It
was, thought Parker, the most conservative of institutions,
more concerned with ritual and with dogma than with life.
Nor need to look to the Church for inspiration or support;
"even the baby-virtue of America," wrote Parker contemptuously, "turns off from that lean, haggard and empty
breast." At the Berry Street Conference Doctor X——
remembered how many infants he had baptized that year,
and Doctor Y—— boasted of the number of tracts they had
distributed in the West. At Worcester the Annual Convention argued the terms upon which Persons should be

admitted to the Communion and debated the grave question, "Have We a Litany Among Us?"; and in 1853 Doctor Lothrop actually hatched a creed studded with silly phrases about "celestial solicitation" and "the withered veins of humanity." That same year Parker peeped in at the Divinity School and concluded that it was a morgue. "The Egyptian embalmers," he said, "took only seventy days to make a mummy out of a dead man. Unitarian embalmers used three years in making a mummy out of a live one." Doctor Ripley's church looked askance at his ideas of social reform, and Chandler Robbins was proud that no social question had ever intruded itself upon the decorum of his services; the Federal Street Church would not allow Doctor Channing to announce an anti-slavery meeting, and Doctor Frothingham found it hard to understand why anyone should wish to improve a society so nearly perfect. Clergymen stood ready to testify to the good character of a Webster or a Choate, and debated whether Emerson was a Christian; there were separate chapels for the poor, where only the orthodox might preach.

The air of Boston was electric with reform, but the windows of the churches were closed. Yet it was not so elsewhere. Out in Worcester Edward Everett Hale vied with Thomas Wentworth Higginson in the socialization of Christianity; in Syracuse Sam Jo May turned his church over to the radicals; and in New York the talented but eccentric Henry Bellows meddled dangerously with profane affairs. But here in Boston the Unitarians had become respectable and conservative. They were gentlemen and not unaware of the fact; they moved in the best circles, their conduct was dignified and their manners refined. They worshipped reason and loved peace, and enthusiasm they thought vulgar. Norton was their scholar and James Walker their philosopher, and they read Holmes more gladly than Lowell. There had been liberals in the church, but somehow they had disappeared, and now Doctor Lothrop and Doctor Frothingham set the pace. Pierpont had talked too much, and Sargent had been too independent, and both, now, were gone. Parker himself was outside the pale, and when James Freeman Clarke invited him into his pulpit, his wealthiest parishioners seceded to more comfortable pews. Emerson had left the church; Ripley had left the church; Brownson had left the church. And Channing was gone, Channing whose greatness of spirit had encompassed the town.

Who was there to take the place of Channing? Who was there now to preach the Dignity of Man and the religion of Humanity? He was, thought Parker, the greatest clergyman of his time, the greatest man of his time. For forty years his presence had been a benediction to the city, and his piety an inspiration to the Church. His saintliness was a challenge to sin, and his holiness a rebuke to iniquity. He took the highest ground and drew men to him; he made the most audacious assumptions and shamed men into granting them. His idealism was inexorable, his faith in the goodness of man was not to be gainsaid, and when men disappointed him, his grief stung them like conscience. He had not great learning, but he spoke with the authority of law; he had neither brilliance nor wit, but his words flew around the earth.

No one had achieved more for reform than had Channing, who was not afraid to descend from seraphic abstractions to homely applications. He had the innocence of Alcott, but he did not suffer fools gladly nor live in a world of his own imagining; he had the serenity of Emerson, but he was not willing to adjourn the present for the future or to insist upon the proper limits of his own responsibility. His tolerance did not paralyze his moral sensibilities nor his magnanimity cool his passion for righteousness. He made heresy plausible and revolution respectable; he lent dignity to every reform, and clothed the most dangerous doctrines in the garments of gentility.

With every year he grew more radical in his thinking and bolder in his action. The Peace Society of Massachu-

setts was organized in his study; and in his study, too,
Dorothea Dix prepared her moving Memorial on the condition of the insane. He championed penal reform and the
abolition of capital punishment, and assured his wealthy
parishioners that the criminal caught the infection of vice
from the upper classes. He was among the first to celebrate
the work of Horace Mann, and he urged the President of
Harvard College to provide democratic education for the
plain people of the country. He gave his name to a form
of Unitarianism, but he had no proprietary interest in the
Church and he was more afraid of conformity than of dissent. He supported Father Taylor and encouraged Brownson and welcomed James Freeman Clarke, and at his death
the Catholic Church honored the man who had befriended
Bishop Cheverus. When Abner Kneeland was jugged for
blasphemy, it was Channing who drew up the petition for
pardon; when Faneuil Hall was denied to the abolitionists,
it was Channing who secured it for them by his Appeal
to the Citizens of Boston. He did not fail to countenance
by his presence the Chardon Street Convention, and from
the platform of Faneuil Hall he denounced the murderers of
Elijah Lovejoy. "I have no fear of revolutions," he said,
"we have conservative principles enough." He was not a
socialist, but no Brook Farmer could have condemned more
severely the sins of property; he was not a non-resistant,
but no pacifist could have painted more blackly the degradation of war; he was not an abolitionist, but his objections to slavery had carried conviction where Garrison's
did not. He was independent of every reform group, but
aloof from none; he belonged to no clique but gave strength
to them all. He was a leader and a symbol, and now he
was gone there was none to take his place.

3

Channing had been a part of Parker's education, and his
influence had been for liberalism. Parker had not known
him well — who indeed had known him well, this frail re-

cluse whom Doctor Dewey found "embosomed in reverence but living in singular isolation"? — but for five years Channing had been something more than an inspiration, he had been a friend and a counsellor. How often, during those West Roxbury years, Parker had wearied of the timidity of Francis and the dogmatism of Norton, and had gone in to see Channing, who was timid only of dogmatism. And Channing had not failed him. He was often wrong, Parker thought, but never unsympathetic or unreasonable. They talked of the most perplexing problems — of intuition and the function of the conscience, of the Platonic element in Christianity (Channing thought Parker was a little hard on Christianity), and of Strauss's new "Life of Jesus." A most useful book, said Channing, and he would not be sorry if some of Mr. Kneeland's disciples should undertake to translate it. Sometimes the conversation would take a more secular turn, and they would debate the respective merits of the Revolutionary Fathers (Channing admired Sam Adams, but Parker held out for Jefferson and "Jefferson stood it best"), or the dangers of industrialism and the growing disparity of wealth. "Oh that we might be a poor people, for the sake of the Highest," said Doctor Channing, and Parker was glad to find confirmation of his own fears. "I felt," he wrote, "there was a broad common ground between us." Channing came not infrequently to Brook Farm, and Parker met him, too, at the Chardon Street Convention. But his closest contact was at those meetings of the Friends in the Tremont House, where Parker saw Phillips and Tuckerman and Follen and where Channing conducted Socratic dialogues such as Plato himself might have written.

Channing could not always approve of Mr. Parker's intemperance of speech and of manner, and he was somewhat startled by the vigor of Mr. Parker's transcendentalism, but when he read the South Boston sermon he wrote: "I wish him to preach what he thoroughly believes. Let the full heart pour itself forth." No wonder that Parker looked upon him as the spearhead of liberalism, and at his death declared, "I have lost one of the most valuable friends I have ever had." How indeed could he estimate the value of that friendship; how could he do justice to the significance of that example? It was the example that was important. It proved to Parker the possibilities of the pulpit, and it justified his conviction that the pulpit commanded every position. No need to follow the example of Emerson and of Ripley when there was the example of Channing.

There had been other influences making for liberalism in those West Roxbury years. There were the meetings of the Transcendental Club, and the eager visits to Doctor Peabody's bookshop, and the faithful attendance upon Comeouter conventions. There were encouragement of Emerson and the friendship of Ripley, and the earnest discussions with Dwight and Stetson and Silsbee. There was the *Dial,* floating in the clouds, and Brownson's *Quarterly,* rooted to earth; Parker contributed to both and thought himself in the swing of things. The very existence of Brook Farm was a challenge to society, a defiance of conventions, and for four years the air that Parker breathed was laden with dissent.

The trip to Europe, too, was not without its value, though it furnished Parker with object lessons rather than with inspiration. He was in England at the height of the Chartist Movement. He talked with Carlyle and Martineau and Newman, and listened to the preaching of Fox. Religious reform was in the air, and the Wesleyan revolt from Anglican orthodoxy was not altogether unlike his own revolt from Unitarian orthodoxy. Old England was grappling with the problems that were soon to trouble New England: education, prison reform, temperance, labor, the position of women and children; these things were agitating the minds of men. Parker visited the teeming slums of Manchester and the wharves of Liverpool, where every boat unloaded a swarm of Irishmen. He saw how industrialism had changed the face of the countryside, and how it had blighted not only nature but man, and he prophesied that "we, the Yankee nation, are going in just the same way as the English, and unless we change our whole system radically, we shall come to just the same result and have the Christian feudalism of gold in Boston as in London. The feudalism of money," he concluded, "is too bad to be borne in a Christian land."

France and Germany were astir with reform, but Parker guessed little of those undercurrents that were to come to the surface in '48. On the Continent he found much to deprecate: the lesson of Germany was the danger of political tyranny; the lesson of the Catholic countries was the tragedy of spiritual tyranny. Yet one thing did impress him, almost in spite of himself: the abundance of simple pleasures available to the poor. However backward the Catholic countries were, he was forced to confess that the people here were happier than in Protestant England. In France there was the theater, — supported by the State, too, think of it! — in Italy there were Carnivals and Holy Days, in Germany music gardens; everywhere there were parks and zoos, and of a Sunday the public gardens were as crowded as were the pubs of Liverpool. How different from the bleakness of England; in the whole of Lancashire there was but one town with a public park, and the Church saw to it that that one was closed on Sunday. On the Continent, the Sabbath was made for man; perhaps Garrison and his friends back home were right in their demand for Sabbath reform. "If we had more of innocent amusements," Parker wrote to one of his parishioners, "we should have less of several things: less intensity of money-making, less political violence, less sectarian bigotry, and less drinking one's self drunk." If Europe taught Parker little of a positive character, it did confirm him in his mistrust of privilege and power whether enjoyed by Church or State or Property.

Yet, for all these influences of person and of place, of Channing and the transcendentalists and Brook Farm, of

Boston and of Europe, Parker came slowly to maturity as a social reformer. He was sympathetic enough, in those early years, but his sympathies rarely flooded over into action; he would join eagerly in any discussion, but he kept aloof from most organizations; he was generous enough with his pen, but not with himself. West Roxbury, to be sure, made no such demands upon him as Boston later made; he was under no compulsion, in this country parish, to set the world aright. But the real explanation was not one of opportunity but of character. His instincts were surer than his intentions, and he knew that he could not hurry himself. He had to have a good cause before he could defend it; he had to have a faith before he could lead a crusade. Grand strategy came before tactics, and he must know the grammar of philosophy before he could speak the language of reform.

So Parker confined himself, during the West Roxbury years, to philosophy and religion, and his energies were given largely to theological disputes. His first task was to clear out the theological underbrush from his own mind and from the minds of his parishioners; his second, to incorporate transcendentalism into his religious thinking and to elaborate a new religious philosophy. He thought, at the time, that he was to inaugurate a new Reformation, and, when he formulated those twenty-eight questions for the Unitarians to answer, he remembered the ninety-five theses which the monk of Wittenberg had nailed on the door of the castle church; it was only later that he came to suspect that the whole controversy had been something of a tempest in a teacup. He was not blind to the social implications of his Natural Religion, but there was time enough to follow out those implications when he had won a hearing for himself. He was not unaware of the intimate connection between religious and social liberalism, but he was not yet ready to embrace the reform program espoused by his liberal friends. He was more anxious to free men from superstition than to free them from poverty or bondage, and he confessed that his method was to "begin the attack a great way off." His preaching, in the Spring Street Church, was as conventional in tone as was the preaching of Doctor Frothingham; he spoke, from the pulpit, of "Tranquillity," of "Inspiration," of "Low Aims and Lofty"; only once did he preach of "The Application of Christianity to Life," and then it was to denounce intemperance and war.

Yet his private correspondence and his journals bore witness to an alert interest in social reform, an interest none the less genuine because it was nourished in the hothouse of his study. "I have lived long enough," he wrote with the disillusionment of thirty, "to see the sham of things and to look them fairly in the face. The State is a bundle of shams. It is based on force, not love. It is still feudal. A Christian state is an anomaly, like a square circle. Our laws degrade, at the beginning, one half of the human race, and sacrifice them to the other and perhaps worser half. Our prisons are institutions that make more criminals than they mend; seventeen-twentieths of crimes are against property, which shows something is wrong in the state of property." He rejoiced in the Fourierist movement because "Our present form of society is irrational and unchristian." He read Brownson's article on socialism and noted that "The present property scheme entails awful evils upon society, rich no less than poor. This question of private property," he added, "is to be handled in the nineteenth century, and made to give its reason why the whole thing should not be abated as a nuisance." Easy enough to write this as he sat in the study of his parsonage; easy enough to denounce property and the State, but was he not himself a beneficiary of the system he so glibly condemned? His own position worried him. "It is a good thing, no doubt," he pondered, "that I should read the Greek Anthology and cultivate myself in my leisure, as a musk-melon ripens in the sun, but why should I be the only one of a thousand who has this chance?" And when he took ship for England he noted the contrast between the comforts of his own cabin and the discomforts of the steerage, and he felt like a criminal. "As the lion in the wilderness eateth up the wild ass, so the rich eat up the poor. There must be a cure for this terrible evil. What is it?"

What was it, indeed? "I look for relief only gradually," wrote Parker, "by applying good sense to religion and religion to life. This is the field in which I design to labor." And he had done what he could in West Roxbury; he had applied good sense to religion — there was a whole shelf of his sermons and writings to prove it: the Levi Blodgett letter and the South Boston sermon, the "Introduction to the Old Testament," the "Discourse of Religion," the two volumes of "Critical Writings." That was the West Roxbury record, and it had carried him triumphantly from Spring Street to the Melodeon. The second part of his task, the application of religion to life, had to be worked out in Boston.

4

So Parker came in to join the Boston reformers, to make his peculiar contribution of applied Christianity. His church had been organized just for him, and under no ordinary auspices, and something more was expected than a performance of ritual or an annotation of the Gospels. Not because of his learning or his eloquence, or even his piety, had it been resolved "that the Rev. Theodore Parker shall have a chance to be heard in Boston," but because he was the one spokesman of transcendentalism among the clergy, the one uncompromising critic of Hunkerism in the Church. No one else could do what he was expected to do, not James Freeman Clarke, not Pierpont, nor Sargent, nor young Starr King, for all their good intentions. Among all the Boston clergy Parker was the only one to associate on equal terms with the lay reformers, with Garrison and Mann, Phillips and Howe. And among all the reformers, he was the only one who found it possible to remain in the Church and to use the pulpit as the vantage ground from which to direct the attack. He had seen the Church become the apologist for the established order, he had seen the leadership in moral progress pass from the clergy to the laity; he remained stubbornly convinced that the Church might yet be made an instrument for social reform, and he was bold enough to assume responsibility for the experiment. He was not a Channing, but he hoped to complete what Channing had inaugurated. Did he anticipate, that winter day of 1846 when he conducted his own installation as Minister of the Twenty-eighth Congregational Society, did he anticipate that preëminence which was to bring him such odium as no other clergyman suffered, such honor as no other clergyman knew, that fame which was to make his name a byword and a benediction? Did he foresee the strange company he was to keep in the coming years, the peculiar causes he was to plead, the power he was to wield? "I did not know what was latent in myself," he wrote years later, "nor foresee all the doctrines which then were hid in my own first principles, what embryo fruit and flowers lay sheathed in the obvious bud." Yet all the future was implicit in that installation sermon on *The True Idea of the Christian Church*.

"A Christian Church," he said, standing there so young and so terribly earnest, so anxious to do justice to his theme and to reach the hearts of the hundreds who had crowded into the great Melodeon, — "A Christian Church should be the means of reforming the world, of forming it after the pattern of Christian ideas. It should therefore bring up the sentiments of the times, the ideas of the times, and the actions of the times, to judge them by the universal standard. We expect the sins of commerce to be winked at in the streets; the sins of the state to be applauded on election day and in a Congress, or on the Fourth of July; we are used to hear them called the righteousness of the nation. You expect them to be tried by passion, which looks only to immediate results and partial ends. Here they are to be measured by Conscience and Reason, which look to

permanent results and universal ends; to be looked at with
reference to the Laws of God, the everlasting ideas on
which alone is based the welfare of the world. If the church
be true, many things which seem gainful in the street and
expedient in the senate-house, will here be set down as
wrong, and all gain which comes therefrom seem to be
but a loss. If there be a public sin in the land, if a lie invade
the state, it is for the church to give the alarm; it is here
that it may war on lies and sins; the more widely they
are believed in and practised, the more are they deadly, the
more to be opposed. Here let no false idea or false action
of the public go without exposure or rebuke. But let no noble
heroism of the times, no noble man pass by without due
honor."

Nothing was beyond the province of the Church, nothing
foreign to its interest or exempt from its control. Its jurisdiction embraced the morals of the State as well as the
morals of men, its purpose was the salvation of society as
well as the salvation of the individual. Its liturgy was social welfare, its sacraments good works, its creed the perfectibility of man. It was Catholic in its authority, Protestant in its attitude. There was no responsibility it could
evade, no duty it could ignore. Every beggar, every pauper,
was a reproach, every poorhouse, every jail, a disgrace, and
it was hypocrisy to pretend to a religion of love and tolerate
the injustices of man to man. For nineteen centuries the
Church had preached the doctrine of Brotherly Love; how
could it explain the persistence of brutal crime and venge-
ful punishment, of iniquity committed in the name of Property, and murder sanctioned by the State? Too long had
the Church been silent in the face of these evils, too long
concerned with dogma and sectarian strife, too long the
refuge of the powerful and the sanctuary of the strong.
What, indeed, had the Church been doing all this time that
the almshouses were crowded and the jails full and harlots
walked the streets of Boston? What had the Church been
doing that slavery was tolerated and war glorified and labor
exploited and woman oppressed and the rich suffered to

lord it over the poor? What had the Church been doing
that the blind were denied light, and the feeble-minded
treated like animals, and children allowed to grow up in
ignorance and want, toiling long hours in the factories and
going to school in crime? "If the church were to waste
less time in building its palaces of theological speculation,
palaces mainly of straw, and based upon the chaff, it would
surely have more time to use in the practical good works
of the day."

This was the heroism of the present, the sainthood of the
future, not the defense of a creed or the punishment of a
heresy, but the philanthropy that toiled for the ignorant
and the needy, for the vagrant and the drunkard, the prostitute and the thief. No need for the Church to seek refuge
in abstractions, to preach nebulous moral sentiments; here
was work enough at hand, here were causes to enlist the
energies of every Christian. War against the crime of war,
war against the crime of slavery, war against intemperance
and vice, against poverty and ignorance and disease. Of
what value the triumph of science and of the arts, if morals
lag behind? But apply religion to life, sincerely, intelligently, and you could make over society, you could work
a real revolution. "We should build up a great state where
there was an honorable work for every hand, bread for all
mouths, clothing for all backs, culture for every mind, and
love and faith in every heart. . . . The noblest monument
to Christ, the fairest trophy of religion, is a noble people,
where all are well fed and clad, industrious, free, educated,
manly, pious, wise and good."

Here was a confession of faith for the church militant,
here was a program of practical philanthropy, a pledge for
reform. Let no one mistake the purpose for which the
Twenty-eighth Congregational Society had been organized,
let no one misapprehend the philosophy which inspired its
minister. He was done, now, with theological polemics,
done with bickering over a Unitarian creed or quarreling
over the privilege of an exchange. He had formulated the
Articles of Faith; now for a Sacrament of Works.

CHAPTER IX

THE SOCIALIZATION OF CHRISTIANITY

PARKER threw himself into the various reform movements of the day with characteristic energy, and soon he was as immersed in the reports of state boards of charities, of prisons, and asylums as ever he had been in the transactions of the philosophical societies. "When I first came to Boston," he remembered later, "I meant to do something for the perishing and dangerous classes in our great towns — for the poor, the drunkard, the ignorant, for the prostitute, and the criminal. But, alas, I did not quite understand all the consequences of my relation to these great social forces, or how much I had offended the religion of the state, the press, the market, and the church. I soon found my very name was enough to ruin any new good enterprise. I knew there were three periods in each great movement of mankind — that of sentiment, ideas, and action; I fondly hoped the last had come; but when I found I had reckoned without the host, I turned attention to the two former and sought to arouse the sentiment of justice and mercy, and to diffuse the ideas which belonged to this five-fold reformation. Hence I took pains to state the facts of poverty, drunkenness, ignorance, prostitution, crime; to show their cause, their effect, and their mode of cure, leaving it for others to do the practical work."

Yet this was a palpable exaggeration; when did Parker ever leave it to others to do work that must be done? His genius lay in agitation, and he gave it full play, but he did what work he could. He served on committees, circulated petitions, organized charitable and social welfare societies, he lectured, he wrote, and he preached. He sought to make his home in Exeter Place a clearinghouse for the reform work of the day, and not without success.

No sooner was he settled in Boston than he issued an invitation to a "Council of Reformers" whose object was to discuss the "General Principles of Reform" and the best means of promoting them. Everyone came: Emerson and Alcott from Concord, Garrison and Phillips who lived near by, James and Lucretia Mott up from Philadelphia and Sam Jo May from Syracuse, Chevalier Howe and Charles Sumner and Edmund Quincy, James Freeman Clarke from the Church of the Disciples, E. H. Chaplin, the eloquent Universalist, and Caleb Stetson, who had delivered the charge at Parker's ordination, but had scarcely contemplated this. For six hours they discussed what Garrison called All the Holy Principles of Reform. They had a sublime faith in discussion, these men; they thought that if only you could get at the truth, the truth would make you free. And when the possibilities of private discussion were exhausted, they had recourse to Conventions.

There was, for example, the Anti-Sabbath Convention of March, 1848. Parker helped to organize it, and it met in his own Melodeon, and for two days the reformers had at each other, hammer and tongs. This question of Sabbath reform was not in itself of great importance (Garrison thought it was, Garrison who hated the enslavement of the spirit as fiercely as he hated the enslavement of the body), but it was important in its implications, in the principles that were at stake. It was not so much that they opposed the old Puritan Sunday, though that was dismal enough; what they objected to were those penal laws which an over-anxious State had thrown around the day and which the Sabbath Union was now agitating with such misspent energy. The laws were innocuous enough, to be sure, rarely observed, more rarely enforced, but even the mildest of

laws represented an assertion of the authority of the State
over the consciences of men. In this matter of religious
observance, they thought, the State had no proper concern.
"Let Sunday and preaching stand on their own merits,"
said Parker. Better empty pews than attendance dictated
by laws or by custom or even by inertia. He preached a
sermon on the matter; history was gutted and philosophy
exhausted to prove that the Sabbath was made for man.

Yet Parker was no extremist. "I have all along," he confessed to a clerical friend, "been a little afraid of a reaction
from the sour, stiff, Jewish way of keeping Sunday into a
low, coarse, material, voluptuous or mere money-making
abuse of it." In the Convention he spoke for moderation (a
rare thing, this), and his resolutions were conciliatory in
tone: "We consider the superstitious opinions respecting
the origin of the institution of Sunday as a day to be devoted to religious purposes to form the chief obstacle to
a yet more profitable use of that day." "But," said another
resolution, "we should lament to see the Sunday devoted
to *labor* or *sport*; for though we think all days are equally
holy we yet consider that the custom of devoting one day
in each week mainly to spiritual culture is still of great advantage to mankind." But the extremists were not satisfied
with these. They represented a compromise, and Garrison
was even less accustomed to compromise than was Parker.
He introduced his own resolutions, twenty of them, and
supported them with argument and poesy, and in the end
all of his were adopted and only four of Parker's. "I was
between two fires," Parker wrote, "*cross*-fires, too."

There was the Anti-Capital Punishment Convention.
"Nothing remarkable," Parker wrote in his Journal, "but
as a sign of the times." And a sign of the times it assuredly
was; not for half a century had men inquired so critically
into the whole problem of crime and punishment or sought
so earnestly to fix responsibility where it really belonged.
Parker had long been familiar with this problem. When he
was a student in the Divinity School he had gone out and

preached to the convicts in the Charlestown prison, and he had never passed up an opportunity to acquaint himself with prison conditions and the statistics of crime. "If I were governor of Massachusetts," he wrote once to John Sargent, "I should know exactly the condition of every jail and house of correction in the state, and of all the institutions for preventing crime and ignorance." He read Plato's "Republic," and was moved to observe that "penal legislation now-a-days has all the effect of the purest injustice, in driving the half-guilty to increased crime, and in making doubly deep the hatred of the revengeful." He visited the Tombs of New York and asked: "How can it be justice to punish as a crime that which the institutions of society render unavoidable? How could anything better be expected of the poor wretches daily brought up to that court, exposed naked as they are, to all the contamination of corrupt society?"

West Roxbury offered little opportunity for a realistic study of the problem of crime, and it was not until Parker came to Boston that his suspicions became certainty and his inchoate idealism a program of action. No sooner had he announced his true idea of a Christian Church than he turned from generalization to particulars, and delivered a series of sermons on the Dangerous and Perishing Classes of society, all of them touching closely this problem of the responsibility of society for crime, poverty, and ignorance, all of them revealing the characteristic alliance of intuition and fact. *A priori* ideas were scrupulously proved, and every moral axiom was appealed to the Census Bureau.

Philosophy and experience, theory and fact, united to point one inescapable moral: it was society, not the individual, that was at fault. Nine tenths of all prisoners, Parker found, came from the "perishing" classes, and seventeen twentieths of all crimes were crimes against property. Over one half of all the persons confined in the Boston House of Correction were foreigners, newcomers gone astray in a strange, a hostile, environment. Of the 547 women on Black-

well's Island in New York, 519 had been committed for
vagrancy — "women with no capital but their person, with
no friend, no shelter." Equally impressive was the correla-
tion of crime and ignorance: in Massachusetts one third of
the criminals could not read or write; New York, of course,
didn't do even that well: at Mount Pleasant six sevenths
of the prisoners were illiterate. The statistics from abroad
merely emphasized the obvious: over ninety per cent. of
all the prisoners in England and Wales, in the year 1841,
were illiterate, and the figures from the Continent were
just as shocking.

The moral was obvious, but Parker did not forbear to
point it. The statistics of crime furnished an index not of
character but of opportunity, and it was inevitable that
our prisoners should be recruited from among the poor
and the ignorant. "The effect of property in elevating and
moralizing a class of men is seldom realized," Parker concluded.

Nor would Parker leave it all to the pleasant anonymity
of "society." Property was at fault, the State was at fault,
the Church was at fault. Men who paid low wages and
high dividends, men who collected exorbitant rentals for
wretched slums or, worse still, for grog shops or houses of
ill fame, men who were willing to pay taxes for war but
not for schools, these were the real foes of society. Bankers
who exacted usurious rates of interest, journalists who reveled in the most loathsome details of vice, lawyers who would
defend, for a fee, the worse of causes, judges who thought it
a crime for anyone to be poor, clergymen who argued the
divine sanction of the gallows, statesmen who made war and
called it honorable, these were the men who organized the
sins of society.

The nation sets the poor an example of fraud by making them
pay the highest on all local taxes; of theft by levying the national income on persons, not property. Our navy and army set
them the lesson of violence; and to complete their schooling, at
this very moment we are robbing another nation of cities and

lands, stealing, burning, and murdering, for lust of power and gold. Everybody knows that the political action of a nation is the mightiest educational influence in that nation. But such is the doctrine the State preaches to them, a constant lesson of fraud, theft, violence, and crime.

Nor did our system of punishment possess even the dubious virtue of efficiency. It neither prevented crime nor reformed criminals. Over half of the offenders haled before the Courts of Boston had already served prison sentences and, within five years, over three hundred criminals had been jailed ten times or more. It was clear that the jails made more criminals than they cured. For all the harshness of the penal code and the horrors of the prisons, the statistics of crime mounted every year. "You may punish the man," Parker said, "but it does no good. You can seldom frighten men out of a fever. Can you frighten them from crime, when all the circumstances about them impel to crime? Can you frighten a starving girl into chastity? You cannot keep men from lewdness, theft and violence, when they have no self-respect, no culture, no development of mind, heart and soul. The gaol will not take the place of the church, of the schoolhouse, of home. It will not remove the causes which are making new criminals. It does not reform the old ones. The gaol does not alter the circumstances which occasioned the crime, and until these causes are removed, a fresh crop will spring out of the festering soil." And when the Reform School at Westborough burned down, Parker wrote, "I am not sorry. It was a school for crime and must graduate villains."

The trouble was that this whole business of punishment rested upon a false philosophy, a mistaken conception of Man. It was based upon hate and revenge, not upon love and respect for the dignity of man. Did it take a transcendentalist to see this, a Bronson Alcott, an Emerson, a Parker? It was so obvious that every man of sense should see it. "How long will it be," Parker asked, with a curious emphasis, "before we apply good sense and Christianity to

the prevention of crime? One day we must see that a gaol
is no more likely to cure a crime than a lunacy or a fever.
A gaol, as a mere house of punishment, ought to have no
place in an enlightened people. It ought to be a moral hos-
pital where the offender is kept till he is cured." And how
illogical this custom of fixed sentences, as if five years of
prison would cure a thief and ten years an embezzler. "It
is wrong to detain a man after he is cured; wrong to send
him out before he is cured." How immoral the fever of the
State to remove men from society, the indifference of the
State to the task of restoring men to society. "I doubt not,"
Parker wrote, "the angel of humanity will beat with her
golden pinions, all prisons to small dust."

If jails were bad, how much worse were the gallows, and
how monstrous that Christian ministers should justify them.
There was the Reverend George B. Cheever, self-appointed
guardian of public morals, who erected a "Defense of Capital Punishment" on the foundations of the Old Testament;
Phillips tried to meet him on his own ground, and presented
a lawyer's brief citing chapter and verse for a different
interpretation of the Scriptures. But Parker would have
none of such truckling to religious prejudices. If the Bible
sanctioned capital punishment, the Bible was wrong. "It
fills me with amazement," he said, "that worthy men in
these days should go back to such sources for their wisdom;
should walk dry-shod through the Gospels, and seek in the
records of a barbarous people to justify their atrocious acts."
And he had no more respect for the authority of the State
than for the authority of the Church. "I know," he said,
"that society claims the right of eminent domain over
person and life not less than over house and land. I deny
the right. Certainly it has never been shown. To me, resting
on the broad ground of natural justice, capital punishment
seems wholly inadmissible, homicide with the pomp and
formality of law. To put a criminal to death seems to me
as foolish as for the child to beat the stool it has stumbled
over, and as useless too."

Easy enough to indict society for its mismanagement of this business, but what was to be done? Some of the reforms were obvious and close at hand. Society must assume responsibility for its own shortcomings; the idea of punishment must be discarded and that of cure substituted. Houses of correction must justify their name, and another Horace Mann should be found to make them institutions of education. The gallows, symbol of vengeance, must go; fixed terms of sentence, symbol of punishment, must go; even prison uniforms must go, for they were degrading. Above all, the attitude of mind that these things represented, must be abandoned.

Nor did the responsibility of the State end when it had discharged its patients. It must see to it that the cure was permanent, that society took back its own. It should maintain a public defender as well as a public prosecutor. It should establish a system of moral police to discover the causes of crime and remove them. It should follow up discharged criminals and see to it that they became useful citizens. Above all it should take care of the children of offenders, protect them from society and from a dangerous environment. This whole business of the care of children had to be changed, and above all the manner of dealing with juvenile delinquents, for here, surely, the fault of society was clear. Reform schools were better than jails, but better still the establishment of state farms where the children could be taught healthy and useful work, or the distribution of children in homes throughout the State. "I wonder," Parker wrote, "men don't see that they can never safely depart from the natural order which God has appointed. Boys are born in *families;* they grow up in *families;* a few in each household, mixed with girls and with their elders." It was a policy that worked well in France; it ought to be tried in America.

Yet these things were palliatives, not cures. "The greater portion of this work," Parker concluded, "is not special and for the criminal, but general and for society. To change the treatment of criminals, we must change everything else. The dangerous class is the unavoidable result of our present civilization, of our present ideas of man and social life. To reform and elevate the class of criminals we must reform and elevate all other classes."

2

More and more Parker came to understand the interrelationship between all social problems, came to see the larger issues behind particular reforms. You could not touch an open wound without irritating the entire nervous system of society; you could not treat an infection without studying social pathology. If you tried to do something about crime and punishment, you ran into the whole question of the ultimate responsibility for crime and the authority of the State; if you tried to grapple with the problem of prostitution, you came up against the Woman Question and the mistaken ideas about sex. Was it pauperism you would eliminate, you would have to face the whole problem of property and property rights. Was it war you would end, you would have to fight down the false notions of national honor and the function of the State. Temperance could not be achieved by regulatory laws, it affected property rights and human rights and demanded a higher conception of the Dignity of Man; the labor question was not merely a matter of hours and wages, but brought up the most far-reaching considerations of the nature of property and the function of labor and of capital in society. Challenge a single wrong and you would find every vested interest arrayed against you; propound a new idea and you would run up against a Chinese wall of inertia, superstition and ignorance.

Take, for example, this matter of prostitution. It would seem so glaring an evil that it would be easy enough to cope with it. No one would defend the institution, yet here were over two hundred brothels in Boston alone. There were laws, of course, but who cared about them? Exhortation was futile, threats worse than useless, and even the practical work of rescue and reform seemed of little avail. All during the Boston years Parker was busy with this practical work. He visited Charles Loring Brace in New York in order to study at first hand the methods of that pioneer welfare worker, and he found a capital friend; the conversations soon drifted away from the conditions of boys and girls in the slums to the Icelandic sagas and Mallet's work on Scandinavian Antiquities. But Parker got something out of it, despite these distractions, and he came back to Boston and tried to do there what Brace was doing in New York. With Phillips and Henry Bowditch and Edward Beecher, brother of the more famous Henry, he organized a society to rescue delinquent girls, instruct them in housework, and place them in homes throughout the State. Sargent, who had been dismissed from the Suffolk Street Chapel for permitting Parker to preach there, was made the agent of the society, and half the reformers of the city enlisted in the crusade.

But it was uphill work, and little to show for it. Parker could not but admire the success of that obscure cobbler John Augustus, who never lost faith in practical philanthropy and who made himself the guardian angel of the poor of Boston. He was a rare person, John Augustus, one of the real Christians of his age; he did not concern himself with social philosophy or theories of reform, but quietly went about his self-appointed task of saving the sinner and the publican. Every day he sat in the police courts, taking care of his own: going bail for the vagrant and the drunkard and the prostitute, for boys and girls who had run afoul of the law. For twenty years he had been a familiar figure in the streets of Boston, this odd, crotchety, wrinkled old man, hurrying around to the courts and the jails and sometimes to the churches, finding money for his wards, getting them work, placing them in homes. Parker knew him well; he had been born in Lexington (Hannah Parker had known his mother, but no one knew his father), and he had found

time and money for his charities there before he moved on
to Boston; and when he died Parker grieved that he was
not there to point the moral of that life. "All the members
of the Supreme Court might die next month," he wrote,
"and the President follow suit, and half the Governors of
the Union, and unitedly they would not be so great a loss
as poor old John Augustus."

Yet for all his admiration of John Augustus, Parker
had little confidence in this hit-or-miss philanthropy. You
could not end prostitution unless you ended the poverty
which drove girls into prostitution and the poverty which
prevented men from marriage. Nor was the question one
of economics only. You could not end prostitution until
you introduced sanity into this matter of sex, broke through
the conspiracy of silence and shame that surrounded the
subject. And behind all these things was the Woman Question, for prostitution, after all, was merely one of the crimes
against Woman, the most flagrant, but perhaps not the most
radical one.

Parker handled the question of sex with a wholesome
robustness that contrasted sharply with the timidity and
priggishness of most of his friends, Thoreau, for example,
or even Emerson. "A history of the gradual development
of the sexual element in mankind," he wrote, "would be a
noble theme. What a deal of prudery there is about the
matter here in New England." His own attitude was a characteristic blend of the scientific and the poetic, and that,
he thought, was the way to understand sex. He had read
something of psychology and physiology as well as the
history of monasticism, and his reading proved what his
common sense affirmed: that celibacy, voluntary or enforced,
was unnatural and dangerous. "If there is a damnable institution on earth," he wrote from Rome, "it is compulsory
celibacy of women; if the men take the unnatural vow
they can break it and, God be thanked, they commonly do;
but it is different with women, they must keep the loathsome vow." And in a long correspondence with the vener-

able Shaker, Robert White, he elaborated this point of view. The body itself, he wrote, was an irrefutable argument for marriage, and the testimony of the instincts was more convincing by far than any of those arguments from Scripture which Mr. White so confidently advanced. And the suppression of these instincts, Parker said, led to terrible evils, to licentiousness, to hysteria and insanity, to vices of the spirit and corruption of the flesh. He was very earnest about it, and in the end even Mr. White was convinced.

But it was not the Catholic Church alone that was at fault; even in America it was generally assumed that the sexual relation was somehow sinful. What was needed, Parker felt, was a frank acceptance of the beauty and power of sex, and the sublimation of the sexual instinct into the spiritual realm. "Those old Greeks," he wrote, apropos of Homer, "were brutes in their lust; for it was not always love. Yet there is something quite æsthetic and graceful about their love adventures. Why cannot old Greek freedom and real, unconventional, love be united with Christian morality, and woman stand in her true position."

Parker knew that it wasn't all a matter of celibacy; there was more than one way of betraying natural law. He knew well enough the psychological rocks upon which so many marriages were wrecked; the unnatural suppression of passion, he thought, was as bad as the unnatural indulgence of lust. "When a noble person marries for the noble end, and then finds it is no marriage, there is horrible suffering; and all sorts of abnormalities of conduct, internal and external, may be expected to take their places. The very eminence of morality in New England intensifies the suffering, for elsewhere the connubial *Abschweifungen* are tolerated, and the disappointed persons find some relief, at least abatement, from their long-continued affliction." Parker didn't know what was to be done about it, and that was one subject he kept clear of in his preaching. More lenient divorce laws might help, though he wasn't at all sure even of that. But "proper notions of marriage and of divorce, can only come as the result of a slow but thorough revolution in the idea of woman."

It was a phrase that he often used, but never defined, this "revolution in the idea of woman." What did he mean by it, what did they all mean by it, Margaret Fuller and Garrison and Phillips and the rest of them? It wasn't only a matter of legal disabilities or political disqualifications (those things worried Phillips), it was more than that. It was a matter of emancipation from those habits of thought that confined her sphere of influence and held her, substantially, in contempt. He wished not only to change the divorce laws, the suffrage laws, the property laws, but to change the attitude of men, and when Wendell Phillips, hot from the Woman's Rights Convention, told him that this was "the most magnificent reform that has yet been launched upon the world," he was not disposed to challenge the exaggeration.

Yet for all of his advocacy of woman's rights, his attendance upon conventions and his sermons and his lectures and his gestures of professional hospitality (the Reverend Antoinette Brown preached from his pulpit, and so did the Reverend Sheba Smith), the Woman Question remained for Parker what it had been in the beginning, a sentiment and an abstraction. He idealized woman, he regarded her as morally superior to man, and his discussions of the subject were sicklied over with romanticism. "I think man will always lead in affairs of intellect," he said, "of reason, imagination, understanding; he has the better brain. But woman will always lead in affairs of emotion — moral, affectional, religious; she has the better heart." And the function of woman, he wrote fatuously, is "to correct man's taste, mend his morals, excite his affection, inspire his religious faculties." No wonder Higginson insisted that Parker never really understood the Woman Question, no wonder Julia Ward Howe jeered at him for his intolerable air of intellectual condescension. He meant well; he knew Elizabeth Peabody and Margaret Fuller and Lydia Maria Child, he worked with

Dorothea Dix and Julia Howe and Lucretia Mott and Frances Cobbe. But when he wrote on the Woman Question he was thinking of his "glorious phalanx of old maids"; when he wrote on the Woman Question he was the husband of Lydia.

3

Nothing took you back to fundamentals as did the labor question, nothing revealed more glaringly the immorality of the whole social order. No sentimentality here, no polite abstractions: Parker saw with dangerous clarity the barbarism and brutality of the industrial feudalism of the nineteenth century, of America, and he lashed out against it in passionate protest. This was no hothouse radicalism; he didn't need the Census Bureau to tell him of the wretchedness and misery of the great cities, he knew his way about the slums of Boston as well as did Father Taylor himself. "See the unnatural disparity in man's condition," he told his congregation, "bloated opulence and starving penury in the same street. See the pauperism, want, licentiousness, intemperance, and crime in the midst of us; see the havoc made of woman; see the poor deserted by their elder brother, while it is their sweat which enriches your ground, builds your railroads, and piles up your costly houses." Years earlier he had written of this, the shouts of the Russell children coming across the field and through his study window as he wrote, "It is common to censure some one class of men — the rich or the educated, the manufacturers, the merchants, for example, as if the sin rested solely with them, while it belongs to society at large." But he was less academic, now, or less tolerant, perhaps, and readier to fix the blame. He had not been in Boston a year before he seared the complacency of the ruling class with a flaming "Sermon on Merchants."

He was a firebrand, he was a demagogue, he was a menace to society. Not even Channing or Brownson had talked like this; no clergyman should talk like this. You would have to go to the socialists or the Fourierites for anything like his description of the bad merchant.

The bad merchant still lives. He cheats in his trade; sometimes against the law, commonly with it. His truth is never wholly true nor his lie wholly false. He overreaches the ignorant; makes hard bargains with them in their trouble, for he knows that a falling man will catch at red-hot iron. He takes the pound of flesh, though that bring away all the life blood with it. He loves private contracts, digging through walls in secret. No interest is illegal if he can get it. He cheats the nation with false invoices, and swears lies at the custom-house. He oppresses the men who sail his ships, forcing them to be temperate only that he may consume the value of their drink. He provides them unsuitable bread and meat. He would not engage in the African slave trade, for that might lose his ships, but he is always ready to engage in the American slave trade, and calls you a "fanatic" if you tell him it is the worse of the two. He cares not whether he sells cotton or the man who wears it, if only he gets his money: cotton or negro, it is the same to him. He would not keep a drink-hole in Ann Street, only own and rent it. He thinks it vulgar to carry rum about in a jug, respectable in a ship. He makes paupers and leaves others to support them. Tell him not of the misery of the poor, he knows better; nor of our paltry way of dealing with public crime, he wants more gaols and a speedier gallows. You see his character in letting his houses, his houses for the poor. He is a stone in the lame man's shoe. He is the poor man's devil. The Hebrew devil that so worried Job is gone, so is the brutal devil that awed our fathers. But this devil of the nineteenth century is still extant. He has gone into trade and advertises in the papers. He makes money; the world is poorer by his wealth. He can build a Church out of his gains, to have his morality, his Christianity, preached in it, and call that the gospel. He sends rum and missionaries to the same barbarians, the one to damn, the other to save, both for his own advantage, for his patron saint is Judas, the first saint who made money out of Christ. He is not forecasting to discern effects in causes, nor skillful to create new wealth, only spry in the scramble for what others have made. In politics he wants a Government that will ensure his dividends; so asks what is good for him, but ill for the rest. He knows no right only power; no man but self; no God but his calf of gold.

Not all the merchants were bad, there were good merchants a-plenty — Francis Jackson, dearest of friends, or George Luther Stearns, or John Murray Forbes who came sometimes to the Melodeon and whom Emerson thought the best man of his generation. But Parker was talking about the merchants as a class, and of the evil that they did. They had established an aristocracy of gold, a feudalism of money. They ruled the State, enacted the laws, appointed legislators, manufactured governments, bred judges. They owned the Church, subsidizing clergymen to preach soft words, building splendid cathedrals to show their piety, hoping to buy their way into Heaven as they bought everything else. They controlled the machinery of society; industry, finance, transportation, labor, and they abused their power. Their morals were the morals of the market place, their politics the politics of peddlers, their culture vulgar and meretricious.

You could denounce their morals but you could not dispute their power. All very well, in the flush of youth, to talk of abating private property as a nuisance; Fourierism had had its day, and the present task was to direct the power of wealth along social channels. There was much that could be done, and most of it of an obvious character. There was this matter of wages: here were the Lowell mills cutting wages ten per cent. and paying extra dividends of twelve; the Massachusetts Mills declaring a dividend of twenty per cent., the manufacturers of Connecticut taking in forty per cent. each year. "When I remember," said Parker, "that all value is the result of work, and see that no man gets rich by his own work, I cannot help thinking that labour is often wickedly underpaid and capital sometimes as grossly overfed. I shall believe that capital is at the mercy of labour when the two extremes of society change places." It was labor that needed protection, not capital. The merchants kept Daniel Webster down in Washington just to see that they were safe from competition, while they brought in wagonloads of girls from the country towns and Irishmen fresh from Limerick to work at starvation wages. "There is no protection," Parker pointed out, "for the carpenter or the bricklayer. Yet if we cared for men more than for money, and were consistent with our principles of protection, why, we should exclude all foreign workmen as well as their work, and so raise the wages of native hands."

There were the hazards of industry, as great as those of war, and as inglorious, and when the jerry-built walls of the Pemberton Mills caved in, hurtling hundreds of men and women to their death, Parker found the cause of the disaster in "human ignorance and cupidity." There were other hazards, less spectacular but even more significant, and he compiled statistics of occupational morality and was not surprised to find that machinists died at thirty-seven and laborers at forty-five, while farmers could expect to live until they were sixty-five. There was the problem of unemployment, bad enough at all times, shocking during those years of acute depression that industry seemed unable to avoid. "What we want," Parker wrote in the black year of 1857, "is work. This time of trouble will make some men consider the chaotic condition of our social system, this antagonistic competition in place of coöperative industry." Organized charity could do something, but that was no answer to the problem. Where charity was organized, beggary was too, and Parker noted that the whole of Boston paddy-land squatted in the anteroom of his own Provident Aid Society. It was downright immoral for industry to make men paupers and then debauch them with charity. What was needed were practical measures: better pay, shorter hours, decent housing (he and Bowditch were trying to get the Legislature to do something about the tenements), lower living costs — free trade was the answer there. These things could be done, by individuals, by the merchant class, by the nation. "If we begin with taking care of the rights of man, it seems easy to take care of the rights of labour and capital. To begin the other way is quite another thing. A nation making laws for the nation is a noble sight." And then that unobtrusive phrase which Parker liked so well and used insistently until it caught the eye of Herndon's friend and was metamorphosed into immortality: "The government of all, by all, and for all, is a Democracy."

4

There were a score of problems that clamored for attention, and all of them went to the heart of things. Parker did not want to be a professional reformer, a common scold; he had no use for that sort of thing. He did not want to dissipate his energies, to spill over every which way. But he could not help himself. There was an interlocking directorate of reformers, and he was in it, for better or for worse. There had to be give-and-take in this reform business as in everything else. He could not take his contributions down to the office of the *Liberator* but that the editor would ply him with Sabbath reform and non-resistance. He could not serve with Phillips on Vigilance Committees without being ensnared into the Movement for Woman's Rights. If he consulted with Sam Howe about some political scheme, the Chevalier would be sure to tax him with neglecting his duty toward society's wards; if he advised with Sargent on the organization of rescue work, the Temperance Question was bound to come up. When he lectured in Worcester, there was Higginson, aflame with indignation over the mistreatment of women; when he lectured in Philadelphia, there were the Motts, James and Lucretia, to ask him why he stood aloof from the Peace Movement. In Ohio, with Horace Mann, it was education that demanded his attention; in Illinois, Herndon would draw him into politics. He would assure them all (he was rather proud of it) that his name would damn any Society, ruin any cause. But that did no good: if he didn't want to work in the open, he could work in private. Every mail brought some new request for aid; every conference divulged some new plan which needed his support. And after all, why not? He was fair game, he did the same thing to the others, posting letters of advice, sending out calls for aid, rallying the reformers to some scheme for the salvation of society. Every Sunday he gathered them in his parlors in Exeter Place, reformers of every stripe, and a hundred conspiracies would be hatched. How could he excuse himself from any of them?

The point was, you couldn't separate these reform movements, or consign these reformers to any one department. There were exceptions, of course: Theodore Weld whom nothing could distract from the struggle against slavery (nothing but the attractions of obscurity), or Dorothea Dix, who espoused one cause and conquered the world. But most of them, however they began, were Universal Reformers. Only monumental arrogance or the most profound humility could account for it, and they were not all arrogant, these men. Who was more innocent than Bronson Alcott, who invited gentlemen to form a "Club for the Study and Diffusion of Ideas and Tendencies Proper to the Nineteenth Century"? Who more modest than Emerson, but he knew that "where a man comes, there comes revolution." No doubt it was amusing that poor old Robert Owen, who ought to know better, should summon a "World Convention to Emancipate the Human Race from Ignorance, Poverty, Division, Sin, and Misery"; but after all there was a truth here that all of them recognized: you could not capture the battlements of Heaven by a series of disjointed raids.

Take Howe, for instance: he had begun life with a quixotic gesture, but his gesture became as reverent as prayer and set the pattern of his life. "I do not like caution," he said, "it betokens little faith in God's arrangement," and he gave himself to making clear God's purpose with man. God intended men to be free, and Howe threw himself with abandon into the struggle for the liberation of the Greeks and of the Poles, and for the liberation of the American slave, and his opponents could bear witness to his lack of caution. God intended men to use their talents, and Howe brought sight to the blind and speech to the mute and knowledge to the ignorant and surcease to those who were in pain. No worthy cause failed to enlist his support: he was director of the Institution for the Blind and his achievements were famous in two continents; he established a school for the feeble-minded and one for the deaf-mutes; he organized the Prisoner's Aid Society and the Board of State Charities; he served on the Boston School Committee and sustained Mann in his work; he fought all through the slavery struggle and was a tower of strength to the less practical abolitionists. His versatility, his coruscating brilliance, his volcanic energy, sprang from an inner harmony: it was the same man who had the infinite patience to work a miracle with Laura Bridgman and the impetuosity to organize the Kansas Crusade. The most generous, the least fanatical, of men, it was faith, not intolerance, that drove him into so many causes. He fulfilled the logic, he justified the philosophy, of reform.

Or, if you wanted the Universal Reformer, there was Wendell Phillips. "Don't shilly-shally, Wendell," his wife would say, and from his first dramatic appearance on the platform of Faneuil Hall to his last outrageous defiance of the Boston aristocracy, as he charged them with recreancy to justice and humanity and flung in their faces the taunt of Henry IV to Crillon, his life was a demonstration of courage. He had a relentless consistency; he was trained to the bar and he followed the logic of reform as a lawyer follows precedents. He had begun, simply enough, as an abolitionist, and before he knew it, he found himself drawn in as defense attorney for every unpopular cause in Boston. Soon he was agitating the Woman Question, peace, temperance, capital punishment, and a dozen other reforms, and with him agitation took on the mantle of dignity. Soon he was execrated on the Exchange and ostracized in the Clubs and his name was anathema in all the best houses, he who had been born on Beacon Street and who could look down his nose at half the families on the Hill. He had enlisted for the duration of the war and for him the war never ended, and it was well that Parker did not witness the tragic isolation of his later years as he stunned a generation of smug conservatives and self-righteous liberals with the revolutionary commonplaces of transcendentalism.

Even Garrison revealed the pervasive, the osmotic, force of the reform movement. How mistaken they were who thought of him as an abolitionist merely. "Our country is the world," he said, "our countrymen all mankind," and he meant it literally. Was it a coincidence that his papers were named the *Genius of Universal Emancipation* and the *Liberator?* "I feel somewhat at a loss to know what to do," he confided once to G. W. Benson, "whether to go into all the principles of holy reform and make the abolitionist cause subordinate or whether still to persevere in the one beaten track as hitherto," and John Humphrey Noyes when he visited him, learned that "his mind was heaving with the subject of Holiness and the Kingdom of Heaven and he would devote himself to them as soon as he could get anti-slavery off his hands." But he did not wait for this consummation of his hopes. He espoused as many reforms as did Noyes himself: he was a no-government man, a no-Bible man, a non-resistant; he was a Perfectionist. He had the intolerance of a fanatic and the benevolence of a philosopher. He antagonized every organization, he flouted every institution, he outraged every convention. He was as dangerous to the established order in New England as to the established order in the South, and they were right who dragged him through the streets of Boston with a halter around his neck. No doubt it was most inexpedient of him to imperil the cause of anti-slavery by mixing it up with woman's rights and non-resistance and Sabbath reform and what not; Theodore Weld and Lewis Tappan thought it was downright wicked. But it was Garrison who was consistent, after all, not they. "No man," said Channing, "should take on himself the office of a reformer whose zeal in a particular cause is not tempered by extensive sympathies and universal love." Regardless of consequences, your reformer had to be an eclectic.

Parker knew this as an axiom of philosophy, but it was not so easy to adopt it as a principle of action. Theology, philosophy, Fourierism, Perfectionism, the Dangerous Classes, the Perishing Classes, war, slavery — sometimes his head was in a whirl. There were so many reforms, there was never any end to the things that needed to be done; and he hurried so desperately, trying to keep up with it all, trudging up and down the streets of Boston (there were parish duties, there were Negroes who looked to him), speaking out at every convention, taking on lecture engagements by the score, scratching out letters in his painful scrawl, hundreds of them in a single month, working fourteen, sixteen hours a day, his beard gray, his health shattered, when he was forty-five. But sometimes it was too much for him. He felt that he was being rushed into things; he needed time to think, to get his philosophic bearings.

Here was this Temperance Movement. All of his friends were in it up to their necks: Chevalier Howe and Horace Mann, Lewis Tappan and Gerrit Smith in New York, the Motts in Philadelphia and Sam May in Syracuse. Phillips thundered from the lecture platform, Pierpont wrote poems about it — and a play too; and Garrison edited a temperance journal. Sometimes Parker was ready to believe that it was one of the vital reforms of the century, and he would speak out with a vigor that shocked even the most lethargic, commingling statistics and aphorisms to prove the dreadful consequences of drunkenness. Sometimes he felt that the whole question was befogged in emotion, that all the temperance reformers had the vapors. He distrusted an incapacity for emotion (nothing worse than the dry-rot of Unitarian intellectualism): the contemplation of social statistics never made a drunkard sober. He distrusted an excess of emotion (nothing worse than evangelical revivals): mass meetings and parades managed by Barnum and Company never kept a teetotaler to his pledge. Temperance was a moral question: Neal Dow and John Gough and lusty John Hawkins were on the right track, and Parker cheerfully signed the pledge, with a gold pen, too. Temperance was a scientific question: he read his French treatises and his German monographs and noted the harmful effects of alcohol here and the beneficial effects there. Temperance was a personal matter, a matter for each man to work out for himself, knowing his own character, answerable to his body and his conscience; all sumptuary legislation was worse than useless, coercion in the realm of morals, inviting all sorts of abuses. Temperance was a social problem, society had the right and the duty to protect itself from drunkenness as from disease or crime, and the Maine law was a good thing.

They have a new law in Maine. It makes the whole State an asylum for the drunkard. . . . The law seems an invasion of private right. It is an invasion, but for the sake of preserving the rights of all. I think wine a good thing; so is beer, rum, brandy, and the like, when rightly used. I think teetotalers are right in their practice *for these times,* but wrong in their principles. I believe it will be found on examination that, other things being equal, men who use stimulants moderately live longer, and have a sounder old age, than teetotalers. But now I think that nine-tenths of the alcoholic stimulus that is used is abused. The evil is so monstrous, so patent, so universal, that it becomes the duty of the State to take care of its citizens; the whole of its parts.

There you had the whole of it, both sides of the question neatly put. If only the agitators wouldn't go to extremes; if only we could have drinking such as he had found in France and Italy and Germany! But the American character was one of extremes, you had to recognize that, after all. If only the reformers wouldn't make drinking a matter of personal morals; he knew perfectly well that there was nothing sinful about drinking, he who, as a boy, had taken Grandmother Parker her daily mug of flip. Yet what was to be done about it all: when he came to Boston there were a thousand grogshops; fifteen years later there was prohibition, but the number had doubled, and every year ten thousand men and women were taken up for drunkenness.

Too bad that the workingman spent his wages at the tippling-house; too bad that the innkeeper flouted the law, dispensing damnation to keep himself and his family alive. But if there were no rich men in the trade, Parker observed, there would soon be no poor ones. It was when you began to trace the infection to its source that you got into trouble. When you described the drunkard's fate your parishioners applauded you, but when you told of the distillers who made the rum and the merchants who sold it, they called you a fanatic and turned you out. Parker had not forgotten how they had treated noble John Pierpont, the cellar of his church filled with barrels of rum, nor how the Unitarians had deserted him, conniving at his dismissal. You could not always gauge the merits of these reforms by the men who advocated them, but you could generally tell something about them from the opposition they aroused. If Parker deprecated the fanaticism of the teetotalers, he was likely to find himself in embarrassing company.

No, it wasn't easy to take sides on all of the reforms, to sign up for every crusade. Here was this question of war. What had Parker to say when Phillips stormed and Garrison declaimed? Here in New England, in his own time, had been inaugurated the greatest of crusades, the crusade to end war: a sailor from Maine and a blacksmith from Connecticut had caught the splendid vision, the great and learned of the world glad to do their bidding. There were peace societies everywhere (even in the South, even in Georgia), and the Legislature of Massachusetts memorialized Congress to arbitrate all disputes, and a million people read Elihu Burritt's "Olive Leaves."

What did Parker think of it all? When Charles Sumner delivered that terrific oration on "The True Grandeur of Nations," standing there so arrogant, so handsome, as he told the representatives of the Army and the Navy, puffed up in their uniforms, that no war was honorable, no peace dishonorable, Parker could not wait to hurry off a note of congratulation. And the next year he was saying the same thing himself, our armies marching on Mexico City, our patriots panting for Darien. "War is an utter violation of Christianity," he said. "If war be right, then Christianity is wrong, false, a lie. Every man who understands Christianity knows that war is wrong." And he proceeded to prove what every man knew. There were fewer classical allusions than Sumner had displayed, but more statistics, and he was churlish indeed who failed to be convinced by this blend of philosophy and figures.

"War is treason to the people, to mankind, to God." But he didn't really mean it, any more than Sumner meant it when fifteen years later the bullets spattered on the ramparts of Fort Sumter. What he meant was that the Mexican War was an infamous war. He would prove it. Here was its genesis, here its secret history, here its shabby purpose. It was conceived in iniquity and prosecuted with brutality and greed. It was a war for slavery, for land, and for money, it was inspired by every ignoble motive, it aroused every base passion. He would prove, too, that it was an inexpedient and unprofitable war. Here is what it cost in men, here is what it cost in dollars, and here is what we might have done with the money. Here were the consequences, too — the effect on the morals of the soldiers, the morals of the nation, on domestic politics and international relations. In short, this war was discreditable and dishonorable, and it should not be sustained. When it came to this war, Parker was as ready to preach the duty of civil disobedience as ever Thoreau was, or Edmund Quincy — Thoreau who would not pay taxes to a government that fought an unjust war, Quincy who turned in his commission as Justice of the Peace rather than serve a government that resorted to force. "What shall we do," Parker asked, "in regard to this present war. We can refuse to take any part in it; we can encourage others to do the same; we can aid men, if need be, who suffer because they refuse. Men will call us traitors; what then?

That hurt nobody in '76. We are a rebellious nation; our whole history is treason; our blood was attainted before we were born; our creeds are infidelity to the mother church; our constitution treason to our fatherland. What of that? Though all the governors in the world bid us commit treason against man, and set the example, let us never submit. Let God only be a master to control our conscience."

All very well for the Mexican War, but what of a war inspired by some lofty motive, fought for some righteous end? What of the war for American Independence (Grandfather Parker there on Lexington Common: "If they mean to have a war, let it begin here.")? What of a war to end slavery? He was ready enough to give money for Beecher's Bibles and for old John Brown; for ten years his letters were filled with the irrepressible conflict, and he did not deprecate it. A war for liberty was a very different thing from a war for greed. "I think," he wrote to Frances Cobbe, "we should agree about war. I hate it, I deplore it, but yet see its necessity. All the great charters of humanity have been *writ in blood*, and must continue to be for some centuries. I should let the Italians fight for their liberty till the twenty-eight million men were only fourteen million."

He was no non-resistant, not he. All very well for the Quakers to make pacifism an article of faith, the gentle Whittier wishing men

> Free, not by blood; redeemed, but not by crime,
> Each fetter broken; but in God's good time.

All very well for Garrison, to whom all government was odious. ("There is such a thing," said William Ladd, "as going beyond the Millennium.") But he was the grandson of Captain Parker, and two muskets from Lexington hung over the desk in his study; he would counsel any fugitive to sell his life dearly, and he was ready to storm the Court House any day if that would save an Anthony Burns.

5

Was he a spiritual Martha, distracted about much serving and troubled about many things? He had abandoned himself to good works, yet every year the state of society seemed more desperate. He had sounded a hundred blasts on the trumpet of reform and the walls of Hunkerdom still stood. What was he about, worrying institutions, exacerbating his fellow men, making a public nuisance of himself? "I am the best hated man in America," he could admit, and to what purpose? Perhaps Emerson was right: "Why so hot, my little man," he had said, and again, "There is a sublime prudence which, believing in a vast future, sure of more to come than is yet seen, postpones always the present hour to the whole life." Parker had been schooled in all the philosophies, even Stoicism, but he had never found Emerson's sublime prudence. A minister, he dwelt in eternity; a scientist, he took a million years in his stride, but he could never postpone the present hour even for the morrow. He had an invincible faith in the future, but he acted as if every moment were the last, as if salvation had to come now, or never.

He knew better. He knew that social institutions were a long and complex growth, that social improvement was gradual, not always to be seen in one generation or even in one century. He subscribed to the theory of Progress and was on familiar terms with the doctrine of Evolution. "It takes a deal of time to accomplish any great work of human progress," he wrote. "It is with men as with the geological formation of the earth." (Did he remember Lyell's book, there on his shelves?) "Enormous periods of time are found indispensable for what we once thought was done in six days. How many thousand experiments must go to one human success in the great departments of our progress. When the civilization you and I dream of is attained, men will find it is underlaid by thick strata full of the organic remains of inferior civilizations, each helpful to the higher one, which itself is no finality, but only provisional for something more grand and glorious." And again, he said to the Progressive Friends: "In the world of matter you find a Plan everywhere, things working out in order." (Did he remember those lectures by Geoffroy St. Hilaire he had thought so brilliant at the time?) "All is orderly, never a break in the line of continuity. In the fossil animals which perished a million years ago you find proximate formations which point to man; nay, yet further back in the structure of the earth, the fashion of the solar system itself, do we find finger-posts which indicate the road to humanity, distinctly pointing unto man."

Things were bound to come out all right in the end. Given time enough, Man would fulfill his destiny. "We have seen only the beginning," Parker assured his friends, "the future triumphs of the race must be vastly greater than all accomplished yet," and it was an echo of Priestley's famous boast, "Whatever was in the beginning of this world, the end will be glorious and paradisiacal beyond what our imagination can now conceive." Yet this faith in the future, this ineffable confidence in progress, did not lead to fatalism, any more than belief in predestination had led to fatalism among the Puritans. Granted that the best was yet to be, the last of life for which the first was made, was that to temper his enthusiasm or paralyze his thought? He himself was part of the evolutionary process; his work of reform in harmony with the plan of the Universe. The doctrine of evolution served merely to authenticate transcendental hope, to justify idealism. It added the experience of all mankind to the experience of the individual man; it brought the support of science to the intuitions of the soul.

So Parker went from philosophy to philanthropy and he justified himself. To his parcel of *a priori* principles and intuitive truths he added this doctrine of evolution; he balanced them all on his shoulders (easy enough, if you knew the trick) and went doughtily on his way. He lived in the wonderful afterglow of the Enlightenment, reason tinged with humanitarianism, realism with romanticism. He lived in an age of faith and of hope, in a country where all things seemed possible. He was the heir of the rationalists, but their skepticism seemed irrelevant, here, in America. He was the heir of the idealists, and their abstractions seemed concrete, here in this brave new world. He was warmed by the first generous winds of science, and they brought certainty, not doubt. He knew that reason would triumph over unreason, that the righteous would be filled. He knew that Paradise Lost would be Regained. All the evils that afflicted mankind would pass away — vice and crime, poverty and ignorance, war and disease.

All evils would pass away — even the greatest of them, even slavery.

CHAPTER X

SLAVERY AND THE HIGHER LAW

"SOUTHERN Slavery is an institution which is in earnest. Northern Freedom is an institution that is not in earnest." So said Parker, pointing the moral cowardice of the North, its insincerity, its futility, its blundering. Here was the North, with twice the population of the South and twice its wealth, celebrating every year the Declaration of Independence, and knuckling under, just as regularly, to the South. Here was the North, dedicated to freedom by Nature itself, schooled in the politics and the philosophy of freedom, but voting the slaveholders' ticket every time. New England went for slavery, the South choosing for her errand boy the favorite son of the Granite State; Massachusetts went for slavery, her greatest Senator speaking for compromise and fastening the Fugitive Slave Bill on the land; Boston went for slavery, Winthrop, Eliot, and Appleton all toeing the line spun by the fine logic of John Calhoun. Faneuil Hall went for slavery, her walls reverberating to the tumultuous applause of Mr. Webster's new doctrine, "the great object of government is the protection of property." State Street signed for slavery, and fifteen hundred merchants volunteered to send Thomas Sims back to his Georgia master. The Press pled for slavery, the *Post* stating, "In every point of view New England seems to have been made for the South and the South for New England. How could either live and flourish without the other?" while the *Courier* and the *Advertiser* urged the proscription of lawyers who dared to defend fugitive slaves. Society sustained slavery, Sumner and Dana and Palfrey ostracized by the first families of the town. Even the Church preached slavery, Brattle Street and Old South taking for their text the "Southside View," and Andover reconciling "Conscience and the Constitution." Slavery in the State House, slavery in the Court House, slavery on Beacon Hill, the city of Hancock and Adams faithless to her past.

It was a singular infamy that Boston could boast. Look through her history these twenty years, from the day she had mobbed Garrison, dragging him through the streets with a rope around his neck, to the day she had welcomed Mason as he stood on Bunker Hill and called the roll of his slaves. When had her men of property and position failed to do the bidding of the slave power? How many abolition meetings had been broken up, how many speakers howled down! Fugitives were hunted in her streets and sent back to the slave pens of the South, her Court House turned into a barracoon, old Judge Shaw crawling beneath the iron chains that were strung around it. When the Fugitive Slave Bill was passed, Boston greeted it with a salute of a hundred guns, and when Webster came out for compromise, 987 men of "property and position" assured him that "he had convinced the understanding and touched the conscience of a nation." ("There never was an event half so painful occurred in Boston," Emerson wrote.) Charles Follen was dropped from Harvard College for his abolitionism, and when he died the Federal Street Church would not allow its own Doctor Channing to hold services for him. Richard Dana espoused abolition and lost his clients; Doctor Bowditch walked arm in arm with Frederick Douglass and lost his patients; Charles Sumner denounced Webster and lost his friends. Well might James Freeman Clarke say, "When I came back to Boston, it was harder to speak of slavery than it had been in Kentucky." Well might Garrison write that here he had found "contempt more bitter, opposition more active, detraction more relentless, prejudice more stubborn, and apathy more frozen than among slave owners themselves."

Northern Freedom was not in earnest, but Parker was in earnest, terribly, implacably in earnest. He came late to abolition, as to social reform, but he made amends for his tardiness. He came fifteen years after Garrison, a decade after Phillips, but within five years from his first appearance in Faneuil Hall he was one of the triumvirate that led the anti-slavery fight, the newspapers of Boston calling on the people of the town to repudiate him, his speeches reprinted in Greeley's *Tribune* as the best that the North had to offer and in Daniel's *Examiner* as the worst. He spoke and his voice rolled like thunder over the land; he hammered and Boston complacency cracked under his blows; he fulminated and reputations shriveled in that terrible flame. He preached in Boston and the Music Hall could not hold the thousands who came to hear of the "New Crime against Humanity"; he lectured in New York, and the Tabernacle was electric with excitement as he described the "Great Battle between Slavery and Freedom"; he carried his message to the people of the country, from the Bay to the Mississippi, and they came to hear him, fifty thousand strong. "I know well," he said that morning when he preached on Anthony Burns — "I know well the responsibility of the place I occupy this morning. To-morrow's sun shall carry my words to all America. They will be read on both sides of the Continent; they will cross the ocean." And it was not boasting or a vain thing that he said.

But these great rugged encyclopædic sermons did not exhaust his passion nor did the pulpit circumscribe his labors. He organized Vigilance Committees and harbored fugitive slaves in his house. He fomented rebellion against wicked laws and offered to lead attacks upon the Court House and the jail. He was indicted for "offending against the peace and dignity of the United States," and so welcomed the indictment that the Judge did not dare let the case go to trial. He helped inspire and finance the Kansas Crusade; he was one of John Brown's secret committee of six, privy to his plans; he incited slaves to insurrection, the disciple of the Prince of Peace counseling violence and bloodshed.

He was a practical man, no non-resistant, but ready for a fight at any time, no anarchist, but willing to use politics and parties to gain his ends. He had no political ambitions, but he was a power in politics all the same, never for a moment to be ignored. He described himself as a humble minister but he spoke with the authority of a Pope. He lashed judges and excoriated Senators and flayed Presidents; he drove Loring off the bench and out of Boston, he gave Curtis a terrible notoriety, he pronounced on Webster the most awful judgment ever read over a great man, and Adams and Dana said that it was just. When Sumner delayed his assault upon the slave power, he explained his delay to Parker; when Chase refused to attack slavery where it already existed, he justified himself to Parker; when Wilson plunged into Know-Nothingism, emerging with political spoils, he apologized to Parker. Seward and Chase and Lincoln, Sumner and Wilson and Hale, read what he wrote and acknowledged his power. "I congratulate you," wrote Seward, "on the awakening of the spirit of Freedom in the Free States. I hope you recognize in this awakening the fruits of your own great and unwearied labors. If you do not, I am sure that I do, and not only I but thousands more acknowledge it."

What was it that Whittier had written, in that dark hour when troops were moving on Mexico and the Whigs stood in Faneuil Hall and voted down Stephen Phillips's anti-slavery resolutions?

Where's the man for Massachusetts, Where's the voice to speak her free?
Where's the hand to light up bonfires, from her mountains to the sea?
Beats her Pilgrim pulse no longer? Sits she dumb in her despair?
Has she none to break the silence? Has she none to do and dare?
O my God for one right worthy to lift up her rusted shield,
And to plant again the Pine-tree in her banner's tattered field!

Did Parker think that he was the man? That same year he too had stood in Faneuil Hall and lifted his voice on behalf of the slave, Joe, carried back from Boston to New Orleans. "I felt like a Hebrew prophet," he wrote, "I have seldom risen so high as that night; never thundered and lightened into such an atmosphere. I did not think of such words; they *came,* and I thank God for it. I did greater than I could counsel, far greater than I knew. My caprice, my personal taste, stood in the background; and my nature — the nature of mankind — and honest blood spoke in me, through me."

2

For fifteen years Parker spoke and wrote about slavery. Yet what did he know about slavery, after all? To hear him talk you would think that he knew everything about it. He knew the whole history of the institution, from ancient times. He could tell Phillips about slavery in Rome, and Sumner about slavery in Gaul, and when Andrew Dickson White came to New Haven to lecture on Russia, Parker astonished him with his knowledge of slavery under the Tsars. He knew the origin of slavery in the New World, and he could trace its progress in minute detail and enlarge upon its law and custom, its economy and its sociology. He could tell you the statistics of slavery in every State of the Union — he was writing a book on the subject, and the whole Census of 1850 was to go into the book. It went into his sermons instead, and Hinton Helper was anticipated by a decade.

He knew everything about slavery. He had read all the books, had most of them in his own library. He had listened to the narratives of a hundred fugitive slaves and he could tell a thing or two to Mrs. Stowe. He knew all the Negroes of Boston, Lewis Hayden and Roger Morris were his parishioners and Frederick Douglass was his friend. When Moncure Conway came to Boston, looking for the husband of a slave-woman, it was to Parker that he was sent, and

Parker took him through the Negro quarters and to the hiding places of the fugitives, and Conway remembered that "every room into which we entered was hushed with reverence as if God had entered." Slaveowners told him their side of the story, Yeadon and Dawson up from Charleston to debate with him; they wrote him long letters of protest, closely written arguments from the Bible and from history, or letters filled with abuse. He subscribed to the Richmond *Examiner* and read *DeBow's Review,* he filled his scrapbook with advertisements for runaway slaves, and convicted the South on its own testimony.

He knew the philosophy of slavery, he had•read Calhoun and the Pro-Slavery Argument, and he could say the Biblical sanctions by heart. Did Abraham have "servants bought with his money," did Paul say, "Slaves, obey your masters"? That argument had no terrors for him, he put no stock in the inspiration of the Scriptures. Abraham lived in a barbarous age, Paul was wrong; it was as simple as that. He had only scorn for Mr. Everett, "A Cambridge Professor of Greek, he studied the original tongue of the Bible to learn that the Scripture says slaves where the English Bible says only servants." A poor thing, Everett, "an *electro-gilder,* you carry him to any piece of metal no matter how base, and he covers it over with his thin tinsel."

He knew as much about slavery as any Yankee could, yet what did he really know? Slavery wasn't something you got at through an encyclopædia or through the Census Reports; slavery wasn't something you learned from fragmentary narratives of escaped slaves, as if you should get at the heart of Catholicism through the stories of Lahey, "the monk of La Trappe." Slavery wasn't something simple and single, a question of profit or loss, a question of progress or decay, a question of right or wrong. It wasn't something the South could put off like a coat; it was something that had grown into Southern society, tied to the South with a thousand sensitive nerves. What could Parker know of slavery? Channing had lived in Richmond and Clarke had preached in Louisville, Birney had owned a plantation in the deep south, the Grimké sisters had come from Charleston, but Parker had never been below Mason and Dixon's line. For all of his apparent realism, his crowding array of facts and figures, he dealt with slavery as an abstraction, and his vocabulary was incomprehensible to the South. His logic was plausible enough, but you might as well try to convert a Hard-Shell Baptist to Catholicism by logic; his statistics were impressive, but suppose you could prove that the family was an extravagant institution, community barracks the most efficient way of raising children — what good were statistics for things like that? His criticism was just, and he could substantiate it, item by item; but who ever heard of a society responding to criticism? His moral appeals were irresistible, if you admitted the premises, but the South did not admit the premises.

Curious what came over Parker when he dealt with slavery. He had balance enough in most things, his feet were on the ground. He made no fetish of temperance, he was no doctrinaire pacifist, he took woman's rights in his stride, he never ranted against property, only against its abuse. He saw the wrongs of industrialism, but he would not topple the factories down, he would not even escape to Brook Farm; he knew the corruption of politics, but he never failed to vote. He had studied the history of the institution of slavery, too, and could write his own "Sociology for the South"; he knew well enough that the planter was not to be blamed for the sin of slavery any more than the State Street banker was to be blamed for the evils of industry. He could distinguish, when he wanted to, between the sinner and the sin, and he took no stock in the doctrine of the depravity of man. But all to no purpose; when he got on the subject of slavery Garrison himself was not more uncompromising, Sumner not more doctrinaire.

He pitched into slavery with a two-pronged fork, and slavery slid in between. He announced that slavery was a moral wrong, a crime against Nature and against Man:

this was an *a priori* truth, an intuitive fact, a transcendental axiom. He announced that slavery was unprofitable and
inefficient, it did not pay dividends, economically or cultur-
ally, and his evidence could not be gainsaid. But what was
the value of evidence to prove a natural law? Suppose Calhoun's dream of a Greek Democracy had come true in the
Palmetto State, suppose Tidewater Virginia were that paradise its planters said it was: would Parker have admitted
defeat and abandoned his position? It was not because Alabama lacked railroads, because immigrants avoided Virginia, because illiteracy in South Carolina was high, that
Parker was an abolitionist; he was an abolitionist because he
hated slavery, and had Alabama been crisscrossed with
railroads, had the Irish crowded into the Old Dominion,
and every Carolinian read Shakespeare, Parker would
have hated slavery none the less. It was the old dilemma
that had troubled him in the past, and he never resolved
it.

Besides, he missed the point, for all of his massive statistics. There were his sermons, his lectures, his pamphlets,
sagging under the weight of evidence. Taken together they
constituted a sociological encyclopædia such as was not to be
found in the whole literature of the controversy: Helper
added little to what Parker had assembled. Here were the
comparative statistics, North and South, for industry and
commerce and trade, for manufactures and inventions and
labor, for population and immigration, for public and private
wealth, public debt and expenditures, for literacy and education and religion too; here they were, all pointing to the
same conclusion, and Parker thought that he had proved his
case. But no such thing. His logic had failed him, his zeal
had led him astray. (He was in good company; who was not
led astray?) His figures were irrelevant, his conclusions
impertinent. All that he had accomplished was to prove that
Negro labor was unprofitable, that ignorant labor was unprofitable. No need to go to South Carolina for that. Boston
could teach him that.

3

What though his statistics were irrelevant; had they been as relevant as the Commandments and as valid as the axioms of Euclid, they would not have been accepted in the South. Parker's argument was, of necessity, addressed to the North, and his appeal there was to morals, not to expediency. He could not hope to wean the slaveholder from his peculiar institution, but he might hope to arouse the freeman from his apathy. His task was to make Northern Freedom in earnest. It was for him to stir up the people of the Northern States, to fight down the aggressions of the slave power, to impeach the Hunkers and exalt the Free-soilers, to nullify the Fugitive Slave Bill, to expose the perfidy of the Nebraska Act, to win Kansas for freedom.

This was the work of a moral agitator, and Parker was on familiar ground. It was not as an economist that Parker made his special contribution to anti-slavery, nor as an organizer, but as a minister. When he hid Ellen Craft from the kidnappers, it was as a minister taking care of his parishioner. When he demanded the nullification of the Fugitive Slave Bill it was as a minister preaching on the "Function of Conscience in Relation to the Laws of Men," when he advised jurors to ignore their oaths and follow their consciences, it was as a minister comparing the "Laws of God and the Statutes of Men." He made abolitionism a religious duty, and gave to nullification the sanction of the Higher Law.

Others invoked the Higher Law, but none so insistently as Parker, none with such cogent logic or such moral fervor. He announced it in his first "Sermon on Slavery," preached in West Roxbury 'way back in 1841. "I know that men urge in argument that the Constitution of the United States is the supreme law of the land," he said, "and that sanctions slavery. There is no supreme law but that made by God; if our laws contradict that, the sooner they end or the sooner they are broken, why, the better." He maintained it in his last formal pronouncement, the letter on John Brown: "The freeman has a Natural Right to help the slaves recover their liberty." He presented it year in and year out, from the pulpit and the lyceum platform, in private letter and in formal argument. He gave it an historical basis, exploring the history of Puritan England and Revolutionary America to prove its validity; he gave it a philosophical basis, justifying it by the logic of idealism and the dialectics of transcendentalism; he gave it a religious basis, finding its sanctions in the injunctions of the Commandments and the Beatitudes.

Parker pointed the way to the nullification of wicked laws, but it was not such nullification as Calhoun prescribed, resting on constitutional metaphysics; he pointed the way to civil disobedience, but it was not such disobedience as Garrison advised, publicly burning the Constitution. It was not revolution that Parker enjoined, for it is not revolutionary to ignore immoral statutes, only to enact them; it was not anarchy that he counseled, for it is not anarchy to conform to natural law, only to flout it. He spoke as the grandson of Captain John Parker and reminded men that their fathers had nullified the Stamp Act and thrown tea into Boston harbor. He spoke as a transcendental idealist and recalled that all men were created equal and endowed by their Creator with certain unalienable rights, life, liberty, and the pursuit of happiness. But it was when he spoke as a minister that he was most effective; even the most orthodox could not find fault with his text: "Thou shalt worship the Lord thy God, and Him only shalt thou serve."

Listen to him as he expounded the "Function of Conscience in Relation to the Laws of Men": "The law of God has eminent domain everywhere, over the private passions of Oliver and Charles, the special interests of Carthage and Rome, over all official business, all precedents, all human statutes, over all the conventional affairs of one man or of mankind. My own conscience is to declare that law to me, yours to you, and is before all private passions or public interests, the decision of majorities and a world full of precedents. You cannot move out of the dominions of God nor escape where conscience has not eminent domain." Hear what he told his parishioners of the Fugitive Slave Act: "When rulers have inverted their function and enacted wickedness into a law which treads down the inalienable rights of man to such a degree as this, then I know no ruler but God, no law but natural Justice. I tear the hateful statute of kidnappers to shivers; I trample it underneath my feet, I do it in the name of all law; in the name of Justice and of Man, in the name of the dear God." When the Ministerial Conference daintily discussed the duty of Ministers toward the law, and clergymen trembled for the Union, Parker reminded them that their loyalty was to God, not man. "O my brothers, I am not afraid of men. I can offend them. I care nothing for their hate or their esteem. But I should not dare to violate the eternal law of God. I should not dare to violate His laws, come what may come — should you? Nay, I can love nothing so well as I love my God."

When Mr. Benjamin Curtis said, "The standard of Morality by which the Courts are to be guided is that which the law prescribes. Your honors are to declare what the Law deems moral or immoral," Parker asked whether it was "moral for the servants of King Pharaoh to drown all new-born Hebrew boys, moral for Herod's butchers to murder the Innocents at Bethlehem." When Justice Peleg Sprague said, "there is no incompatibility between the will of God and the laws of Man," Parker reminded him of the law of King Ahab that the Hebrews should serve Baal, and the law of the Scribes and Pharisees that "if any man knew where Jesus were, he should show it that they might take him," the law which Judas obeyed. When Judge Curtis cried him down for advising jurors to ignore the law, and, standing in Faneuil Hall, asked "the Reverend Gentleman in what capacity he expects to be punished for his *perjury*,"

Parker rose in the gallery. "Do you want an answer to your question now, Sir?" he shouted. Mr. Curtis did not; but Parker answered him anyway, from his pulpit: "Suppose a man has sworn to keep the Constitution of the United States and the Constitution is found to be wrong in certain particulars, then his oath is not morally binding, for before his oath, by his very existence, he is morally bound to keep the law of God as fast as he learns it. No oath can absolve him from his natural allegiance to God."

He had often been called an Infidel and an Atheist, but here was real infidelity — infidelity to the laws of God; here was practical atheism, the denial of the laws of God. "To say that there is no law higher than what the State can make," he asserted, "is practical atheism. It is not a denial of God in His person; this is only speculative atheism. It is a denial of the functions and attributes of God; that is real atheism. If there is no God to make a law for me, then there is no God for me."

It was something for him to turn the tables on his critics, it was something to show who were the real heretics — Nenemiah Adams taking his "South Side View" and Moses Stuart joining in unholy union "Conscience and the Constitution" ("All Southern men of intelligence and fairness admire your pamphlet," wrote Webster); President Lord of Dartmouth, posting his "Letter of Inquiry on Slavery," and Francis Wayland of Brown, proving "Slavery, a Scriptural Institution"; Orville Dewey of New York, who boasted that he would return his own brother to slavery if the law required it; and Hubbard Winslow, who deplored all agitation of the painful subject. "It seems amazing," said Parker, "that American Christianity of the Puritanic stock, with a philosophy that transcends sensationalism, should prove false to the only principle which at once justifies the conduct of Jesus, of Luther, of the Puritans themselves. For certainly if obedience to the established law be the highest virtue, then the Patriots and Pilgrims of New England, the Reformers of the Church, the glorious company of the Apostles, the goodly fellowship of the prophets, and the noble array of martyrs, nay, Jesus himself, were only criminals and traitors."

The magistrates went for atheism, making an idol of the law and asking people to bow down and worship it. A new philosophy of government was announced (new for America, new for Massachusetts), and it was the philosophy of materialism. "Here is the first maxim," said Parker — " 'There is no Higher Law.' That is the proclamation of objective atheism; it is the selfish materialism of Hobbes, De la Mettrie and Helvetius, gone to seed. You have nothing to rely on above the politicians and their statutes; if you suffer, nothing to appeal to but the ballot-box. Here is the next maxim — 'Religion has nothing to do with politics.' That is subjective atheism, with a political application. If there be no law inherent in mind and matter above any wicked statute of a tyrant, still the instinctive religious sense of man looks up with reverence, faith and love, and thinks there is a God and a higher law."

But perhaps the orthodox would argue that Parker was not competent to test things by religion: he had abandoned religion. So thought Andrews Norton, for example. "It is lamentable," he said, on the occasion of Parker's first speech in Faneuil Hall, "that what is put forward most prominently is a speech by one disgraced in the eyes of good men as an infidel clergyman." But Parker's argument was based on history, too; and here no one could impugn his credentials. "When a small boy," he wrote, closing his "Defence" in the case of The United States *versus* Theodore Parker — "When a small boy my mother lifted me up, one Sunday, and held me while I read the first monumental line I ever saw: SACRED TO LIBERTY AND THE RIGHTS OF MANKIND. Gentlemen, the Spirit of Liberty, the Love of Justice, was early fanned into a flame in my boyish heart. That monument covers the bones of my own kinsfolk; it was their blood which reddened the long green grass at Lexington. It is my own name which stands chiselled on that stone; the tall Captain who marshalled his fellow farmers and mechanics

into stern array was my father's father. I learned to read
out of his Bible, and with a musket he that day captured
from the foe, I learned also another religious lesson, that
REBELLION TO TYRANTS IS OBEDIENCE TO GOD."

He was in the American tradition, in the tradition of Otis
and Adams and Jefferson. He was at home in Faneuil Hall,
he and his doctrine of the Higher Law, more at home than
Webster, who advised Massachusetts to "conquer her prejudices" for liberty, more at home than Everett, who invoked
the "patriotism of all citizens to abstain from discussion" of
slavery, more at home than Curtis, who stood on its platform
and encouraged the crowd to howl down the Higher Law.
The pretensions of the Government did not impose on him;
he knew the history of Stuart England and of the Protector-
ate — "That which concerns the mysterie of the Kings
Power is not lawful to be disputed," said James I, but Crom-
well said, "There is one general grievance, and that is the
Law." The presumption of the Courts held no terrors for
him; he knew the use that despotic governments made of pliant judges, Judge Kelyng arguing, "If a company of people
will go about any public reformation, this is high treason,"
Chief Justice Finch sustaining the Ship-money, Jeffreys and
Scroggs doing the bloody work of James II. He knew the
history of independency in Puritan Massachusetts and of
the Charter Oak in Connecticut, he was familiar with the
philosophy of the Revolution and of the Declaration of Independence and could fling the words of Otis and Adams and
Jefferson in the teeth of those who denied the Higher Law.

And how fitting for a transcendentalist to espouse the
Higher Law! It was idealism applied to politics, intuition in
the realm of social ethics. Parker could take out those sermons and articles on religion and he wouldn't have to change
a single idea. He could write "State" where he had said
"Church," change "Bible" to "Constitution," and "pharisees" to "politicians," substitute "Higher Law" for "Conscience," and there you were. He had always taught the
ultimate authority of the soul, the sufficiency of intuition,

the validity of *a priori* truths. He was an old hand at nullification; he had nullified the Scriptures where they were
contrary to the teachings of Nature; he had nullified social
institutions where they ran counter to the principles of
justice. Now he was ready to nullify the laws of slavery because they stultified the Higher Law, and when his friends
in Syracuse spirited a slave, Jerry, out of jail, Parker wrote
to them: "Injustice mounted on a statute is not the less unjust, only the more formidable. There are some statutes so
wicked that it is every man's duty to violate them."

It was an impregnable position that he occupied, as impregnable as the Declaration of Independence; in any argument he was bound to have the best of it. Challenge his
facts and he would face you down; slavery was a fact that
couldn't be gainsaid, and all qualifying facts were, in the last
analysis, irrelevant. Show him the statutes and he would
deny that they were binding. Ask for his own authority, and
he would refer you to "the law which God wrote ineffaceably
in the hearts of mankind."

There was only one way of meeting this argument from
the Higher Law: you could charge that, in effect, it led
to anarchy. If every man is to judge for himself what is the
law, then there is no law, and no authority, and society is
back in a state of nature. Jefferson had faced this same problem, and had met it, not with logic, but with common sense:
he had appealed to prudence, that laws should not be nullified for light and transient causes, and had called on experience to prove that "mankind are more disposed to suffer
than to right themselves by abolishing the forms to which
they are accustomed." The Higher Law abolitionist had to
meet the same argument, and he did it as best he could. He
entered an objection as to facts and another as to logic.
"If we do not obey this law (it is said) we shall disobey all
laws. It is not so. There is not a country in the world where
there is more respect for human laws than in New England,
nowhere more than in Massachusetts. Even if a law is unpopular, it is not popular to disobey it. . . . Who is it that

oppose the fugitive slave law? Men that have always been
on the side of law and order and do not violate the statutes
of man for their own advantage. This disobedience to the
fugitive slave law is one of the strongest guarantees for the
observance of any *just* law. You cannot trust a people who
will keep a law *because it is law;* nor need we distrust a
people that will only keep a law when it is just."

And by what right did Hunkers charge abolitionists with
disrespect for law? The accusation should have palsied
their tongues. By what logic did magistrates show so fine
a frenzy for the enforcement of the slave law; there were
laws enough on the statute books flouted and ignored, if
they wished to make a name for themselves. Parker was not
one to stand on the defensive; he raided the enemy's camp.

Are the laws of Massachusetts kept in Boston, then? The
usury law says, "Thou shalt not take more than six per cent on
thy money." Is that kept? There are thirty-four millions of
banking capital in Massachusetts and I think that every dollar
of this capital has broken the law within the past twelve months,
and yet no complaint has been made. There are three or four hundred brothels in this city of Boston, and ten or twelve hundred
shops for the sale of rum. All of them are illegal; some are as
well known to the police as is this house, indeed a great deal more
frequented by some of them than any house of God. Does anybody disturb them? How many laws of Massachusetts have been
violated this very week, in this very city, by the slave-hunters
here, by the very officers of the State? What is the meaning of
this? Every law which favours the accumulation of money must
be kept, but those which prohibit the unjust accumulation of
money — by certain classes — they need not be kept.

Tax Parker with disrespect for the law! The only laws
he cared to respect were the laws of human nature. Indict
him for contempt of court! There was only one Judge whose
authority he acknowledged; black-robed judges could not
scare him. Confront him with the prohibitions of the Constitution, he pointed to the guarantees. Charge him with in-
citing rebellion, he would reply that "rebellion to tyrants

is obedience to God." To the argument of the Higher Law there was no effective answer; even force was not effective.

Here, then, was Parker's philosophy of freedom and his program of abolition. It was a philosophy which assumed as intuitive truths that freedom was right and slavery wrong. It judged slavery by its own ideal standards, and found it morally indefensible. It was, at the same time, a pragmatic philosophy which taught that slavery was a failure. It judged slavery by its fruits and found that they were demonstrably rotten. It was inspired by idealism and sustained by faith; it was rooted in experience and bottomed on fact. Its premises were general and timeless; its data were particular and circumstantial. It was no sudden inspiration, no theory hastily concocted to meet an emergency, but it was broad enough to embrace any emergency and realistic enough to cope with any crisis. Its formulation was independent of measures or men, but its application was immediate and opportunistic. So Parker always had his speeches ready; the particular illustrations might change, but the general principles never. So he was always ready to fight; the tactics of each foray differed, but the grand strategy remained the same.

CHAPTER XI

FUGITIVE SLAVES: TRUMPETS
AND ALARUMS

ONE evening, late in October of 1850, Parker returned from Plymouth to find Doctor Howe waiting for him, chafing with impatience. It was barely a month after the passage of the Fugitive Slave Bill, and Howe had come to tell Parker that the kidnappers were in town, hunting for Ellen and William Craft. The Crafts were parishioners of Parker's, and friends too; they had won their way from Georgia north to Boston, and come to his house; the narrative of their escape staggered the imagination. He was responsible for them, he was minister-at-large to all the fugitive slaves of the city. Besides, had he not drawn up the resolutions of the Vigilance Committee, publicly advising fugitives to stay in Boston — "For we have not the smallest fear," he wrote in his folly, "that any one of them will be taken from us and carried off into bondage." Now what was to be done? There was a hasty meeting of the Vigilance Committee; Doctor Bowditch was there, and Ellis Gray Loring, who could always be relied on for legal aid, Francis Jackson and Samuel May, Phillips and Charles Ellis, and Howe, of course, who was chairman; and there were two Negroes: Lewis Hayden whose house was a notorious depot on the Underground Railroad, and Frederick Douglass, the "Swarthy Ajax" of abolition. With doors locked and blinds drawn (for when would Howe forgo the dramatic gesture, he who had fought with Byron and known Lafayette?), the committee discussed the crisis. A bold stand, that was best. Let them scare the kidnappers out of Boston, not the Crafts.

Who should speak for the Committee, intimidate the ruffian Knight, and Hughes, the burly jailer? Parker's name was suggested and one member said that this was no business for a clergyman. "Gentlemen," said Parker, "this committee can appoint me to no duty I will not perform."

So the Committee swung into action, Parker in charge. They armed William, — a revolver, a pistol, and a dirk —, and Lewis Hayden gave him shelter. Ellen they sent out to Loring's place in Brookline, Parker and Miss Stevenson driving her there in the small hours of the morning, clattering through the silent streets, the cab swaying over the cobblestones, jolting the hatchet in Parker's hand. A week later there was a new scare; Parker hurried out to Brookline and sent Ellen in to Number 1 Exeter Place; Bowditch, who had heard of the danger and dashed out ready for any emergency, met him walking cheerfully along the Mill-dam road, munching an apple. It was not the first time, nor the last, that Parker harbored a fugitive slave, and for a week he wrote his sermons with a pistol on his desk, loaded and ready for use.

The Crafts were safe; now to hound the slave-hunters out of Boston. Parker led the Vigilantes, sixty strong, down to the United States Hotel. They stamped into the lobby and ranged themselves along the stairways, while Parker and Ellis paced sentry-like back and forth along the corridor; they refused to leave until the unhappy landlord had produced his guests. "I told them," said Parker, "that they were not safe another night. I had stood between them and violence once, I would not promise to do it again. They were considerably frightened." Well they might be: Boston had disappointed them. They had alleged that William Craft stole the clothes on his back, and Ellis Loring had clamped a warrant on them and arrested them for slander, and the Boston merchants had to go bail for them, ten thousand dollars. They could not show their faces on the streets but a crowd would gather, swinging caps and shouting: "Slave-hunters, slave-hunters, there go the slave-

hunters!" Mr. Parker was right, they were not safe in
Boston; one fellow had smashed in the door of their carriage
and threatened their lives. Yet they tried to bluster it out;
they were prepared for violence; they would make no
promises, not they. But that same afternoon they took the
train for New York. Parker did not forget them. A year
later he noted with satisfaction that jailer Hughes had been
killed in a drunken brawl, and he pointed the moral like
any Puritan divine.

It had all been melodrama so far: the perilous flight from
Georgia north, the happy interlude, the appearance of the
villains from the South, the hue and the cry, the closed doors
and drawn shades, the wild ride in the night, the dirks and
revolvers, the storming of the hotel, the ruffians slinking
away, imprecations of good men ringing in their ears. Nothing was lacking but a romantic ending, and Parker furnished
that. Ellen and William Craft were already married, as
well as slaves could be, but it was not enough. They must
be married on free soil, according to the laws of Massachusetts, and by Parker. So he married them, in a boarding
house on Nigger Hill, the Vigilance Committee standing
by.

"Then came the marriage ceremony," — it is Parker
telling the tale, — "then a prayer such as the occasion inspired. Then I noticed a *Bible* lying on one table and a sword
on the other; I saw them when I first came into the house and
determined what use to make of them. I took the Bible, put
it into William's right hand, and told him the use of it. . . .
I then took the *sword;* I put that in his hand and told him
if the worst came to the worst, to use that to save his wife's
liberty or her life, if he could effect it no other way . . . I
put into his hands these two dissimilar instruments, one for
the body, one for his soul at all events."

Then he went home to prepare his speech for the meeting
that should welcome George Thompson back to America; he
didn't get a chance to make it, hoodlums howled him
down while he stood and pointed at a portrait of Washing-

ton. He went home to read the Diary of old John Adams; he noted that then, too, most of the men of property and most of the clergy were on the side of tyranny, and the thought gave him comfort. He went home to write a letter to President Fillmore; he told the President the story of the Craft escape and challenged him to enforce his monstrous law. "I send you," he wrote, "a little sermon of mine."

It was not the first time Parker had acted on behalf of fugitive slaves, though it was his first rescue. There was the Latimer case, back in 1842; its echoes had reached even West Roxbury and Parker had preached a sermon on it, though he decided against reading a petition from his pulpit. Doctor Bowditch and young William F. Channing had stopped off from their professional work to bring out the *Latimer Journal,* and Parker had sent in a contribution. Latimer had gone free, after all, and Whittier had flung the defiance of "Massachusetts to Virginia" —

> No slave-hunt in our borders, no pirate on our strand!
> No fetters in the Bay State, no slave upon our land!

and sixty thousand persons had petitioned the legislature to make the boast come true.

Then, four years later, came the case of the slave Joe. He had made good his escape; a free man, he walked the streets of Boston, and within twenty-four hours he was recaptured and shipped back to New Orleans. No slave-hunters had done this, but the captain of a Boston ship, acting under instructions from a Boston merchant, and without a shadow of legal right. The abolitionists were indignant, and not only the abolitionists. Emerson, who had rebuked them ("Does he not do more to abolish slavery who works all day steadily in his garden than he who goes to abolition meeting and makes a speech?"), Emerson was shocked out of his aloofness. "I feel the irreparable shame to Boston of this abduction," he wrote. There was an indignation meeting, at Faneuil Hall. John Quincy Adams presided, tremulous with age, but gallant to the end; it was the last time he spoke in that Hall, his picture and his father's picture hanging from its walls. The list of speakers was an impressive one: Charles Francis Adams and Charles Sumner, Wendell Phillips and Stephen Phillips, Chevalier Howe and Edmund Quincy, and young John Andrew to read the Resolutions. And here was Parker too, a new name in this company, better known as a heresiarch than as an abolitionist, but the fittest representative that the Church could send. He spoke of the Higher Law and scored politicians who embraced expediency and forgot principles. "A low, unprincipled, buffoon speech," Andrews Norton called it, but Parker himself thought that it was the greatest effort he had ever made. It was the first time he had stood on the platform of Faneuil Hall, the first time he had been publicly associated with Phillips and Sumner and Howe. It was his formal confirmation to Abolition. He never forgot the ceremony nor repudiated his vows.

2

But all this was before the Fugitive Slave Bill, before Mr. Webster "stamped his foot, and broke through into the great hollow of practical atheism which undergulfs the State and Church." Slave-hunters, who had regarded kidnapping in New England as a bad business and Boston as a sink of freedom, took courage from the new law and prepared to vindicate their rights in the shadow of Bunker Hill Monument, and forty blacks left Boston within a week, while the Vigilance Committee prepared to nullify the law. The Craft case was the first test of strength, and Freedom proved itself in earnest. But it had been badly managed by the Georgians and by the magistrates, too; it had never come into court, it had proved nothing but that the Vigilantes were cleverer than the kidnappers. The South was not willing to acknowledge defeat: it had been successful elsewhere, success in Boston was essential. The Hunkers were not willing to admit defeat: they wished to vindicate their loyalty to the Union, to express their affection for Mr.

Webster, to prove their contempt for the Higher Law. There was a great meeting of the conservatives in Faneuil Hall, and they cheered tumultuously when Mr. Benjamin Curtis said, of fugitives, "With the rights of these persons Massachusetts has nothing to do. It is enough for us that they have no right to be here."

Soon there was a chance to vindicate these fine words. Frederic Wilkins was a fugitive from Virginia. He had come to Boston and found work in the Cornhill Coffee House; he knew his Bible and had taken the name of "Shadrach." On the morning of February 18, 1851, he was seized by Marshal Riley and, the use of the jail being forbidden by Massachusetts law, he was lodged in the Court House. Dana hurried to defend him; he applied to Chief Justice Shaw for a writ of *habeas corpus,* but the great man put him off, his objections "frivolous," his manner "insulting," and Shadrach stayed in jail. But not for long. That very day Lewis Hayden rounded up his friends from Nigger Hill. They crowded past the guards and pushed into the courtroom where Shadrach sat. "Shoot him," Riley screamed; but no one shot. Twenty Negroes seized Shadrach and flung him into a waiting carriage, which drove madly off, across the Charles to Cambridge, out along the historic road through Lexington and into Concord, fresh horses there, and west to Leominster, west and north to Vermont, north to Canada and freedom. "I think it the noblest deed done in Boston since the destruction of the tea in 1773," said Parker, who had hurried down to the Court House himself, and found that he was no longer needed. The next morning Parker preached to a crowded hall: "When I came among you I expected to have to do and to hear some hard things, but I never expected to be asked to read such a note as this: 'Shadrach, a fugitive slave, in peril of his life and liberty, asks your prayers, that God will aid him to escape out of bondage.' But he does not need our prayers. Thank God we have heard of him safe, far on his way to freedom." "There was a moment of perfect silence," wrote one who was there that day, "then one spontaneous shout of applause reëchoed through the building."

But that wasn't the end of the matter. President Fillmore issued a proclamation directing "prosecution to be commenced against all . . . aiders and abettors of this flagitious offence." Lewis Hayden was indicted, and the fabulous Elizur Wright — George Ticknor had predicted a brilliant future for him if he would stick to French literature and turn out more of those translations, but he preferred to edit the *Chronotype* and sit in on the councils of the Bird Club and rescue fugitive slaves. The case came to trial, and Parker charged that the jury was packed. "All that Boston influence and the money of the United States could do," he wrote, "all that shameless impudence could do, has been done." The Judge sustained the constitutionality of the law, and the Government had a clear case, but the jury was unable to agree and the case was dropped. Parker congratulated himself that he had touched the consciences of men, but two years later one of the jurors told Dana the inside story of that trial. The jury had stood eleven to one for conviction; he alone had held out for acquittal; he was the man who had driven Shadrach from Concord to Leominster!

Shadrach had escaped, he had vindicated his Biblical name. But now the Government was aroused. "So far as depends on me," said President Fillmore, "the laws shall be faithfully executed and all forcible opposition to them suppressed." Webster called the rescue treason, and Clay wanted to know whether "the government of white men is to be yielded to a government of black." It was clear that next time there would be neither rescue nor escape. On the night of April 3, 1852, a Negro boy, Thomas Sims, was seized. He was held in the Court House, five guards behind him, one on either side, while a dozen policemen guarded the narrow stairs. Iron chains were strung across the Court House doors and old Chief Justice Shaw bent low as he crawled beneath them, while Longfellow wrote in his Journal, "This is the last form of degradation. Alas for the people who cannot feel an insult."

In vain the Vigilance Committee exhausted the technicalities of the law; in vain Dana and Sewall and Rantoul and Loring argued the unconstitutionality of the Fugitive Slave Bill, the applicability of the Personal Liberty Law, the insufficiency of evidence, the fact of false arrest, the right of *habeas corpus*, and a trial by jury. All these were denied. George Curtis knew the Constitution; he had just finished his series of lectures on its history, and besides he had the advice of his brother Benjamin and a written opinion from the incomparable Rufus Choate. There was no salvation that way.

The law failing, the Executive Committee of the Vigilantes took charge. There was an excited meeting in the office of the *Liberator,* Higginson proposing desperate remedies while non-resistant Garrison sat calmly by, writing editorials. There was a meeting in the Tremont Temple which Horace Mann addressed, and another in Parker's study. Wild schemes were broached. Higginson wanted to rush the Court House, and Parker was with him there — one hundred brave men and the trick was done. Loring thought that they might filch the record of the Southern Court from the Commissioner's desk. Parker was all for an attack upon the boat that would carry Sims back to Georgia — old Captain Bearse of Barnstable could manage it, he was not afraid of a little piracy. But all the plans fell through. There were two hundred policemen in the marshal's guard, there were chains across the doors and bars across the windows. This time the Government meant business.

Perhaps an appeal to the moral sense of Boston might stir things up, and on April 10, while Sims still lay in his cell, Parker launched against Curtis such a philippic as had surely never before been heard in a Boston church. He called the roll of the monsters of history to find for him a fit companion; he reviewed every act of tyranny to discover one as gross as this; he evoked religion and morals to witness the enormity of the Commissioner's crime. "You have placed the Commissioner in an immortal pillory to receive the hootings and rotten eggs of the advancing generation," Charles Sumner wrote him, and from Howe came a letter addressed to The Reverend Thunder and Lightning Parker: "I have no language to describe the effect upon me of your sublime discourse. Had not God stored up in your soul a great store of wrath and indignation . . . we should never have witnessed such a storm and whirlwind as that in which you have come down upon the wicked."

But neither hootings nor verbal whirlwinds would make Sims free. At three o'clock of the morning of the thirteenth, Doctor Bowditch was aroused from his bed, and hurried down to the Court House Square. The Commissioner had given his verdict and now they were taking Sims to the ship, sneaking him off in the night while the city was asleep. But not all the city was asleep. Parker was there, pacing sadly back and forth, and William Channing, and the Negro preacher Grimes, and a faithful handful of the Vigilantes standing by for the Death Watch. At four the marshal's guard formed, Sims in their center. They moved into Court Street, down State Street, past the spot where Crispus Attucks fell, and to the Long Wharf where the *Acorn* was moored. Sims stepped aboard. The flying jib was hoisted, the anchor was weighed. "And is this Massachusetts liberty," he said. It was dawn now, the stars were gone. The Reverend Foster offered up a prayer, and the little group struck up Bishop Heber's hymn: —

> From many a Southern river
> And field of sugar cane,
> They call us to deliver
> Their land from slavery's chain.

3

Thomas Sims was landed at Savannah and publicly whipped on the nineteenth of April; he was the first slave

Massachusetts had returned since she had made that date memorable. Who was responsible for this crime? Was it the owner of Sims? He had published a card in the Boston papers thanking the merchants "conspicuous in their efforts to serve us." Was it Marshal Devens, who had taken Sims down to the wharf and put him on the boat? He had acted from a tortured sense of duty, and he tried desperately to buy Sims back: years later he was to make amends. Was it Commissioner Curtis? Parker had already dealt with him.

There was one whose responsibility was greater than that which even Curtis bore: Daniel Webster. But for him there would have been no Fugitive Slave Law. He had urged the law with specious logic and defended it with meretricious rhetoric. He did not apologize for it as a necessity but defended it as a right. He had disparaged instructions against it and with brazen effrontery he had flaunted it in the face of the whole North. He had made the Seventh of March as awful as Good Friday. Not since Lucifer had there been so great a fall.

Mr. Webster was responsible: it was his doing, this odious law and all its consequences. Mr. Webster was responsible, and his mail brought him hundreds of letters of congratulation from men of property and position (a letter from William Corcoran, too, with canceled notes for six thousand dollars and a check for a thousand more). He would sit down at his desk and answer them: "It is grateful to receive in a letter so respectably and so numerously signed, opinions so decidedly concurring with my own," he would say, or "Such a letter, with such names, assures me that I have not erred," or, "I have no doubt, Gentlemen, that you and the great body of your fellow citizens of Massachusetts approve these sentiments and opinions and will sustain those who honestly act upon them." But old Judge Hoar, said Emerson, "had never raised his head since Webster's speech."

He was sure of himself, Mr. Webster, he was exalted with virtue. ("Since the 7th of March," he wrote, "there has not been an hour in which I have not felt a crushing weight of anxiety and responsibility.") Massachusetts would sustain him. He had rejoiced at the election of Mr. Eliot to the House — a great victory, it was; but Winthrop, who was appointed to Webster's Senate seat, had voted against the Slave Bill. Yes, Massachusetts would sustain him — but it was Charles Sumner who was elected to fill his seat, after all. ("The papers are ringing with Sumner! Sumner! and the guns are thundering out their triumph," wrote Longfellow.) And the last time Webster stood in the Senate it was to hear the new Senator from Massachusetts, as handsome as himself and as eloquent, denounce the Fugitive Slave Bill and the Compromise. Mr. Webster had stood in front of the Revere House, and he had said in his lordly tone that agitation had its foundations in "unreal, ghostly abstractions"; but Ellen and William Craft went free, and Shadrach too, was that an abstraction? "I omit," he said, "to notice the blustering of Abolition societies as unworthy of regard," but Emerson was no abolitionist, and he wrote: "This filthy enactment was made in the nineteenth century, by men who could read and write. I will not obey it, by God." He had his letter from 987 merchants, but the Alderman denied him the use of Faneuil Hall, and he left the city in a huff. He went to Buffalo and said, "My sympathies, my love of liberty, for all mankind, are the same as yours," and Emerson confided to his Journal: "The word *liberty* in the mouth of Mr. Webster sounds like the word *love* in the mouth of a courtezan." He went to Syracuse and told them, ever so arrogantly, that "the Fugitive Slave Law will be enforced in spite of all opposition; even in this city, even in the midst of your abolition conventions," and within a year he had to eat his words: the Negro Jerry was rescued out of the Syracuse jail and Gerrit Smith stood up in court and defied the authorities to arrest him. All the newspapers assured Mr. Webster of their devotion, and sixty boys in Groton Academy signed a paper pledging their affection and their support for the Presidency, but in the convention of 1852 he received twenty-nine votes, and not one vote from the South. He had brought out a six-volume edition of his Works, but perhaps it was too big; the people of the North were reading, instead, those lines by the Quaker poet: —

Of all we loved and honored, naught
Save power remains;
A fallen angel's power of thought
Still strong in chains.

All else is gone; from those great eyes
The soul is fled.
When faith is lost, when honor dies
The man is dead.

Then pay reverence of old days
To his dead fame;
Walk backward, with averted gaze,
And hide the shame.

Whittier was right. It was on the seventh of March that Webster died; two years later his body confirmed the death sentence passed on him then. There were a thousand funeral orations, for how could the Church forbear to point the moral of this man's life? Parker went out to the country, to such a place as Webster himself had loved, there to meditate on his subject. He came back, and in four days he had written a book, and when he had read it, keeping his congregation long after the accustomed hour, Julia Ward Howe hurried breathless home. "Do not scold me," she cried, "I have just heard the greatest speech I shall ever hear."

"Of all my public trials," Parker said, as he picked up the bulky manuscript that Sunday morning, "this is my most trying day." It was no easy matter to pass judgment on Daniel Webster. He had his own prejudices to overcome as well as those of others. He had loved Webster, all New England had loved Webster, and gloried in him. He was, said Parker, an institution. He was a power, and a symbol of power. His word could inspire hope or despair. His pen wrote the history of the State. His life was an epic and a tragedy; he had known such splendor as no other man of his time, he had experienced, at the end, bitterness and despair. He had been called Godlike and he had been called Lucifer. No moralist who concerned himself with the character of the American people could avoid the responsibility presented by the death of this man.

Into his "Discourse on Webster" Parker poured all of his love for New England, all of his passion for the slavery struggle, all of his learning and his wisdom. He told the story of Webster's boyhood and youth, and it might have been his own: the pious family, the little country town, the back-breaking work of the farm, the hunger for learning, the schooling, gained at such cost, the ambition of the boy to conquer new worlds and the conquest, against such odds. He followed the story of Webster's political career: how he had come to Boston and made it his bailiwick, Massachusetts his pocket borough; how he bestrode all New England like a colossus, how he had chosen Presidents, written laws, drafted treaties; how he had defended the Constitution and saved the Union. He reviewed the slavery struggle, and Webster's part in it: his early devotion to freedom, and the great betrayal. He analyzed Webster's character, his mind and his morals and his conscience, the forces that fashioned him, the ideas that inspired him, the ambitions that bedeviled him.

That "Discourse" was a tremendous thing, as grand and roughhewn as Webster himself. It had the immediacy of death and the finality of the last Judgment. It was designed alike for the exigencies of the moment and the edification of the future. It had eloquence and beauty and the clean penetration of poetry, it had the passion and power of Webster's own oratory. It poured forth like a cataract, tumbling and swirling and eddying and foaming, its roar drowning out all the threnodies and the elegies that marked the day. What life, indeed, offered a grander subject for a homily?

He had such talents as no other man of his age; how nobly he had used them, how ignobly he had misused them. Heaven itself had favored him beyond other men, endowing him with a body as impressive as his mind. "He seemed," said Parker, "made to last a hundred years. Since Socrates there has seldom been a head so massive huge, save the stormy features of Michael Angelo. Since Charlemagne, I think there has not been such a grand figure in all Christendom. A large man, decorous in dress, dignified in deportment, he walked as if he felt himself a king. Men from the country who knew him not, stared at him as he passed through our streets. . . . His countenance, like Strafford's, was manly black. What a mouth he had. It was a lion's mouth. Yet there was a sweet grandeur in his smile, and a woman's softness when he would. What a brow it was! what eyes! like charcoal fire in the bottom of a deep, dark, well. His face was rugged with volcanic flames, great passions and great thoughts."

He had a massive intellect, but comprehensive rather than penetrating. He had great learning but not philosophy, his genius was for reason rather than for wisdom. He had eloquence beyond that of any public man, yet it did not seduce you by its beauty but bludgeoned itself through your mind. "He was not a Nile of eloquence, cascading into poetic beauty, now, then watering whole provinces with the drainage of tropic mountains; he was a Niagara pouring a world of clear waters adown a single ledge." His genius was critical rather than creative, he organized and marshaled his facts, but no great ideas were original with him. "He had not the instinctive genius which creates a beautiful whole by nature," said Parker, "as a mother bears a living son, nor the wide knowledge, the deep philosophy, the plastic industry, which forms a beautiful whole by art, as a sculptor chisels a marble boy."

He was great intellectually rather than morally. He had power, he was power incarnate, but he lacked courage. "His life has been one long vacillation. Ere long men will

ask for the historic proof to verify the reputation of his
power. It will not appear." He was cankered with ambition,
he loved office for its own sake, he attached himself to no
great moral principle, unless his passion for the Union partook of morality. He loved not money, but display and extravagance, he loved the easy way of life, his pleasures
were sensual and lavish rather than discriminating. He
lacked spiritual as well as physical abstemiousness, intellectual and moral as well as physical fastidiousness. So he
fell an easy prey to the money power, and was the paid attorney for the merchants of Boston.

His cardinal defect, indeed, was of character; he lacked
integrity, and it was a fatal flaw. He wanted stability and
independence; he followed the dictates now of prudence, now
of expediency. He never overcame his lawyer's training,
and his arguments were ingenious, as for a client, rather
than ingenuous, as for truth. He did not know that a straight
line was the shortest distance between two points, but took
a course as crooked as a drummer's. He did not, for all of
his origin, trust the people; his theory of government was
not democratic but imperial. He was fearful of consequences,
he put his faith in forms of law rather than in the instincts
of men. So he could commit himself to the principle that
the purpose of government was the protection of property,
and cry down the Higher Law.

No living man has done so much to debauch the conscience of
the nation, to debauch the press, the pulpit, the forum, and the
bar. There is no Higher Law, quoth he, and how much of the
pulpit, the press, the forum and the bar, denies its God. He
poisoned the moral wells of society with his lower law, and men's
consciences died of the murrain of beasts, which came because
they drank thereat.

Yet he had many popular qualities. He was open-handed
and lavish. He loved the company of men of all kinds, he
was a good neighbor and a good townsman. His affections
were strong and deep. He had a passion for nature, for the

mountains of his native New Hampshire, and the ocean beating on the shores of his Marshfield farm.

He was a farmer, and took a countryman's delight in country things, in loads of hay, in trees, in turnips, and the noble Indian corn, in monstrous swine. He had a patriarch's love of sheep, choice breeds thereof he had. He took delight in cows, short-horned Durhams, Herefordshires, Ayrshires, Alderneys. He tilled paternal acres with his own oxen. He loved to give the kine fodder. It was pleasant to hear his talk of oxen. And but three days before he left the earth, too ill to visit them, his cattle, lowing, came to see their sick lord; and, as he stood in his door, his great oxen were driven up, that he might smell their healthy breath, and look his last on those broad, generous faces, that were never false to him.

It was slavery that was the divining rod, and it discovered his weaknesses and exposed them. It was his apostasy of the Seventh of March that men could not forgive, that Parker could never forgive, and he launched a terrible invective.

Mr. Webster stamped his foot and broke through into the great hollow of practical atheism, which undergulfs the State and Church. Then what a caving in was there. The firm-set base of northern cities quaked and yawned with gaping rents. "Penn's sandy foundation" shook again, and black men fled from the city of brotherly love, as doves, with plaintive cry, flee from a farmer's barn when summer lightning stabs the roof. There was a twist in Faneuil Hall, and the doors could not open wide enough for Liberty to regain her ancient Cradle; only soldiers, greedy to steal a man, themselves stole out and in. Ecclesiastic quicksand ran down the hole amain. Metropolitan churches toppled, and pitched, and canted, and cracked, their bowing walls all out of plumb. Colleges broken from the chain which held them in the stream of time rushed towards the abysmal rent. Harvard led the way, *Christo et Ecclesiae* in her hand. Down plunged Andover, *Conscience and the Constitution* clutched in its ancient failing arm. New Haven began to cave in. Doctors of Divinity, orthodox, heterodox, with only a doxy of doubt, "no settled opinion," had great alacrity in sinking, and went down, as live as ever, into the bottomless pit of lower law . . . Fossils of theology, dead as Ezekiel's bones, took to their feet again, and stood up for most arrant wrong. "There is no Higher Law of God," quoth they, as they went down, "no golden rule, only the statutes of men."

Mr. Webster was not alone at fault, Boston was at fault, Boston that had bribed him; the Hunkers of the North were at fault, they had corrupted him; politics was at fault, its morals were unclean; the churches were at fault, they had renounced the Higher Law and called him good. Slavery, above all, was at fault, and Webster's catastrophic end showed how slavery contaminated all things that it touched. Parker's prose swung into poetry, indignation crowding the Miltonic lines: —

Slavery, the most hideous snake which Southern regions breed, with fifteen unequal feet, came crawling North, fold on fold, and ring on ring, and coil on coil, the venomed monster came: then Avarice the foulest worm which Northern cities gender in their heat, went crawling South; with many a wriggling curl, it wound along its way. At length they met, and twisting up in their obscene embrace, the twain became one monster, Hunkerism; theme unattempted yet in prose or song; there was no North, no South, they were one poison. Northward and Southward wormed the thing along its track, leaving the stain of its breath in the people's face; and its hissing against the Lord rings yet in many a speech. Then what a shrinking there was of great consciences, and hearts and minds.

A tragic figure, Daniel Webster, and his tragedy was the tragedy of a nation false to its past. He was, said Parker, "the saddest sight in all the Western World. I have long mourned for him as for no living or departed man. He blasted the friends of men with scornful lightning; him, if I could, I would not blast, but only bless continually and evermore."

And in his Journal Parker wrote, "A sad and dreadful day." Others thought so too, but for different reasons.

While all Boston was honoring Webster, repeating "Say no evil of the dead," Parker had committed this outrage. Felton considered it a disgraceful performance, and so did Doctor Lothrop. But Richard Henry Dana, who loved Webster, wrote in his Journal, "Strange that the best commendation that has appeared yet, the most touching, elevated, meaning eulogy, should have come from Theodore Parker. Were I Daniel Webster I would not have that sermon destroyed for all that had been said in my favor as yet." And Charles Francis Adams wrote in a prophetic vein: "Yours is the only independent and thorough analysis that will be made of that gentleman's life."

4

Twice Boston had flouted the Fugitive Slave Bill, but Webster had lived long enough to see Sims sent back to Georgia. Was the future to be with the Higher or the Lower Law? Let us "discountenance all agitation," said the Whigs, and nominated Mr. Scott; let us "resist all attempts at renewing agitation," said the Democrats, and nominated Mr. Pierce. The Compromise had settled everything; the question was closed. No sooner was Mr. Webster laid away in his grave, there in the Marshfield earth he loved so well, than the country went to the polls and sent Young Hickory of the Granite Hills to the White House (any man is in danger of being made President now, said Parker). The Free-Soil candidate polled only one hundred and fifty thousand votes, and eight thousand Whigs voted for Webster dead rather than the hero of Chapultepec alive. The Compromise was approved, the issue settled. "I fervently hope," said Mr. Pierce (no notes for him, no manuscript, he knew his piece by heart), "I fervently hope that no fanatical excitement may again threaten the durability of our institutions." No more excitement, no more agitation; nothing to do now but build railroads and annex Cuba and put Austria in her place. (*Boo!* said Mr. Pierce.) The slavery question was at rest, and when Mr. Sumner moved for the repeal of the Fugitive Slave Bill there were only four Senators to support him. In his first message President Pierce congratulated the country on "a sense of repose and security to the public mind." Just one month later, on January 4, 1854, Mr. Douglas rose in the Senate and introduced his Nebraska Bill, and the card-house of security was scattered as by a sirocco. In vain the Appeal to the Independent Democrats, in vain the resolutions of the Legislatures of the Northern States. March 3, the Nebraska Bill passed the Senate; and May 22, the House. The news reached the country the following day, and Colonel Suttle, on his way from Alexandria to Boston, read it with satisfaction. Another day and all over Massachusetts men and women knew that on application from Colonel Suttle the marshal had seized, on the streets of Boston, a fugitive slave. His name was Anthony Burns.

It was Anniversary Week in Boston when Burns was seized, the city was filled with men in from the country towns, every hall housed a convention and every church a conference. The Anti-Slavery Convention was meeting that week, and Parker had prepared an address for it. "Slavery is to perish out of America," he had written in his confidence. "Democracy is to triumph." It was a fit time to test the validity of this conviction; it was three years since Massachusetts had returned a slave.

It was night when Burns was arrested, on a trumped-up charge, and lodged in the Court House. Assailed by six ruffians, charged first with robbery, confronted by his owner, denied access to his friends, the wretched prisoner had confessed to his identity, and the next morning Commissioner Edward Loring was prepared to give his decision. But not so fast, Loring, the news is out. Here is young Dana, a thorn in the side of respectable society, and Ellis with him, two able lawyers to intercede for the fugitive. Here is the mighty Phillips, pushing his way past the guards, and here is Parker, breathless with haste, his mouth set in that grim line that all men knew. "May it please your

Honor," it is Dana speaking, "time should be allowed to the prisoner to recover himself from the stupefaction of his sudden arrest, to consult with friends, to determine what course he will pursue." Did the prisoner want counsel, did he wish to offer any defense? He thought of the whipping post in Alexandria, and the auction block, and kept silent. Parker went up to him, "These men are your friends," he said, "do you want a defense?" And, catching his breath, the prisoner said "Yes." Loring had to lecture at Harvard, and the case was put over for two days, and Parker rushed home to prepare the first of those incendiary placards that were designed to arouse Boston to violence.

KIDNAPPING AGAIN!!

A Man was Stolen Last Night by the Fugitive Slave Bill
Commissioner
He will have His
MOCK TRIAL
On Saturday, May 27, at 9 o'clock, in the Kidnapper's Court
Before the Honourable Slave Bill Commissioner
At the Court House in Court Square
SHALL BOSTON STEAL ANOTHER MAN?
Thursday, May 26, 1854

and another, the same day: —

SEE TO IT THAT NO FREE CITIZEN OF MASSACHUSETTS IS DRAGGED INTO SLAVERY

See to it indeed. How was it to be done? The Vigilance Committee was in continuous session and there were a dozen plans. Higginson was down from Worcester, hot for a fight, as always, a scheme already hatching in his brain; Martin Stowell was coming on with a crate of axes; old Captain Bearse was all for a rescue at sea. How was it to be done? The conspirators were in and out, no plan, no direction, only indignation and talk. But the posters were up for a meeting in Faneuil Hall, and time pressed.

All Boston flocked into the hall that Friday night, and the Cradle of Liberty seethed with excitement. Every seat was taken, the aisles were filled, the galleries crowded, the stairs packed tight, the very windows jammed with men, all kindling ready for the spark. And on the platform sat the speakers: Chevalier Howe and Wendell Phillips, Francis Bird and young John Swift, Theodore Parker, and Russell of West Roxbury to preside.

There they sat, whispering among themselves. What was afoot that night? Did Parker understand the plans, did Phillips know his cue? Frank Bird was introduced (he needed no introduction, the Bird Club was famous throughout the State), and he told the story of the capture. John Swift, a voice like thunder, asked them, "What are you going to do about it?" and from all over the Hall came the answer, "Fight, Fight!" Howe read the Resolutions, and Phillips, never grander, spoke for action.

"Parker, Parker!" The galleries caught up the cry, and Parker took the floor.

"Fellow subjects of Virginia . . ." he said, and the crowd cried, "No, No, take that back."

"I will take it back when you show me that it is not so. Men and brothers, I am not a young man; I have heard hurrahs and cheers for liberty many times; I have not seen a great many deeds done for liberty. I ask you, are we to have deeds as well as words?" (What are you about, John Swift — why don't you speak up?) "They have got no soldiers billeted in Faneuil Hall, as in 1851. They think they can carry this man off to-morrow in a cab."

"They can't do it. Let them try!" (Why doesn't the signal come?)

"There is one law, the slave law; it is everywhere. There is another law, which is also a finality, and that law is in your hands and arms, and you can put it in execution just when you see fit." (Lash them some more, Parker, whip their emotions up.) "Gentlemen, I love peace, but there is a means and there is an end. Liberty is the end, and sometimes peace is not the means to it. Now I want to ask you, what are you going to do?" (This is your moment, Higginson; it is now or never.) "What are you going to do?"

"Shoot, shoot."

"No, there are ways of managing this matter without shooting anybody." (Not for long, Parker, not after tonight.) "These men who have kidnapped a man are cowards, every mother's son of them." (He was marking time, now, something had gone amiss.) "Let's pay a visit to the slave-catchers at the Revere House. Shall it be to-night? Put that question." (A forest of hands; they wanted action, these people; but it would never do.) "It is not a vote."

"To-night, to-night!" — but Parker's voice drowned them out:

"It is not a vote. We shall meet at the Court House to-morrow morning at nine o'clock."

And this was all, Parker. What a famous fiasco. Dear God, had all the plans gone wrong? Too late now; the game was up. Phillips rose to speak, the turbulent crowd sat back, and there was quiet. It would be to-morrow then, a peaceful protest, that was best. It would be folly to do anything to-night.

There was a shout from the door. "To the Court House! to the Court House!" The signal had come at last. The Hall was in turmoil. Empty your seats now, Faneuil Hall, turn out your galleries, burst open your doors. There is Howe, he never ran so fast before, and young Channing by his side. There is the faithful Bowditch, and tall Phillips, and Parker, his short legs clumping along the cobblestones. Faster, faster, you never did such work as this, farm boy from Lexington.

Too late, Parker. Too late, Higginson. Too late, Anthony Burns. Everything had gone wrong that night. ("The attack was planned deliberately, cautiously, and most judiciously," Higginson wrote.) Phillips hadn't heard the plans, and Parker hadn't understood. The signal hadn't been given on time, and when it came, some thought it was a trick.

The Hall was too full; the crowd got out of hand. Stowell had lost his axes, and the raiding party was disorganized.

Yet there had been a gallant attempt.

They were a score of men, Negroes and whites, Higginson and Lewis Hayden in charge. They had ripped the banister off the stairway of the Museum, and battered in the Court House door. It swung loose, on one hinge, there was death on the other side. (Where was Howe, now; where was Parker?) A Negro sprang up the steps and pushed through the door, a black Arnold Winkelried, Higginson close behind. The policemen swung their clubs and blood spurted from Higginson's chin. Come, men, up the stairs and in, help is on the way. There was a shot and a scream, and the attacking party fell back. "You cowards, will you desert us now?" Higginson cried, but the Hall was brightly lighted and the police were crouching on the stairway, pistols pointing through the rails. Still no reinforcements. There was a moment of silence, and frail Bronson Alcott stepped forward, cane in hand, and up the steps to the shattered door. "Why are we not within?" he asked. There was a pistol shot, and no one moved. From a distance came the tramp of many feet, and a company of soldiers wheeled into the Court House Square.

Alcott turned, and came slowly down the steps; he was bathed in transcendental calm. The crowd from Faneuil Hall was streaming into the Square, now, but it was too late. "Mister, I guess you've left your rumberill," said a boy to Higginson, and Higginson took his umbrella and went off to have his chin sewed up. Sullenly the crowd fell back, and the soldiers took command; they were there by accident, but no matter. There had been murder that night, and treason. James Batchelder was dead. A shot from Hayden's gun had narrowly missed Marshal Freeman. "Why didn't he hit him?" cried Parker, and wrung his hands.

That very night Marshal Freeman telegraphed for authority to call out the soldiers, and soon President Pierce himself wired back: "Incur any expense deemed necessary to insure the execution of the law." Incur any expense, and the Columbian Artillery were stationed in the Court House Square. Incur any expense, and two Companies were called in from Fort Independence and the marines from the Charlestown Navy Yard. Incur any expense, and a marshal's guard of one hundred and twenty-four, the sweepings of the slums, was sworn in to keep the law. Incur any expense: it cost one hundred thousand dollars to send Burns back, but that was only the beginning. The real bill came later, and it was paid in blood.

For ten days Boston was in a state of siege, while Loring ruled on points of law. For ten days the granite Court House was a Bastile: soldiers guarded the doors, soldiers lined the stairs, soldiers peered out of the windows. Three cordons of police were strung around the court, and two more of soldiers. For ten days the business of the regular courts was suspended; and when Francis Jackson and Samuel May tried to gain access to the court they were stopped by soldiers. Every day the crowds milled around the Square. "Go home," said Mayor Smith, "the law will be maintained." And the troops marched in from Portsmouth and from Newport, and Colonel Amory rallied his Independent Cadets. And the marshal's guard swaggered down the streets of the town, flaunting their incongruous authority in the faces of decent men.

A precious crew, this marshal's guard: jailer Andrews recognized among them forty-five of his regular customers. While they served, said Dana, Boston was reformed. "The people have not felt it necessary to lock their doors at night, the brothels are tenanted only by women, fighting dogs and racing horses have been unemployed, and Ann Street and its alleys and cellars show signs of a coming Millennium." Parker's description was as graphic and as unflattering. "Marshal Freeman," he said, "raked the kennels of Boston. He dispossessed the stews, bawding the courts with unwonted infamy. He gathered the spoils of brothels; prodigals not penitent who upon harlots wasted their substance in riotous living; pimps, gamblers, the succubus of Slavery; men which the gorged gaols had cast out into the streets scarred with infamy; fighters, drunkards, public brawlers; convicts who had served out their time, waiting for a second conviction; men whom the subtlety of counsel or the charity of the gallows had left unhanged."

What a ferment there was. Rumor flew round the city like an epidemic: there would be another attack upon the Court House; the Virginians would be hounded out of town; Wendell Phillips would be shot; Garrison would be mobbed; Parker would be arrested. What a ferment there was: law-abiding men carried pistols and respectable women stood on the street corners and hissed the guardsmen and the soldiers as they passed by. Boston was never so crowded; every train brought a delegation from some country town and there were nine hundred in from Worcester alone. Colonel Suttle was being entertained by the Harvard professors ("I do not like to think that the natural instincts of Massachusetts are all snobbish," wrote Lowell), and twelve men had been arrested for the murder of Batchelder, and the churches of the city sent up prayers for the fugitive. And in the Courtroom, bayonets lining the walls, Dana and Ellis pled for the life of Anthony Burns.

They had a good case, so they thought. Could it be proved that Burns was indeed the fugitive described in the affidavit? The identification was inaccurate and incomplete. Could it be proved that Burns owed service to Colonel Suttle? The Colonel brought no such proof nor did he offer to procure any. Could it be proved that Burns had escaped from service? Mr. Brent swore that Burns had been in Virginia on the twenty-fourth of March and there were six witnesses to swear to his presence in Boston on the first of that month.

But Burns had confessed. He had answered to his name, he had admitted his identity, he had expressed his willingness to go back. So said Colonel Suttle and Mr. Brent, and so said the guard on duty by his cell. What court would accept, under such circumstances, a plea of guilty — a confession extorted by intimidation, made not to the court but to the parties in the litigation, supported by *ex parte* evidence? Colonel Suttle could not prove a case; the law was with Burns.

But Loring thought otherwise, and he ruled against the prisoner on every point. He was acting in an executive, not a judicial, capacity and did not have to consider questions of constitutionality, or the right of the great writs of *habeas corpus* and replevin. He was concerned only with the identity of the prisoner, and since the law forbade the fugitive to testify, he accepted Burns's confession and called it "evidence." He allowed the claimants to take action, first, under the sixth section of the Fugitive Slave Law, and then, that failing, under the tenth. He ignored every technicality through which Burns might gain his freedom and embraced every technicality through which he might be returned to slavery.

This was bad enough, but it was not the sum of his infamy. He prejudged the case, urging upon Phillips, before the trial commenced, the futility of any effort on behalf of the prisoner. He violated judicial proprieties by drawing up a bill of sale for Burns while the case was still in court and Burns still presumably a free man. He acquiesced in the intimidation of witnesses, he connived with the claimants in outwitting the lawyers for the defense. And, at the end, he told his decision to Suttle and Brent twenty hours before he gave it in court.

A brief decision, Loring, and to the point. With the wisdom or even the validity of the Law you had nothing to do; your function was ministerial, not judicial. You were satisfied that the prisoner was the fugitive, Anthony Burns; for proof, the "evidence" of Burns himself. The claim was granted, and the prisoner surrendered to his claimants.

That decision was to cost you dear, Judge Loring. The women of Woburn sent you thirty pieces of silver, and you could travel the length of the Cape by the light of your burning effigies. Phillips arraigned you as a fit companion to

Jeffreys and Scroggs, and Parker charged you with the murder of James Batchelder. Your students deserted your
classes, and Harvard College would not have you on its
faculty. Soon the legislature moved for your dismissal from
the bench, and within three years Boston knew you no
longer.

It was on Friday morning, the second of June, that Loring read his decision, and the word flew over Massachusetts
and darkened the skies like an eclipse. "That man *must* not
be sent out of Boston as a slave," wrote non-resistant Whittier, but Dana knew better. "I firmly believe," he said,
"that in the providence of God it has been decreed that
one cup more should be put to our lips, and that it should
not pass away until we had drained it to the dregs." And
stern Ezra Gannett, who kept the law and who asked "What
is one man set against the safety of the Union?", Gannett heard the news and flung himself sobbing into a chair.
"God forgive this guilty nation!" he said.

The Courtroom was cleared, all but the marshal's guard,
roistering on the floor. The soldiers mustered in the Court
House Square. A cannon rattled over the streets and was
planted by the door of the Court House, a six-pounder, it
was, with forty rounds of shot, its muzzle pointing toward
the crowds beyond. At noon a column of soldiers marched
down State Street, clearing the way for Burns; a cordon was
drawn on both sides of the Street, the soldiers gripped their
muskets and stared stolidly down, closing their ears to the
taunts and jeers of the crowd. Boston had never known such
a day: the sun so bright, not a cloud in the sky, all about
the warm loveliness of June; twenty thousand people lining the streets, sunk, said the Reverend Mr. Beckwith, "in
a funereal sadness."

At two, the soldiers formed in the Court House Square
and began their long procession. Call the roll of the Companies, what famous names they bore: The New England
Guards, the Pulaski Guards, the Independent Fusiliers, the
Washington Light Infantry; the Columbian Artillery, the

American Artillery, the Bay State Artillery, and the Webster, too, dragging the cannon along. There were the Marines from Charlestown, the Mounted Dragoons and the Lancers, and Colonel Amory and his Independent Cadets, and in the center the marshal's guard, with Anthony Burns decked out in a new suit of clothes. Down the street the long procession came, no martial music here, only the dull tramp of the soldiers' feet and the clatter of the horses' hoofs, and the groans and hisses of the vast throng, crowding the sidewalks, filling the doors and windows of the shops, the balconies, and even the roofs. "There was lots of folks," said Burns, "to see a colored man walk down the street."

Down State Street, past stores and offices, draped in black. Flags at half-mast, flags hung in crape, flags Union down. As the soldiers passed Washington Street, marching under a coffin labeled LIBERTY, there was a commotion and some cheers; the crowd had caught sight of old Thomas Garrett, carpetbag in hand; he had sent a thousand slaves into liberty. Howe was there, the tears streaming down his face "for sorrow, shame and indignation"; Higginson was there with his Worcester guard, his chin swathed in bandages; Parker was there, the lines for his next sermon forming in his mind. Two boys were there with famous names, Charles Lowell and Henry Lee Higginson. "Charley," said Henry, "it will come to us to set this right." (Easy enough, Henry; just ten years more and Lowell will be dead at Cedar Creek and you left for dead on the field of Aldie Gap.)

The procession turned into Commercial Street. The crowd surged forward, and bayonets drove them back; a drayman blocked the way, his cheek was cut open with a sword. The soldiers struck up a tune. "Carry me back to old Virginny," they sang, and on, past the Custom House, to the back of Long Wharf. The steamer *John Taylor* was there, ready to carry Burns out to the revenue cutter *Morris*, and they put him aboard. It was just three o'clock. The great bells of Brattle Street began to toll, and all up and down the Bay the bells caught up the mournful sound, from town to town the dirge was heard, in Pilgrim Plymouth and in ancient Salem where another Higginson once preached, northward to Haverhill, you could hear them in New Hampshire, and south where the spirit of Williams was not banished from Narragansett Bay and out in Worcester where Daniel Shays once fought, the bells tolled the return of Anthony Burns.

5

Parker had not heard the last of the Burns case. That same month he wrote in his Journal: "What shall I do if I am sent to gaol?" His answer was characteristic: —

1. Write one sermon a week, and have it read at Music Hall, and printed the next morning. Who can read it? Write also prayer, etc. 2. Prepare a volume of sermons from old MSS. 3. Write Memoirs of Life, etc. 4. Vol. I of "Historical Development of Religion," i.e., the Metaphysics of Religion. 5. Pursue Russian studies.

But it was not to be, more the pity. The State would have done scholarship a service had it jugged Parker for a year: the "Historical Development of Religion" remained a massive fragment, and Parker was never satisfied with his Russian. The Grand Jury met, and Judge Curtis charged them to find bills against all who were guilty of obstructing the execution of the Fugitive Slave Law. But the Grand Jury was recalcitrant, and there were no indictments; and Parker wrote to Desor, "I should be sorry if a Massachusetts jury should disgrace the State by such meanness; but I should have liked the occasion for a speech."

Indeed he would, and ostentatiously he placed a chip on his shoulder. "Perhaps the Court will try again," he said with cheerful impudence, "and find a more pliant Grand Jury, easier to intimidate. Let me suggest to the Court that the next time it should pack its jurors from the Marshal's guard." It was an excellent suggestion. The Court did try again. A new Grand Jury was impaneled, and on it Mr. William Greenough, brother-in-law to Judge Curtis. Mr. Greenough didn't like Mr. Parker; meeting him in a bookstore Mr. Greenough had snubbed Mr. Parker, and Parker cherished the snub for future use. Sure enough, this time the Grand Jury was more pliant: referred to the Attorney General for instructions, it found indictments against Parker, Phillips, Higginson, Stowell, and others who had talked that night at Faneuil Hall and fought at the Court House. Mr. Greenough, so Parker was informed, was "very active in his endeavors to procure an indictment."

This was better. November 29, as Parker was writing his Thanksgiving sermon, he was notified of his arrest. "This is a very disagreeable business, Mr. Parker," said the man who served the warrant. "I make no doubt of it," said Mr. Parker with unction, and went out to arrange for bail. Back in his study he dusted off the "Defence" he had prepared in June — "The main lines all marked out, the fortifications sketched, the place of the batteries determined." Then he wrote to his friends and to his counsel. "I think it quite a serious affair," he confided solemnly to Sam Jo May. "It is the Freedom of Speech which is assailed through me." And he read with satisfaction this note from Charles Sumner: "I regard your indictment as a call to a new parish, with B. R. Curtis and B. F. Hallett as deacons, and a pulpit higher than the Strasburg steeple."

It was indeed a call, and Parker answered with enthusiasm. Things couldn't have been better. A minister, he was to be tried for preaching the Bible — as he understood it; the grandson of Captain Parker, he was to be tried for speaking on behalf of Liberty from the platform of Faneuil Hall. The jury was packed (remember, there was Mr. Greenough who had snubbed him), the Judge was prejudiced (the Curtis family had tried to oust him and his Society from the Music Hall that very year). And as for Mr. Curtis' charge to the grand jury — it was bad law and worse logic; you could drive a team of oxen clean through it. "Not only those who are present, but those who, though absent when the offence was committed, did procure, counsel, command, or abet others to commit the offence, are indictable as principals." So said Mr. Curtis. And what was it to "procure, counsel, command or abet"? Listen to this: "Such procurement may be . . . by evincing an express liking, approbation or assent to another's criminal design. . . . It need not appear that the precise time or place or means advised were used."

"So every man in Boston," said Parker, "who on that bad Friday stood in the streets of Boston between Court Square and T Wharf was 'guilty of a disdemeanor.' All who at Faneuil Hall stirred up the minds of the people in opposition to the fugitive slave bill, all who shouted, who clapped their hands at the words or the countenance of their favorites or who expressed 'approbation' by a whisper of 'assent' are 'guilty of a misdemeanor.' Well, there were fifteen thousand persons 'assembled in the highway' of the city of Boston on that day opposed to kidnapping; half the newspapers in the country towns of Massachusetts 'evinced an express desire' for freedom and opposed kidnapping; they are all 'guilty of a misdemeanor,' they are all 'principals.' Nay, the ministers all over the State who preached that kidnapping was a sin; those who read brave words out of the Old Testament, or the New; those who prayed that the victim might escape; they were 'guilty of a misdemeanor,' liable to be fined three hundred dollars and jailed for twelve months."

So Parker and his fellow conspirators prepared for the trial. They were sure of themselves, but they took care to engage good counsel all the same: Senator Hale and Charles Ellis, and young John Andrew, the coming politician of the State. "At the trial," said Parker, arrogant as ever, "it was optional with us to beat the Government on the indictment before the Court, or on the merits of the case before the Jury." So they decided to do both, and Parker to help them. "I thought it best to take an active part in my own defence," he wrote, "for the matter at issue belonged to my previous studies and general business." And to Sumner, so learned in the law: "We will fight them inch by inch . . . Tell me of any examples of bad Judges, of tyrannous Courts, etc., of perversions of Law to serve Power."

April the third came the trial, Judge Curtis himself on the bench — "an eye on the Chief Justiceship," wrote Parker, "so I expect no justice." Most of the defendants took the matter lightly enough, and Phillips did not bother even to come to court; but Parker was there, and Higginson remembered him "busy with his terrible note-book, so that he seemed as important a figure in the scene as the presiding judge himself."

Here was martyrdom. "I stand now in as important a position as my honored Grandfather at the Battle of Lexington." But alas, no Pitcairn here, to cry "Disperse," no violence, no tyranny, no shot heard round the world, only the droning of the lawyers as they argued "that the said indictment does not allege and set forth fully and sufficiently the authority and proceedings whereon the alleged warrant and order were based, or facts sufficient to show that the alleged process and order were lawfully issued by any person duly authorized, and his authority and jurisdiction . . ." Then the Attorney General was indisposed, and there was a recess; the Court convened again to hear "that the writ of venire for the jury that found said indictment was directed to and returned by Watson Freeman, the Marshal, who was not an indifferent person, and it was not served and returned as the law directs." No thunder here, no torrential eloquence, only the wrangling over technicalities. And before they had properly begun, Parker thumbing through his notes on the history of judicial tyranny, the whole thing was over. There was no proper legal averment that Commissioner Loring was actually such a Commissioner as was described in the law of 1850, and the indictments were quashed. "You have crawled out of a very small hole this time, Mr. Parker," said the Attorney General.

"I will make a larger hole next time, Mr. Hallett," said Parker.

But how? That was the rub. It was a trick, thought Parker, the judges were afraid. But he wasn't to be cheated out of his chance after all: that summer he prepared his "Defence" for the printer, and he found that he could write a good many things that the judge would never have permitted him to say in court. Page after page of manuscript; that was another thing, he had more space this way, more elbowroom, and besides, he could put in his footnotes; then even the most unsophisticated reader could see what a monument of learning it was.

Gentlemen of the Jury [he wrote, though there was no jury now, only the public], it is no trifling matter which comes before you this day. You may hereafter decide on millions of money and on the lives of your fellow men; but it is not likely that a question of this magnitude will ever twice be brought before the same jurymen . . . Your verdict concerns all the people of the United States; its influence will reach to ages far remote, blessing or cursing whole generations not yet born. It is not I, merely, now put to trial. It is the unalienable Rights of Humanity.

So much for the importance of the case. It was a trial between Slavery and Freedom, so in went the history of the encroachments of the Slave Power; it was a brazen attempt to establish judicial tyranny, and here was a history of wicked judges, from Stuart England to nineteenth-century America, with a hundred instances of judicial usurpations; it was an effort to destroy the independence of juries, so Parker included a history of the jury system, with some remarks on the duty of juries to follow the guidance of their conscience rather than the instructions of the Court. These preliminaries out of the way (fifty thousand words, no less), it was time for an examination of the special case of The United States *versus* Theodore Parker, for all history converged on this. First a history of the Fugitive Slave Bill and its enforcement, with remarks on the Curtis family that would surely have been contempt of court; then a review of Parker's opposition to the bill. Did the Court want evidence of his "offending against the peace and dignity of the United States, to the evil example of others"? He would give them, he said, "their bellyful," and he found space for a review of the Craft Case and the Shadrach Case and the Sims Case, for quotations from his sermons and his speeches, for a history (discreet, of course) of the attempt to rescue Burns.

"Gentlemen, I must bring this defence to a close. Already it is too long for your patience" (five hundred pages of manuscript now) "though far too short for the mighty interest at stake, for it is the Freedom of a Nation which you are to decide upon." A brief recapitulation, another fling at the Curtis family, an eloquent reference to Lexington and what happened there, and he was done.

It was a powerful thing, eloquent and moving, irrefutable if you subscribed to the Higher Law, irrelevant if you did not. From Herndon and from Sumner came congratulations, and Howe assured him, "It is a wonderful monument of power, learning, wisdom, labour, zeal, and humanity." It was, indeed; but it was something of an anticlimax, after all. Anthony Burns was free again, now, a student at Oberlin — and it was Kansas men were talking about.

CHAPTER XII

THE POLITICAL LEADER

THE North was awake, at last. Parker had chalked up ten
victories for Slavery and but two for Freedom, but now
all that would be changed. There were new Generals, and
a new board of strategy. Away with the Fabian tactics of
the past; the North was on the offensive, here was a party
pledged to fight and leaders who were bold. "You have no
idea of the change of feeling here," wrote Howe to Horace
Mann, and Dana could tell Sumner that "There are few
Compromise men left in Boston." All over the North there
were stirrings of revolt. Massachusetts sent Henry Wilson
to the Senate, Maine sent Fessenden, and from the President's own State came John Parker Hale. Ohio took Chase
for Governor and put rough Ben Wade in his Senate seat,
and all the genius of Douglas could not prevent the choice
of Lyman Trumbull as his colleague from Illinois. Anthony
Burns had done his work, and Douglas, with his Nebraska
Bill.

At last Freedom was in earnest. Did Douglas speak for
Squatter Sovereignty and the South, in its folly, applaud?
Even while the Nebraska Bill was being debated in the
Senate, Eli Thayer out in Worcester moved to beat the slave
power at its own game. "It is much better," said Thayer,
"to go and do something for free labor than to stay at home
and talk of manacles and auction blocks and bloodhounds."
So the Massachusetts Emigrant Aid Company was organized, and the board of Directors read like a roster of State
Street merchants: Amos Lawrence and J. M. S. Williams
and George Luther Stearns and Samuel Cabot; and from

Providence John Carter Brown — think of it. Pierce's signature was hardly dry on the Nebraska Bill before the first
company of crusaders entrained for Kansas, men everywhere reading Whittier's new poem: —

> We cross the prairie as of old
> The pilgrims crossed the sea,
> To make the West, as they the East,
> The homestead of the Free.

All that year and the next little bands of emigrants set out
for the Missouri, Sharpes rifles in hand, and Parker went
down to the station to see them off. They had a new song,
now: —

> 'Tis Freedom calls us hither,
> For Freedom's sake we roam
> 'Mid Western wilds, in Freedom's cause
> We'll make our happy home.

Parker wanted to go with them; he too heard the call, he
wanted to roam. Higginson was out there (Jim Lane had
made him a Brigadier General), and his faithful Martin
Stowell, and Howe, of course — you couldn't keep Howe
away from any excitement. But Parker had his work cut
out for him at home: he organized committees, he raised
money, he circulated petitions, he counseled politicians, he
preached and lectured, he had never been so busy. One
great sermon after another rolled off his pen: "The New
Assault upon Freedom in America," "Some Thoughts on
the Progress of America," "The Dangers which Threaten
the Rights of Man in America," "The Consequences of an
Immoral Principle and False Idea of Life," "The Great
Battle between Slavery and Freedom" (it took two read-
ings to cover that, each from a manuscript of twenty thousand words). There seemed to be no end to the demands
upon him: lecture engagements poured in, he had to turn
down two out of every three. He was becoming downright
popular; for once he was on the winning side, he didn't
know what to make of it.

They had slavery on the run now, he had never known such excitement. Garrison didn't approve at all, nor Wendell Phillips, they spent their time inditing jeremiads, but this was no time for non-resistance nor for nullification, and when the radical abolitionists called a secession convention at Worcester, Parker would not attend. In 1855 he swung out into Ohio, where Chase and Wade had the upper hand; the next year he was in Illinois and met Herndon, and heard Douglas: "He was considerably drunk," Parker wrote to Hale, "and made one of the most sophistical and deceitful speeches I ever listened to." He was up to his neck in politics, now, working tirelessly for the election of Frémont, though he had little faith in the Pathfinder, and less expectation of success. But that was no great matter: Buchanan would be elected, but he would be the last slavery President, of that Parker was convinced.

They had slavery on the run, and the slave power was desperate. What was the assault upon Sumner but an act of desperation, what was the sack of Lawrence but a confession of defeat? *"The North are Up,"* Herndon wrote exultantly to Parker, and every day his verdict was confirmed. Kansas had pointed the way, Kansas had revealed the temper of the North. Too bad that the first victory of freedom over slavery should be won with Sharpes rifles instead of with pulpit arguments, but that's the way it was. Preaching and speechmaking were all well enough, and burning the Constitution was a fine gesture, but John Brown, not Garrison, was the man of the hour.

A wonderful man, this John Brown, a man after Parker's heart. He was in earnest; he made all the Bostonians look like dilettantes, and they were glad to enlist under his leadership and to help him, no questions asked. Parker recognized in him a kindred spirit: Brown thought that this thing of slavery had to be settled, in the end, by the sword, and so did Parker; he was not afraid of a fight, nor of a little bloodshed, nor was Parker; he did not recoil from an insurrection of the slaves, but encouraged it, and in the end

Parker was with him even there. "I should like of all things," he told Sarah Hunt, "to see an insurrection of the slaves. It must be tried many times before it succeeds, *as at last it must*."

There was something about this man Brown: all of them felt it, even gentle Emerson, even hardheaded Lawrence. He came on to Boston and hypnotized them all. He stood up there, so tall and grizzled, and talked like a prophet out of the Old Testament, fanaticism staring out of his eyes. "Without the shedding of blood," he said, "There is no remission of sins." Was he mad, as he told of the sack of Lawrence and the murders at Osawatomie and talked of vengeance? It was a time for madness, men had been sane too long. Were his plans chimerical, desperate? Even a gesture would be some measure of success. "I doubt," said Parker, "whether things of the kind will succeed. But we shall make a great many failures before we discover the right way of getting at it. This may as well be one of them."

It was money that Brown wanted (he would do the fighting, leave that to him), and he came East to get it. Gerrit Smith of New York (Bronson Alcott turned Maecenas), the Reverend Mr. Higginson in Worcester, Frank Sanborn teaching school in Concord, audacious Howe, wealthy George Stearns, and Theodore Parker, these were the men for him. He was in Boston that winter of '56, and Garrison met him at Parker's house, and all evening long they discussed non-resistance, Brown citing the Old Testament, Garrison the New. Higginson had him up before the Massachusetts Legislature; they were trying to get a grant of one hundred thousand dollars to aid Bleeding Kansas, — little Vermont had voted twenty thousand, — and Brown was to persuade them; but for once his eloquence failed. His own demands were almost as extravagant: thirty thousand dollars was what he needed, but he was willing to take less. Parker and Sanborn and Higginson did their best, but money was hard to get, that spring of '57, and Brown was in despair. He prepared to leave, he called Mrs. Stearns in to hear him read "Old Brown's Farewell to Plymouth Rocks, Bunker Hill Monuments, Charter Oaks, and Uncle Tom's Cabins." It was a moving document, and Mrs. Stearns hurried home to persuade her husband to do better by Old Brown.

So Brown went back to Kansas with seven thousand dollars from George Stearns ("One of the noblest men in Boston," Parker called him), and more from other members of the Kansas Committee. But it wasn't enough, and soon Parker was reading another appeal for funds. "My particular object in writing is to say that I am in immediate want of some 500 or 1000 dollars, for secret service, and no questions asked." Somehow the money was raised ("I have friends," said Parker, "who will give me money without asking any questions"), and there was much ado out in Tabor City, Iowa, a new drillmaster training the men; but nothing happened after all, and next spring Brown came on to Peterboro, New York to divulge his latest scheme. "I have nearly perfected arrangements," he wrote Parker, "for carrying out an important measure in which the world has a deep interest, as well as Kansas, and only lack from 500 to 800 dollars to enable me to do so. It is my only errand here, and I have written some of our mutual friends in regard to it, but none of them understand my views as well as you do, and I cannot explain without their first committing themselves more than I know of their doing." But explain he did, to Frank Sanborn and Gerrit Smith, and all that afternoon the young philanthropist and the old trudged the country roads discussing these new disclosures, while the shadows of the hills slanted along the snow. "You see how it is," said Smith at last. "Our old friend has made up his mind to this course of action, and cannot be turned from it. We cannot give him up to die alone; we must stand by him."

But Sanborn was not so sure, and he asked Brown to come to Boston and consult with the rest of the Kansas

Committee. Parker met him at the American House, and Brown told his plans for an invasion of the South. He needed trained soldiers, and he asked Parker to compose an "Address to the Officers and Soldiers of the United States Army on the Duty of a Soldier." The Duty, Mr. Parker should say, was to desert the army and join up with Osawatomie Brown. But Parker would have none of this; he sent, instead, General McClellan's new "Report on the Armies of Europe." Nor was the Committee more encouraging. The new drillmaster was making trouble now, everyone seemed to be in on the secret; better by far to postpone action for another year. Discouraged, the old man set out for Kansas. It was the last time Parker saw him.

So far it had all been rather fun, and the Committee had enjoyed it — the hatching of plots, the secret meetings, the code ("How goes our little speculation in wool?" they would write, slyly), the purchase of arms, the tall talk and the rodomontade, matching the Southerners word for word. It had all been a game, outwitting the Government (that legerdemain about the arms — that was clever), outwitting the villainous drillmaster, outwitting the Border Ruffians; and when Brown ran off with eleven slaves, all the way from Kansas to Canada, they thought of the slaves they too had rescued. They had heard of the bloodless Wakarusa War, but they never understood the meaning of Potawatomi, and an invasion of the South they were not ready to approve.

But John Brown meant business. Potawatomi had not been a game. And Harper's Ferry was no game, the dead lying in the streets of the little town, the arsenal a shambles. This was no fine adventure, no swashbuckling over the plains of Kansas, or talking so bold in Concord meeting with Emerson there to applaud. When old Gerrit Smith heard the awful news ("We must stand by him," he had said) his mind gave way. Howe rushed off to Canada, — it was his health, he said, — with Sanborn on his heels. Higginson alone stood his ground. Soon Sanborn was back, and when they tried to arrest him Judge Hoar was ready with a writ of *habeas corpus* and the citizens of Concord ran the Federal marshals out of town. Parker was in Rome when he read of Harper's Ferry and the sentence passed on Brown, his own death sentence just as sure. "I could not help wishing I was at home again," he wrote to Francis Jackson, "to use what poor remnant of power is left to me in defence of the True and the Right." And he went on to show what was True and Right — to show that slaves had a right to revolt, and that freemen had a right to help them, "and as a means to that end, to aid them in killing all such as oppose their natural freedom." And he reverted again to his hope of a slave insurrection — it might have been Brown himself who penned the words: —

The South must reap as she sows; where she scatters the wind, the whirlwind will come up. It will be a pretty crop for her to reap. The Fire of Vengeance may be waked up even in an African's heart, especially when it is fanned by the wickedness of a white man: then it runs from man to man, from town to town. What shall put it out? *The white man's blood.*

2

When it was the Slave Power crowding Kansas with Border Ruffians or striking down Sumner in his Senate seat, Parker was sure that that South was desperate, and he wrote, "The Devil is in great wrath because he knoweth that his time is short." Was the North, too, in despair, that it had to resort to Sharpes rifles and to massacre in Potawatomi and that good men applauded the raid on Harper's Ferry? Parker did not really face this question. The aggressions of freedom, he felt, were justified by a different philosophy. These things were no confessions of moral bankruptcy, as with the South. It was not that John Brown's way was the only way. Neither persuasion nor politics had been abandoned, this was merely another expedient: if the South could not understand Garrison or Sumner, perhaps it could learn to understand men like John Brown. "We want all sorts of weapons to attack slavery with," Parker wrote to Thayer, when that deluded philanthropist proposed the colonization of the South itself, "the heavy artillery and the light horse which cuts the lines asunder and routs a whole column before they know the enemy is upon them."

He was convinced that only war could settle this matter of slavery, but he did not embrace a foolish consistency and abdicate politics. He was convinced that the Union would not hold together, but he would not go along with Garrison and Phillips in working for its dissolution, not as long as four million Negroes were slaves. War would come, there was no doubt of it; he had been predicting it ever since the Compromise, and because he was so sure of it, he helped to bring it on. He preached the inevitable conflict, he talked of appealing from the parchment of the Constitution to the parchment on the head of a drum, he struck fine gestures and assured his friends that he bought no more books — he needed his money for cannon.

War would come, and within a few years, too, but sufficient unto the day was the evil thereof, and meantime there was some hope in politics. "I think we live in a time when it is a man's *Duty* to attend to political affairs," he had written, and he was never one to neglect his Duty. He was up to his neck in politics, now, and he fancied himself a power behind the scenes; he took himself seriously and he was taken seriously. He went barnstorming around the country and men forgot his heterodoxy and listened to his politics; only Beecher could command a greater audience, only Greeley was more widely read. His acquaintance was immense, it embraced all of the radical politicians of the North, and he did not hesitate to presume upon it. Not since the days of the Puritan theocracy had any clergyman used so lordly a tone. He knew the place of religion and of politics; he knew that it is less worthy to serve Cæsar than to serve God. He could tell all the politicians what to do and ignore the consequences; what had he to do with consequences? When Sumner was elected to the Senate, Parker sat down and wrote him a letter.

You told me once that you were in morals, not in politics. Now I hope you will show that you are still in morals, although in politics. I hope you will be the *senator with a conscience*. I expect you to make mistakes, blunders; but I hope they will be intellectual and not moral; that you will never miss the Right, however you may miss the Expedient . . . I hope you will build on the Rock of Ages, and look to eternity for your justification. You see, my dear Sumner, that I expect much of you, that I expect heroism of the most heroic kind. The moral and manly excellence of all our prominent men is greatly over-rated by the mass of men. You see I try you by a difficult stand-ard and that I am not easily pleased.

And Sumner, the proud Sumner, humorless and didactic, listened courteously to this sermon (he was used to sermons, he wrote them himself), and tried to be the *senator with a conscience*.

When Wilson went to the Senate, Wilson, the Natick cobbler who justified democracy, Parker warned him that he think more of principles and less of political advance-ment: —

There is only one thing which made me prefer Charles Francis Adams or S. C. Phillips to you. You have been seeking for office with all your might. Now I don't like this hunting for office in foes and still less in my friends. But for this you would have been my first choice for the senatorship . . . Now let me tell you what I think are the dangers of your position, and also what noble things I expect of you.

And Wilson, who was to disappoint so often those expecta-tions answered meekly: "I sometimes read over the letter you were so kind as to send me. You dealt frankly with me in that letter, and I thank you for it, and I hope to be better and wiser for it. I shall endeavor while in the Senate to act up to my convictions of duty, to do what I feel to be right." But it was not enough, and soon Sumner had to intercede for Wilson: "I fear you are too harsh upon Wilson, and I fear that you and others will help undermine him by furnishing arguments to the lukewarm and the Hunkers. Bear this in mind and be gentle."

But it was not in Parker to be gentle when moral issues were at stake, and Sumner himself was to feel the flick of his whip more than once. "I thought you did not quite do your duty in 1850–51," Parker wrote him, and when he did not speak at Parker's bidding, Mason of Virginia taunted him: "I see my friend Theodore Parker is after you." And so he was, letter after letter, egging him on, and to Howe, "Do you see what imminent deadly peril poor Sumner is in? If he does not speak, he is *dead — dead — dead*." But Sumner was not dead, and soon he found an opportunity to make the speech that was expected of him, and Parker was quick to write his approval — and careful to qualify it. "You have made a grand speech," he assured the Senator. "It was worth while to go to Congress to make such a speech. You have done what I have all along said you would do, though I lamented that you did not do it long ago." But there was mutual respect behind all of this, and affection too, and when Sumner was assaulted by Brooks, none grieved more deeply than Parker. "I wish that I could have taken the blows on my head," he wrote, but his sympathy for his friend did not becloud his understanding of the significance of the attack. "Slave holders are not fools," he pointed out. "The South never struck down a Northern advocate of a tariff or a defender of the Union. It attacks only the soldiers of freedom, knowing that the controlling power of the North also hates them."

Sumner and Wilson were Parker's Senators, and he had a right to counsel them, but he did not confine himself to the Senators from Massachusetts: he was father-confessor and spiritual adviser to all the leaders of the Free Soil and Republican parties. Did Seward understand the situation, Seward, whom he was grooming for the Presidency? "Dear Sir," Parker wrote him, "It seems to me that the country has got now to such a pass that the people must interfere and take things out of the hands of the politicians who now control them. Allow me to show *in extenso* what I mean."

And he did, in one long letter after another, and soon Seward was in Boston, canvassing the political situation with Parker, and on his return to Washington he wrote: "I assured Mr. Sumner and Mr. Wilson that I considered Massachusetts at least organized to the cause of Human Nature. In my own thoughts I have constantly supposed that consummation if speedily attained, was to be due to your restless and sagacious and vigorous ability." And when Parker came to New York he told his audience, "There is not at this day a politician so able, so far-sighted, so cautious, so wise, so discriminating, as William Henry Seward," — and this even though Mr. Seward had "no drop of Puritan blood in his veins."

With Chase he was on a more familiar footing. "What a noble man Chase is," Parker exclaimed. "He called to see me yesterday. His face is a benediction to any audience; what a fine eye he has." And to Chase himself: "I *do* consider you a great man and a great statesman. If you are not a great statesman, then who is?" Chase could not answer this question, but, not to be outdone, he assured Parker: "I always like to read your heroic utterances." But their relations were not always on this idyllic plane. When Chase failed to rescue the poor fugitive Margaret Garner, Parker tore into him: "I thought the anti-slavery Governor of Ohio would get possession of that noble woman, either by the hocus-pocus of some legal technicality, or else by the *red right arm of Ohio*, and I confess that I was terribly chagrined that it did not turn out so." And he went on to New York and told his audience there, "If three and a half millions of slaves had been white men, do you suppose the affair at Cincinnati would have turned out after that sort? Do you suppose Governor Chase would have said, 'No slavery outside of the slave States, but inside of the slave States, just as much enslavement of Anglo-Saxon men as you please'?" Chase hadn't said any such thing, and he did not hesitate to tell Parker so, and to tell him how wrong he was in this and in other matters. Was Parker disposed to criticize his conduct? He was not satisfied with Parker's conduct, either, and sometimes Parker threw him into despair by his willful intermixing of religious with political radicalism. "Shall I not say to you frankly," Chase wrote, "how much I regret that on the great question of the Divine Origin of the Bible and the Divine Nature of Christ your views are so little in harmony with those of almost all who labour with you in the great cause of Human Enfranchisement and Progress." Yet their friendship weathered these recriminations. When Chase came to Boston he did not fail to attend the Music Hall, however much he disapproved of the theology which he heard there, and when Parker invaded Ohio he visited the Governor in Columbus and saw his own picture hanging in the dining room and his sermons lying on the table of the Executive Office.

He knew them all and he made his influence felt. He could see things that the politicians could not see, for he was a philosopher; he could say things that the politicians could not say, for he had no career to consider. "The non-political reformer," he pointed out, "is not restricted by any law, any Constitution, any man, nor by the people, because he is not to deal with institutions; he is to make the institutions better. The non-political reformer is to raise the cotton, to spin it into thread, to weave it into web, to prescribe the pattern after which the dress is to be made; and then he is to pass the cloth and the pattern to the political reformer, and say 'Now, Sir, take your shears, and cut it out and make it up.' " Easy enough for Parker, he was good at spinning thread and weaving webs, and better still at prescribing the patterns for the politicians to cut. "Now a word about Kansas . . ." he would write to Senator Hale, and there would follow pages of illegible manuscript for Mr. Hale to decipher. And, "now *my* way of dealing with the nation is this . . ." he would inform Governor Banks (a broken reed, this Banks) and there would be a long disquisition on the character of a political party and the duty of the Republicans to abolish slavery everywhere. Or to William Herndon on the Ottawa debate: "Mr. Lincoln did not meet the issue. He made a technical evasion. That is not the way to fight the battle of Freedom." Parker knew how to fight the battle of Freedom, and he lectured them all on grand strategy and on tactics — Bancroft and Birney, Palfrey and Mann, Adams and Julian, as well as the great leaders of the party. "Among all my old friends, there is not one that I can consult with the same confidence I can you," Birney assured him; and from Herndon came a letter to Lydia, "He is about the only man living who can hold me steady."

But it was not all a matter of writing letters or of preaching sermons. He tried his hand at practical politics; in '54 he was busy getting up a convention of all the Free States, and the next year he was circulating petitions throughout the North for the removal of those Federal Judges who had ruled wrongly on the Fugitive Slave Bill. When Sumner was attacked, Parker told Hale, "I shall go to the State House as soon as the House meets to see if I can stir up that body to action," and when the Republicans declared that it was not their intention to attack slavery in the States, he wrote, "It is *my* intention as soon as I get the power." His study was a clearinghouse of radical opinion; here men like Chase and Hale could find out for themselves how relevant were the arguments of Garrison and Phillips. Parker knew what was going on in every State, and everywhere he held up the hands of the radicals and cried down compromise. A political realist, he saw the economic bases of politics; an idealist, he refused to recognize them or to accommodate himself to them. He knew that the Whig Party was no less subservient to vested interests than was the Democratic Party to slavery, and he warned his friends of the attempt of the money power to get control of the new Republican Party. He saw even the effect of the new railroads upon the struggle for freedom in the West, but his perspicuity did not lure him into the compromise fatal to Rantoul, nor bring him over to Douglas, and his abiding fear of that statesman was not without effect in heading off the consummation of Greeley's plot to swing the Little Giant over into the Republican Party.

How much influence did Parker exert, after all? Did Sumner need his prodding or Hale his encouragement? Did Seward benefit by his advice, did Chase profit by his warnings? The task of the non-political reformer, he had said, was to create sentiment, to advance ideas, to suggest modes of action. He had stirred up sentiment enough, and he was generous with ideas, but the only mode of action he could suggest, in the end, was agitation, and that led to war, which is what the politicians were trying to avoid. Yet it was something to be in advance of the politicians without breaking the lines of communication as Garrison had broken them. It was something to rebuke timidity and reject compromise and formulate a policy of aggression, to recall men to fundamental principles and denounce a policy of expediency. It was something to be the Conscience of a Party.

3

Sometimes, though, the Party got along famously without a conscience, and Parker was discouraged. "I opened my eyes when I went out west," he wrote to Sarah Hunt, in November, '56, "and saw that the hands of the republicans were not yet quite clean enough to be trusted with power. There has a deal of bad stuff come over to the republican party." Perhaps he wasn't as important as he liked to think: Sumner didn't really need any conscience but his own, and Chase consulted other oracles, and Banks preferred to junk morals and principles altogether, and then Parker wondered whether all of his preaching and lecturing and letter-writing had any value. But there was one who never failed him, who confided in him and counseled with him and yielded to him — William Herndon of Illinois, junior law partner of Abraham Lincoln.

It was a curious friendship, this between the frontier lawyer and the Boston scholar, sustained by a mutual passion for freedom, a mutual recognition of the interdependence of politics and morals. Herndon was a Southerner, but as radical as any Yankee. The Illinois politicians were all too tame for him, even Lincoln, whom he loved. It was to men like Sumner and Phillips and Parker that he looked for right counsel. A queer man, Herndon, wild and passionate, and shrewd; a backwoods pantheist, who fancied himself a philosopher and read all the deep heavy books he could find, yet genuine, downright, and sincere. He was always stumbling, himself, upon some great truths, and confiding his discoveries to Parker; he was so enthusiastic, so boyish, so easily dashed. He told everything to Parker, letter after letter, politics, religion, philosophy, he was so anxious to show how deeply he thought about these things, how much he knew of life and of men, how cleverly he combined the practical and the ideal. It was from Herndon that Parker learned all about Illinois politics, about Lyman Trumbull and Abraham Lincoln, about the machinations of Douglas and the vacillations of the Greeley Republicans. And it was Herndon who advertised the fame of Parker, spread his ideas broadcast over the State, pressed his sermons and speeches on his friends.

It was the sermons that had first attracted Herndon's attention: they had taught him natural religion, rescued him, so he said, from infidelity. Better still the addresses on politics: when Christianity was applied to politics Herndon could understand it. This clergyman was more eloquent even than Garrison or Phillips, whose speeches Herndon had been collecting. "Every time a good speech on the great issue was made," he wrote later, "I sent for it. Hence you could find on my table the latest utterances of Giddings, Phillips, Sumner, Seward, and one whom I considered grander than all the others — Theodore Parker." Herndon was already in touch with many of the anti-slavery leaders, and when he read Parker's speech on the Nebraska Act he decided to add Parker to his list. Soon he was writing in a strain that was almost embarrassing. "May I say you are my ideal — strong, direct, energetic, charitable," and he sent Parker some of his own speeches. "If you see any expressions in these pieces which are yours in essence," he wrote, "remember you impressed the hard steel upon a softer plate."

It was wonderful how they agreed on everything. Herndon saw it all as Parker would have seen it — how perspicacious he was. Parker thought war inevitable, and Herndon wrote: "I am for war. The more I think of this question and the more I know of Phillips' and your position, the more I am convinced that this people will have to meet this issue on the only field that you point out." Parker did not fear a war. "If north and south ever do lock horns," he said, "there is no doubt which goes into the ditch," and Herndon, who was from the South and doubtless knew what he was talking about, assured him that the Southerners were cowards. "They will cringe and crawl away. They can bluster and swagger, but there is an unboastful calmness in Northern bravery which paralyzes their heated and inflated courage." Just so, thought Parker, he had often suspected as much. And here was a letter about Douglas. "Douglas is — what shall I say — an unscrupulous dog. He is a hybrid; Nature says to him, Perish and Rot." So Parker himself might have said; how well Herndon knew Douglas, and Nature! Or here was a letter warning Parker against Greeley; and Parker had always distrusted Greeley, ever since the Brook Farm fiasco. Now Herndon told him that Greeley was planning to scuttle the Republican ship — he was going to carry the party clean over to Douglas. "There is an agreement," Herndon wrote, "to lower the Republican flag, so that all gray-headed, cowardly, sniveling, conservatives, North as well as South, may gather upon a degraded plank." Seward and Weed were in on it, and Henry Wilson too. Soon there was another letter, agitated with italics. "Greeley is *already lowering the Republican flag*. Greeley has done us *infinite* harm here in this State." And Parker, who had just received a letter from Wilson asking support for this nefarious scheme, wrote back, "Greeley's conduct I think base. I had never any confidence in him," and "Greeley is not fit for a leader. He is capricious, crotchety, full of whims, and as wrong-headed as a pig."

Sometimes Herndon would write about his friend Lincoln. Lincoln will take care of Douglas, he would say, or Lincoln asks to be remembered to you, or Lincoln has read your last address and thanks you for it. He wrote Parker all about the great senatorial compaign, and sent him a copy of the "house divided" speech, and Parker thanked him for it; "I think I shall congratulate you on his Senatorial dignity next winter." Illinois was to be the battleground of freedom and slavery, Herndon explained; it was all-important for Lincoln to win (no mention of the Presidency: Seward was their candidate, or Chase), and he had to be careful, and sometimes Herndon had to apologize for his friend's moderation. "Stump orators," he admitted, "will take higher and more lofty grounds. Prudence is written all over the political world, and we cannot help it. Do not blame us for not jumping higher just now. Remember your great law of the historic continuity of the development of ideas, and then you will say 'all is right.'" But Parker didn't always say, "all is right." When he read the reports of the Ottawa debates he wrote Herndon that "Mr. Douglas had the best of it. Lincoln did not meet the issue. That is not the way to fight the battle of Freedom."

But it wasn't all politics. Herndon had to show that he was interested in more than politics. He, too, was a philosopher, after a fashion, a prairie Thoreau: —

I am at this moment in my office — bodily so; yet I am in the woods. I got tired of town and books; and so I thought I would take a ramble in the forests with my dog and gun, and see what I could see. The day is very cold. . . . The keen wind whips

round the sharp corners of the hills. I am now in the deep woods;
and stealthily creep along the underbrush, now moving this bush,
now that limb, that impedes my way. Man is the lord of all he
surveys. He is king! And yet he bows down humbly to the out-
stretched arm of briar and bush. Great lord, he.

Page after page of this, yet it was all interesting enough,
for this was Lincoln's country, this was the prairie West
that Parker knew so little about. It was better, certainly,
than those excursions into philosophy that Parker was supposed to appreciate. Here was one on Law in Nature:—

Come and go to the nuclei of the winds and the water currents and what do you see? Nothing but the constant modes
of operation, paths, not Laws, which speak in the eloquence of
Gulf Streams and Simoons. Come let us leap up into the un-
columned air and rest upon the spongy foundation, and there let
us see satellite, planet, and sun; sea, air, and land. What do you
see? Co-existences and successions, powers and forces, and consciously God — no Laws . . . This is my philosophy. Am I
wrong? I would say to the philosophers, "Drive the ultimates
upwards and downwards around the circle till they meet in
God. . . ."

It was all too much for Parker, this driving of ultimates
upwards and downwards. Herndon did better when he stuck
to politics. Then Parker could write, "Your letters rejoiced
me very much. I honor the noble spirit which breathes in
them all," and Herndon would be delighted. "Friend, let
us be candid. Your compliment did me no harm but *great
good*. I do love the approbation of good men." He was so
eager for appreciation and understanding, so eager for Parker's friendship! Do come out West, he urged him, and
eventually Parker came and lectured at Springfield, and the
whole thing was a fiasco — a small and unsympathetic audience, and a smaller fee. Poor Herndon cut a sorry figure,
awkward and confused; it was all so different from what he
had imagined, and he wrote, "Friend, pardon all — forget
and forgive." and Parker assured him, "Don't think I had

any hard thoughts about the lecture at Springfield. I was more concerned with the smallness of the audience than aught besides."

Soon it was Herndon's turn to complain. He had gone to Washington to see the politicians, and to Boston to meet the abolitionists, and he ran up against Boston respectability and Boston frigidity. He was so anxious to meet all the great men, but they hadn't time for him, he was neither amusing nor important nor rich, he was just friendly and pushing and rather crude, a Southern poor white, an Illinois pettifogger, trying to come up in the world. They didn't call on him, and when he tried to see them, they snubbed him; no such hospitality here as he was used to in Kentucky or in Illinois. Even Parker disappointed him; Sumner repelled him. Only Garrison, of all men, was generous and friendly. "Your men are generally cold," he told Parker, later, "probably not more selfish than other men but they are *cold*. But your women are spontaneously good, generous, and loving. And now I say, God save you all."

But the trip was not unprofitable. He had talked with Seward and Greeley. ("Douglas is a brave man," said Greeley, "forget the past and sustain the *righteous*.") He had "looked Douglas in the eye." He had heard Parker at the Music Hall, he had met Phillips and Garrison, he had told Banks that Illinois would never support Douglas, and wherever he went, he had talked about Mr. Lincoln. He took back with him Prior's new "Life of Edmund Burke" (a wretched affair, Lincoln thought) and a book on Southern economy by Hinton Helper, and a batch of Parker's anti-slavery sermons. No sooner was he home than Parker sent him another of these sermons: "The Effect of Slavery on the American People," it was called, and Herndon read it eagerly. "Democracy is direct self-government, over all the people, for all the people, by all the people," Parker said. It was a good definition, thought Herndon, and he underscored that passage. It might interest Mr. Lincoln.

4

It was hard work being a public figure, a preacher, a scholar and a politician all in one. Sometimes Parker couldn't get around to answering all the letters that came to him. "I didn't answer before," he apologized to Herndon, "for I had no time, and a hundred letters now lie before me not replied to. When I tell you that I have lectured 84 times since November 1 and preached at home every Sunday but 2 when I was in Ohio, and never an old sermon, and have had six meetings a month in my own house, and have written more than 2000 letters, besides a variety of other work belonging to a minister and scholar, you may judge that I must economize minutes."

It was all too much for him, preaching, lecturing, politics, reform, yet with every year the demands upon him increased. It seemed as if, after all these years, his radicalism had become respectable, and he was no longer openly proscribed, even by the Church. In 1856 he took on an independent church in Watertown, and every Sunday for a year he drove out to that town, which he remembered so well from his youth. It was hard work, preaching twice a day, but he owed Watertown something, he owed something to Francis and to his young friend John Weiss. Then the Progressive Friends asked him down to their place in Chester County, Pennsylvania, and he was glad to go (an earthly Paradise, he called it), and he preached a series of sermons on the "Testimony of Nature to God." He thought they were the best things that he had ever written, massive, learned, deep, an analysis of the evolution of religion and the relation of religion to science. The Friends liked Parker; transcendentalism was nothing new to them, it was the Quaker doctrine of the inner light, with a fancy name. Other congregations of Friends wanted him to come and preach for them, and he promised that he would (he could never learn to say No) — but the promise was never fulfilled.

He was doing a good deal of writing now, too; people

seemed more interested than ever in what he had to say. In 1856 there were two volumes of "Speeches and Sermons," and the next year a new edition of his first book, the "Discourse of Religion," and two years later a third edition of the translation of De Wette — there was some call for that book, after all, even if the American scholars did ignore it. Then there were these new lectures at the Music Hall — the "Fraternity Lectures," they were called — and Parker had promised to start them off with a series on Historic Americans, and soon he was ready with lengthy biographies of Franklin, Washington, Jefferson, and John Adams. It meant an immense amount of work, reading the writings of these men and the biographies and the histories, and perhaps it wasn't worth the effort. Jefferson and Washington he wasn't able to understand; John Adams he understood so well that he could not be impartial or objective; he was successful with Franklin alone: curious that the transcendentalist should feel such admiration and affection for the most pragmatic of American statesmen.

His writing was hurried now, and a little superficial. The new *Atlantic Monthly* had invited a contribution (think of it! Lowell was going to make a splendid editor), and Parker sent in one of his weakest efforts, an essay on Henry Ward Beecher that said nothing about Beecher, nothing worth saying. Then the *Examiner* reopened its pages to him, after all these years, and in went two long, hard, articles: a review of Buckle's "History of Civilization in England," and an essay on the "Condition of the People of Massachusetts." Parker thought well of Buckle's book, the greatest book of the century, he said, the greatest since Bacon's "Novum Organum," but what a pity the bibliography was so faulty. Mr. Buckle was pleased with the review, and with Parker, whose works he had just read, and he told Parker that he regarded him as "the most advanced leader of opinion in one of the two first nations of the world." He was going to write a book on American civilization, soon, and Parker's works would indicate "the highest points of

American civilization." Parker told him what else to read about the United States, and Mr. Buckle was grateful for the suggestions, only he couldn't make out the names of any of the books. But all that would be cleared up when he came over to America; they would have much to talk about.

No doubt about it, Parker was becoming both respectable and popular. His congregation was larger than ever, his influence more extensive. The politicians were coming around to his point of view, the reformers found that he was the man to work with; even the Church was catching up with him, what with all these young men like Higginson and Hale and Starr King and Weiss and Wasson and Kimball and Fish and Frothingham and half a dozen more preaching Parkerism all over the country. But his very success showed how dangerous he was; they were still afraid of him out at the Divinity School, and when one class, more courageous than its predecessors, invited Parker to give the graduation sermon, the faculty promptly put a stop to that nonsense.

That was the year, too, of the great revival. It had come with the hard times; no wonder men turned to religion when everything else seemed to fail, the mills closed down and the banks shut and men and women walking the streets of the towns, begging for work. All that winter and into the next spring the revival went on, the churches never so full, the clergymen never so eloquent, the whole country one vast prayer-meeting, a million souls saved, a million men shouting the battle hymn of the new crusade: —

> Stand up, stand up, for Jesus
> Ye soldiers of the cross.

It was nothing new to Parker; he had already seen two of these revivals, one when he was a young teacher in Boston and Lyman Beecher had been called in to describe the torments of Hell and save Boston from Unitarianism; one when he was preaching out in West Roxbury and the great Finney had come on from Oberlin to remind Boston-

ians of the fate of Sodom and Gomorrah. But Boston would
not stay revived; a backsliding city, Boston, what with so
much of wealth and worldliness, what with pale Unitarians
indifferent to salvation, and smug Episcopalians sure of salvation, and proud Congregationalists who were bent on being saved their own way, what with Theodore Parker
there in his Music Hall every Sunday, thousands of people
crowding to hear his blasphemies.

It was from Parker that Boston had to be saved. He was
the infidel, the blasphemer, he was, one might suppose
from the sermons at the Park Street Church, the Anti-
Christ, the Beast of the Apocalypse. He was the foe men
thought of as they sang

> From victory unto victory,
> His army shall they lead,
> Till every foe is vanquished,
> And Christ is Lord indeed.

There would be letters from pious clergymen: "Sir," wrote
the Reverend Luther Griffing, "I take the liberty to state
to you that your clerical robes are too transparent to conceal the viperous serpents that nestle in your bosom and
twine around your heart." There were sermons by indignant clergymen: "Hell never vomited forth a more blasphemous monster than Theodore Parker," said the Reverend
Mr. Burnham, "and it is only the mercies of Jesus Christ
which now preserve him from eternal damnation." From all
over the city the prayers went up, "O Lord, if this man is
beyond the reach of the saving influence of the Gospel, remove him out of the way and let his influence die with him."
And, "O Lord, send confusion and distraction into his
study this afternoon, and prevent his finishing his preparation for his labors to-morrow, or if he shall attempt to dese-
crate the Holy Day by speaking to the people, meet him
there, Lord, and confound him." One clergyman prayed that
"God will put a hook in this man's jaws, so that he may not
be able to speak," and another asked, pertinently enough,

"O Lord, what shall be done for Boston if thou dost not take this and some other matters in hand?"

But it took more than songs and prayers to stop Parker, and there was no hook in his jaws as he preached the first of his three sermons on the revival. "A False and True Revival of Religion," it was called, and it showed neither confusion nor distraction, but hard sense and power.

What an idea of God is offered to man. Can any one love such a God. I do not wonder men and women go mad. The idea of Christ — what blasphemy against that noble man who said religion is love of God and love of Man. What an idea of religion here, and of heaven, hereafter. My friends, piety is not delirium.

And then a final fling at the old enemy, the Church: —

The churches need a revival. No institution in America is more corrupt than her churches. No thirty thousand men and women are so bigoted and narrow as the thirty thousand ministers. The churches — they are astern of all other craft that keep the intellectual sea. The people mean a revival of religion, but the ministers will turn it into a revival of ecclesiastic theology, — the doctrine of the dark ages, which we ought to have left behind us centuries ago.

He was back in the early days of his ministry, fighting the old battles over again, fighting the old enemy, restating the simple truths of natural religion. A pity that twenty years had brought so little advance in the popular theology, so little religion in the churches. A pity that Boston was still unredeemed, for his labors.

Yet there had been some advance, after all. He had spoken to his Unitarian brethren before; now his own Church was coming around to him, and he spoke to the whole country. The Music Hall was as crowded as the Park Street Church, and the revival sermons sold by the bushel — ten thousand in ten days, and the presses couldn't keep up with the demand.

5

These were his last forays into the field of theology, the
sermons to the Progressive Friends and the sermons on the
revival. He was a sick man, now; the prayers of the re-
vivalists might be answered after all. He didn't know what
to make of it, he had always been so strong, able to walk
thirty miles in a day, able to do the work of three men.
That was the trouble, of course, too much work, too much
worry. He had been reckless of his health, he had not
used good sense: all of this traveling about the country in
wretched cars, putting up at wretched taverns, eating
wretched food, all of these long hours and late hours. He
had always presumed upon his health and his strength; even
as a boy on the farm he had strained himself, building
stone fences and working in the field, and then, later, when
he was a teacher in Boston and a student at the Divinity
School, living on a diet of bread and milk while he studied
fifteen hours a day. A wonder his health had held up this
long, it was more than he had a right to expect.

Yet it was not all a matter of work. He hadn't enough
fun, enough relaxation; even when he went off on his vacations he would cart along a bag full of books and work
like a Trojan. He knew what was the matter with him; way
back in the West Roxbury days he had written to Hannah,
"My candle stands in a current of air and so, I suppose,
will burn away faster than if all about it was still. I don't
know that I need rest; I think I need fun, which I can't
easily get." And a little later he was telling Desor, "Here
and now my life has not enough of society, of conversation,
and joy in it. What you Germans call *Heiterkeit*, I have too
little of . . . If at twenty-five I had joined a club of good
fellows, and met with them to talk, laugh, dance, bowl, or
play billiards, once a fortnight ever since, I should be a
wiser and a happier man."

Then, as he got up into the forties, his health became a
serious problem. "I write and work more with a will than

by the spontaneous impulse which once required the will to check it," he admitted, and, a little later, "I am 47 by the reckoning of my mother, 74 by my own internal account. I am an *old man.*" And so he was, his head bald, his beard white; it was all very becoming, and he was almost handsome, now, but he looked as old as Josiah Quincy himself. "I don't know what is to come of it," he wrote. "Sometimes I think of knocking at earth's gate with my staff, saying 'Liebe Mutter, let me in.' " Soon it was more than weariness. There was a breakdown in '55, and another in '56, when he all but fainted on the lyceum platform, yet that year he managed to lecture over one hundred times. The next spring came a more serious illness. Lecturing in upstate New York, stranded overnight in an icy car, he came down with pleurisy; there was an effusion of water on the lungs, and he was eight months recovering. It was a nuisance, but, he said, "It did not much interfere with my work."

His friends were alarmed, now, and they took him off for the summer on a cruise around the Cape, through Long Island Sound and up the Hudson, while Emerson and Phillips and young Sanborn supplied the pulpit at the Music Hall. He was, he thought, "likely to recover," but he wasn't sure of it, and he began to look into his health. He knew so much about it; he knew all about his family, how many of them had lived to be old men, how many had died in infancy or youth, how many of them had been consumptive. Now he watched the ups and downs of his own health with an interest that was almost impersonal; he had studied a little medicine, a little physiology, a little chemistry, he knew all about his ailments and the treatments that were prescribed for him, he could talk it all over with the doctors as one man of science to another. He began to calculate his chances. If only he could get through to the fifties, then he would be all right, he was sure of that.

But it was as hard as ever to persuade him to take care of himself. He slowed up a little that year when he had pleurisy — only seventy lectures that year, and the next winter he felt a little better. But in the spring of '58 he was sick again, and the Church gave him another long vacation, and with his new friend Joseph Lyman (Hannah called him "the lover") he went off on a long wagon trip through New England and New York, two Yankees as pleased as Punch over the trim New England countryside and the ragged appearance of New York. When he came back there was an operation for a fistula. He was on his back for three weeks, and then he felt better, and he wrote, "I have weathered the Cape . . . I think I have conquered the last of my physical enemies." He went to a funeral, strained himself, and there was a relapse, and when he had finished his sermon for the first Sunday of the new year, he turned to his Journal and wrote: —

This is the first New Year's Day that I was ever sick. Now I have been a prisoner almost three months, living in my chamber or my study. The doctor says I mend, and I quote him to my friends. But I have great doubt as to the results. It looks as if this was the last of my New Year's days upon earth. I felt so when I gave each gift today; yet few men have more to live for than I.

But he preached that Sunday, leaning for support on the pulpit, his hands gripping the lectern: that was the safest place for him, he felt, nothing cured him like church. He spoke on a well-worn subject, "What Religion May Do for a Man." An old theme, this, but ever new; there was so much that needed to be said, and he was always coming back to it. For the next Sunday he promised a sermon on "The Religion of Jesus and the Christianity of the Church"; it was as if he were back in those early days in Boston, those fighting days, when every Sunday he had hurled himself against the citadels of orthodoxy. His whole life had gone into this fight; and now here he was, twenty years later, preaching the same truths.

But his congregation waited in vain that morning, and as

they sat in the Music Hall looking for that familiar figure, so awkward and heavy and gray, to come out on the platform, fear swept over them. At last there was someone coming up the platform steps; it was Deacon Manley, and he had a slip of paper in his hands. "Well-beloved friends," he read, "I shall not speak to you today; for this morning a little after four o'clock I had a slight attack of bleeding from the lungs or throat. I intended to preach on The Religion of Jesus and the Christianity of the Church, or The Superiority of Good-Will to Man over Theological Fancies. I hope you will not forget the contribution for the poor, whom we have with us always. I don't know when I shall again look upon your welcome faces, which have so often cheered my spirit when my flesh was weak.

"May we do justly, love mercy, and walk humbly with our God, and his blessing will be upon us here and hereafter, for his infinite love is with us for ever and ever."

CHAPTER XIII

I HAVE FOUGHT THE GOOD FIGHT, I HAVE FINISHED THE COURSE, I HAVE KEPT THE FAITH

THIS was the end, and Parker knew it. Consumption was far advanced; he had one chance in ten, the doctors told him, and he said those were just the odds for him, he was used to such odds. But it was the end. There were weary months ahead, and futile gestures, the West Indies and Switzerland and Rome, a silly business, all of it. Better to die in Massachusetts and be buried with his people out in Lexington, better to die with his boots on. But Lydia would not have it so, nor Hannah, nor his friends. He knew that you couldn't run away from death; he was not even sure that he wanted to run away from death. There was work to do, to be sure: there was the fight for freedom coming, a real war, and he wanted to be there; there were books to write, he was almost ready for them now. Vanity, all of it; he should know better than to tempt fate or to plan for the future. Now he was tired, incredibly tired. He was ready to let others write the books, fight the war. What was it he had said, just a year ago? "Sometimes I think of knocking at Earth's gate with my staff, saying 'Liebe Mutter, let me in.'"

The game was up now, but there were still a few conventional moves before the game was over: doctors and nurses, medicine and diet, a sea voyage, a warm climate for the winter. Lydia was managing all that, Lydia and the doctors, so many of them he could scarcely keep track of them

— Doctor Cabot and Doctor Jackson and Doctor Bowditch and Doctor Flint, and Howe, who was a doctor too, and there would be a lot more abroad, specialists in Paris and in Rome. One chance in ten; it wasn't worth all this fuss, the doctors didn't know what they were about anyway. He would do what he could, of course. It wasn't that he wanted to die, but "when I see the inevitable," he said, "I fall in love with it."

He still had strength for a few letters, and he tried to scrawl off notes to his friends. He had never known that he had so many friends; now that he was sick everyone was writing to him or calling on him, leaving flowers and kind messages. It seemed as if they didn't want him to die, after all, didn't want him out of Boston. Perhaps he was not the "best hated man" in the North; perhaps it had all been a mistake, all that bitterness that he had hugged; perhaps Howe had been right in rebuking him for his sharpness and his attitude of martyrdom.

He couldn't begin to thank all these people who had written to him: a card in the *Tribune* would take care of that, so they would not think him ungrateful. But there were some to whom he had to write. There was George Ripley — what fun it had been in those early days when they were going to conquer the world; if they could lie together once more under the trees in West Roxbury, all would be right again: "Many thanks, my dear George, to you. I count your friendship as one of the brightest spots in my life which has had a deal of handsome sunshine." There was Sam Andrews, who had always been faithful to him: "You and I have had many a good time together, and I had hoped that we should enjoy many more. I am not well enough to see you; it will make my heart beat too fast." He could not leave without a word to Francis; what would he have been without Francis? It was easy to forgive all that timidity and indirection; what he remembered now was that Francis had encouraged him and brought him books and set standards of scholarship and written him the most interesting letters in the world. And Francis's sister, Lydia Maria Child — did she ever know how she had helped him? He thanked her, now, "for cheering words to a young fellow fighting his way to education." There were all the men who had stuck by him when the Unitarians were trying to oust him from the Church, Sargent and Clarke, and Bartol too; Bartol had never agreed with him, but "in all our long acquaintance you never *did* or *said* or *looked* aught that was unkind." Then all his friends from politics and from reform, how could he ever get around to them? But he managed to write to a few — Herndon, of course, and Chase and Garrison. No one like Garrison, he was the best of the lot, when you came right down to it, the greatest man of his age, and Parker wrote him a farewell letter. "I value integrity above all human virtues. I have never known you to fail, no, nor even falter. God bless you for it. But it is getting late and I must write no more, or Dr. Cabot will ask, What brought your fever up so high?"

The doctors wanted to hurry him away, but he found time for a few calls — Uncle Jonas Clarke, who had been so good to him when he was a boy, and Lydia's aunt, in whose house they had lived, and Charles Ellis, who had brought him to Boston in the first place. Then early in February they were ready to go: Lydia and Hannah, and George, who would leave them at New York, and Sam and Julia Howe, who were going all the way to Cuba with them. For the last time his friends and parishioners came to call, crowding into the house where they had been so often before, looking to see for themselves how sick he really was. He tried to speak to each of them, but he could not, and he read instead the forty-second psalm.

Why art thou cast down, O, my soul, and why art thou
Disquieted in me. Hope thou in God
For I shall yet praise Him for the help of His countenance.

Good-by now to Boston that he had loved, and to all the things that were dear to him. Good-by to the old houses fronting the pleasant streets, the gracious houses of Summer Street and the proud houses of Franklin Square, their doors had been closed to him, but that was nothing, now. Good-by to the bookshops where he was known, and to the Common with its playing boys and girls, and to the wharves. Good-by to Faneuil Hall and to the Court House, they had seen stirring days, and dreadful days, too, but that was forgiven; Boston would yet redeem herself. Good-by to this old house, the pleasant rooms and the steep stairs, the bears hugging the mantelpieces, the books, they were like his children, the little alley with its plaster Flora, the light winking over at him from the study of Phillips's house. Good-by to the Music Hall where he had preached, it was Parker's Music Hall, it could never be anything else, and he knew it so well, the rose-tinted walls and the blue diamonds in the ceiling, the organ with its queer Egyptian figures, and the great bronze Beethoven looming up behind him. He remembered when they had dedicated the statue, and what the choir had sung: —

> Freude, schöner Götterfunken,
> Tochter aus Elysium,
> Wir betreten Feuertrunken,
> Himmlische, dein Heiligtum.

2

Here he was now aboard the *Karnac* bound for the West Indies. A long tedious voyage, but he didn't mind that; he did not want any excitement, he wanted merely to be alone, to lie out there on the deck buried beneath blankets and coats, his slouch hat over his eyes. The Howes were with him, but that was not much fun, for Howe was sick too, and just as grumpy as he himself was. But the sea air was a tonic, and soon both of the invalids were up and about. Yet it wasn't for long that he could enjoy Julia and the Chevalier; they were leaving at Havana, would he ever see them again? So thought Julia, too, and when the time came,

and they had gone down the gangplank and into their little craft, she looked back, and there was Parker, "bending
over us, between the slouched hat and the silver beard, the
eyes that we can never forget, that seemed to drop back in
the darkness with the solemnity of a last farewell."

There were still a few things that he wanted to do, as
soon as he could find the strength. There were some letters
to write, there was some business to put in shape. But
these things were not really important. Most of all he
wanted to render up an accounting of his ministry, to make
a report to his church. Ever since that night in January
when he had been taken sick, this matter had weighed on
his mind, and during the long sleepless nights he had thought
what he was going to write. It was something to think
about now, too, as he lay on the deck of the *Karnac*, the
air so soft, the breezes scented with the tropics. "Theodore
Parker's Experience as a Minister," he would call it: that
was impersonal enough. Too bad that it had to be the report of a sick man, but that couldn't be helped, now; he
had waited too long, and he would have to take the consequences.

Soon he was well enough to do a little writing, a wonder that any one could read it, but Lydia could, and she
and Hannah copied it off as fast as he wrote it. "Theodore
Parker's Experience as a Minister," it took a lot of writing to cover that subject, but his mind was full of it, and
his pen raced as fast as ever over the pages as he relived
the West Roxbury and the Boston years. Finally it was
finished, and he sent it off to his church, dated from Santa
Cruz, April 19, a bulky manuscript of forty thousand
words, not bad for a sick man.

Here it was then, the whole of his public career, all neat
and tidy; not impartial, perhaps, but honest. Here was an
account of the work that he had done and the work he
had meant to do, the obstacles that he had met and overcome, and some that he had not overcome. Here was the
whole story: the intellectual background, the social fore-

ground, the ferment of thought in which he had lived and worked, the philosophical history of a whole generation. Here was his own philosophy, nicely analyzed — what he had taught from the pulpit and preached from the platform, what he had taken over from the Germans and the English, and what he had added that was his own. Here was his program of social reform, all neatly itemized, and the history of the greatest of reforms, the struggle against slavery. It was as good a biography as any man could want, none better.

But what did it tell about him, about the essential Theodore Parker who had been a farmer boy and had lived for fifty years and was dying now? It told of his ministry, and that was what was important about Theodore Parker; it told of his work for the regeneration of society, and that was what would last; it told about his books, and that was how he would be remembered. It was filled with all the particulars of his public life, so that men could say, there is the Parker we heard at the Music Hall, there is the Parker who barnstormed through the West, there is the Parker of the Vigilance Committee. It was a faithful report; to read it, you would think you were hearing him again, the pithy Anglo-Saxon words, the sharp epigrams, the powerful generalizations, the sweep and bigness of it all, the prose-poetry, the words marching to martial music, the unconquerable optimism.

But Parker knew that this Letter was not himself. He had planned to write an autobiography, if he had the strength, and he did manage to get down a few pages of it. It was harder to do than the more formal report, and he did not get very far. What could he say about himself, about his mind and his character, about the things that were intimate and personal and really important? What could he say to explain how it had happened that the little boy who had played with corncobs in the kitchen of a Lexington farmhouse had become the Great American Preacher? What could he say to explain how it was that life had been so rich, so various, so good, and that he had had such happiness as comes to few men?

He had had a goodly inheritance, physical, moral, intellectual. He had grown up in a large family, had learned to adjust himself to people, had never wanted for affection. He had learned how to work, and how to play, too, though he had almost forgotten that. He had grown up on a farm, lived simply and frugally, come to like plain things, plain food and clothing and furnishing, plain speech, plain men and women. He never learned sophistication, there was always a rusticity about him, about his features, his hands, his broad shoulders, his firm, sturdy walk. He handled himself well; there was awkwardness, but no uncertainty. His speech, too, was colloquial and direct, no subtleties, no fine phrases; sometimes this was almost an affectation. There was an earthiness about him. He never seemed quite at home in Boston, in his study, in his parlor. He liked to lie in the grass, to mow hay, to chop trees; he liked to walk along country roads or cut across the fields. Nothing better than a long walking trip, so he could get close to the country and to country people, note the line of the hills and the look of a village in the distance, stop at some farmhouse for a glass of milk, sit in a country tavern and listen to talk about cattle and crops.

He was provincial, he was a Yankee. He was never really happy outside Massachusetts. All that traveling, all that foreign learning, never changed his provincialism. He thought New England customs were best, New England people best. He knew that Europe was the home of culture, but it wasn't the kind of culture that he cared for. He was impatient with people who went into ecstasies over St. Peter's or Notre Dame; Europe could show nothing like the cattle shows and mechanics' fairs of New England, and for real beauty there was nothing like a reaper cutting a swathe through a field of wheat. No town in all Europe could compare with Boston, no picturesque German village gave you the sense of well-being that you found in Lexington. No, he wasn't comfortable outside of New England. He knew that the West was the home of democracy, but he didn't like the West, it was coarse and heavy and unfinished, not civilized like New England. He had said many bitter things about the ruling classes of New England, but they were the best people in the world, after all; where else could you find such intelligence, such morality, such material well-being? He loved to read New England history, to remember the Puritan tradition: no other war in history was so glorious as the American Revolution, no folk-movement so splendid as the Puritan migration. He mistrusted foreigners, he looked with fear upon the influx of the Irish and the French Canadians. He mistrusted imported religion, imported ideas, even, and he was not happy until he had Americanized them.

He was a practical man, knew how to use his hands, could make things grow and build things, repair tools and handle machinery. He never forgot what he had learned in his father's shop and on the farm. He was practical in his outlook, looked to the use of things, liked useful things and useful people. He liked to talk with farmers, they knew the realities of life; he liked women who could bake bread — that came closer to real art than did all the twaddle of a Margaret Fuller. He was proud of the things he had made for himself, he was proud of Lydia because she was so good a housekeeper, so neat and clean and thrifty. He knew things that city-bred men didn't know — when the apple and the cherry and the peach trees would blossom, and where to find water-lilies and where columbines and anemones, and when the birds would fly South, and he could tell the song of the chickadee and the hermit thrush and the white-throated sparrow. He knew how to feed cattle, and to milk cows, and to harness a horse and shoe it too; he knew how far apart you should plant potatoes, and how to plow a straight line over a hill, and how to prune trees. He knew how to manage, he had always managed well, on the farm, in school, as a preacher in West Roxbury and in Boston. He had earned his way, and made a good living, he had more than enough for his needs and for Lydia. He had never needed to ask for help, he had helped himself. He owned the best library in Boston, and he had bought every book himself, not like these Ticknors and Prescotts and Adamses who were born to riches and to culture. He was thrifty and frugal, smart about money, able to help his brother Isaac and his nieces, and young men in college, and ministers in need; he even advised people about investments. He was, he said, too rich to be mean, too poor to care about money.

He could stand on his own feet, independent, though not self-sufficient. He did not need anyone to take care of him, though all the ladies fluttered about wanting to take care of him, and sometimes he liked it well enough. He was no dear absent-minded parson, he knew what he was about all the time. He wasn't easily imposed upon or taken in by sentiment or by helplessness; he did not suffer fools gladly. He liked such men as Garrison and Howe, he couldn't abide Bronson Alcott with his foggy ways: once out at Emerson's he had lost his temper, and Emerson remembered that "he wound himself around Alcott like an anaconda: you could hear poor Alcott's bones crunch." He was robust and wholesome and straightforward, and he distrusted eccentricity and subtlety, sophistication and prudery.

He was a realist, in religion, reform, and politics. He had his feet on the ground. He understood the psychology of religion, the sociology of reform. He knew how the political wheels went around. No use talking to him about the sacred principles of the parties, that buncombe didn't go down with him. He saw through all the fanfaronade about Manifest Destiny and the bombast about patriotism and the sententious devotion to the Union; what men were really talking about was their balance at the bank. He knew the realities of economics, how the protective tariff worked and how the railroads got their charters and how

industry brought in immigrants to depress the labor market. He saw how the Church had been roped in by the
vested interests, how clergymen did the bidding of wealthy
parishioners, how religion was subservient to wealth. He
was downright and honest and shrewd.

He was, for all of his transcendental idealism, a utilitarian.
He judged the tree by its fruit, institutions by their consequences. He thought that men and institutions should pay
their way. He believed that religion and morals should
justify themselves. Even religion was a matter of practical
ethics; it was the consequences of religious doctrines that
he looked to — how they affected men in their daily life,
how they affected society. His quarrel with dogma, with
theology, was not so much intellectual as social. This was
why he was so anxious to authenticate intuitive truths by
facts of demonstration, this was why he appealed so insistently from the teachings of the heart to the teachings
of science, from abstract principles of justice to the irrefutable testimony of the Census Bureau. His thinking was
concrete. He suspected all theological abstractions. He detested the doctrine of Sin: there were particular sins, but
no general Sin. He thought Unitarians made fools of themselves when they talked about Grace and Salvation, Inspiration and Revelation. He didn't believe in abstract
atheism or infidelity: practical atheism — the denial of a
Higher Law, or practical infidelity — treason to human
nature, that was another thing.

He was utilitarian in his interpretation of art and science
and scholarship. Art for art's sake was a vain thing; when
he looked at a picture or a statue he drew from it a moral.
"I had much rather be such a great man as Franklin than
a Michael Angelo," he told Ripley, "if I had a son I should
rather see him a great mechanic like George Stephenson in
England than a great painter like Rubens who only copied
beauty." He had little use for dilettantes or littérateurs;
when he spoke of a certain class of men as "weak and literary," young Andrew Dickson White began to look with

some misgivings upon a literary career. He was vastly interested in science, but it was botany and zoölogy and physiology and geology that attracted him, not mathematics or
astronomy. He bought books for use, not for show; he was
not consistent in this, he pretended that he would have
some use for many a book that was mere self-indulgence,
but he had to keep up the pretense. He was not interested
in a large private collection; his own library was to go to
the people, and to the public library in Boston rather than
the scholar's library in Cambridge. He thought that scholarship should pay its way as well as art and letters. What
was the use of history if it did not teach some lesson, if it
did not judge the past and illuminate the future? So, too,
with novels and poetry, his yardstick was a moral one;
he could not forget that Rousseau was a bad man and
Byron a libertine and Goethe without moral standards.

Education, too, should be of the practical sort. He had
once thought otherwise, and he had the scholar's delight
in antiquarianism, but he learned, in time, the lesson that
Wendell Phillips learned: the best scholars were not the
best men, scholarship estranged men from their fellow men.
He saw that the scholars of New England were in alliance
with the Hunkers, that all their learning did not teach them
the things that every farmer and every mechanic knew,
did not teach them democracy and humanity and justice.
"Our colleges," he said, "are institutions for the general
Hunkerization of young men. In the last forty years no
New England college, collective faculty, or pupils, has shown
sympathy with any of the great forward movements of
mankind." That was the trouble with the Divinity School,
and with Harvard College, too, they turned out scholars,
not men. If he had a son, he said, he would send him to
Harvard — "juxtaposition is something!" What was needed
was moral education and vocational education, culture of
the hand and the heart as well as of the head.

Scholarship and education should be democratic; the
lyceum platform was worth a dozen colleges, and the Lowell

Institute as good as Harvard College. His own life had been given to the democratization of learning, he was the greatest popularizer of his time, the journalist of scholars. Sometimes he thought that he had a philosophic mind, that he was born for dialectics and metaphysics. But his instinct was surer than his ambition, and when the times called for a stump speaker, he answered the call. He had no tricks of oratory, his voice was harsh, his gestures awkward, he lectured from a manuscript, but he was one of the great orators of his generation. He did not condescend to his audience, but gave them the hard, gritty truth, and learning too. He could marshal his facts like an army and maneuver them with brilliance. He handled words superbly, no polish, no subtlety, but an elemental force, a vividness of imagery, a richness of texture that no one could match, not even Phillips, not even Beecher. He relied on the spoken, not the written word, his vehicle was the newspaper and the pamphlet, not the book, which was more exclusive. What he wrote for the pulpit or the platform was not designed primarily for publication; it was rich, overflowing, verbose, there was a rhythm to the words that had to be heard.

To the end he hoped that he might find time for the fulfilment of his scholarly plans, and they were grandiose. There were a dozen books that he wanted to write: when he was fifty he would stop all this lecturing and get down to the business of scholarship, when he was sixty he would withdraw from public life and be a philosopher. Perhaps he was right, perhaps no one else could do these books; but he was right, too, he thought, in putting them off. His work was for the plain people of the country, not for the scholars; his work was for the present, not for the future. He left little that was of permanent value, little but the record of his life, and that was everything.

He had vast learning, no man in America was more learned, more widely read. He took pride in his reputation as a scholar, he was vain of the number of languages with which he was familiar, he exaggerated his reading, he was not sure enough of himself to forbear an occasional display. His mind was encyclopædic rather than discriminating, his scholarship copious rather than exact. He knew a little of everything and a great deal about many things; all was grist that came to his mill. Yet he never took time to assimilate what he knew, he spent it all as soon as he got it, he was prodigal of his scholarship as of his energies. His learning did not make so much for wisdom as for analysis, he was a better critic than he was a philosopher. His memory was prodigious, he was quick to acquire and tenacious to retain, he was alert, nimble-witted, and impressionable. He never missed anything, he took in his surroundings, his society, his reading, his experience, and kept them all for future use.

He had intellectual as well as moral integrity. He was a popularizer, but no vulgarizer, he did not spare himself nor did he take refuge in generalizations or abstractions or anecdotes. He always knew more than he could say, he was always pressed for time. His sermons and lectures and articles had substance, none of your clerical vapors for him. No man in all America worked harder. He did not have to spur himself on to work, he had to restrain himself. He was not happy unless he had more to do than any man could do. He had an inexhaustible nervous energy, a passion for activity; he could no more stop working than a cataract could stop its flow. He did not know what leisure was, he could never loaf and invite his soul. Even when he was resting his mind was busy with a hundred projects. He could not lie under an apple tree but he must speculate on the law of gravity; he could not walk along a country lane but he must fill his terrible notebook with observations on the soil and the crops; no sooner had he begun to collect little bears for Lydia's mantelpiece than he wrote off for all the monographs on bears. "Your life," Dwight had written him, "seems a succession of convulsive efforts." He acted as if everything depended upon him, and every

demanded every virtue in a book, he expected perfection in his friends. Buckle's book was the greatest book of the century — but the bibliography was inadequate, the material wretchedly organized, and Mr. Buckle had too low an opinion of morality. Emerson was the foremost man of letters that America had produced — but his poetry was sorry stuff, and his Oriental mysticism was nonsense. Channing was the first of American preachers — but he lacked courage and originality. John Quincy Adams was a statesman of integrity and ability, but guilty, nevertheless, of many things that "deserve the censure of a good man." Horace Mann was one of the three great Americans of his generation, but he was materialistic, narrow and unforgiving, and guilty of duplicity. And so it went. It had always been so: even in youth he had been a captious critic. He had admired his professors, but he could see their faults: Norton was dogmatic, and besides, he couldn't translate German; Francis was timid and narrow; Palfrey was too much of a popularizer, too diffuse; Furness didn't keep up with the progress of scholarship abroad. Something was wrong with all of them, you would have to go to Europe for your scholarship, though it was well to remember that the Germans couldn't write and the French were superficial and the English lacked imagination and spirituality. He knew so much, he could always catch others in errors; he had read so widely, he could always think of some book men had not consulted; his moral ideas were so absolute, he could always point to the shortcomings of others. No wonder men thought him ungenerous and bitter, no wonder that Samuel Bowles wrote of his "gross conceit and bigotry," and Howe warned him of his carping spirit, and even Julia Howe, who loved him, prodded him for

> Saving the perilous souls of the nation
> With holiest, wholesomest vituperation.

"I have the reputation," he wrote once, "of washing down my dinner with nice old sulphuric acid and delighting to spear men with a jest and to quarrel with all sorts of people." He knew that his reputation was undeserved — but there it was. He did not mean to be captious, he did not love controversy, or criticism that was destructive merely. He wrote harsh things, but he wept as he wrote them. It grieved him to attack Curtis and Hallet as he did, and when he delivered his oration on Webster, it was a "dreadful day." But all this was a matter of principle: he could not take the easy way, flatter people, acquiesce in mediocrity. He had a great responsibility, he was the reformer in scholarship, the scholar in reform, he was the moralist in politics. It was because he was an idealist, an optimist, that he expected so much; it was because he believed so ardently in the divinity of men that he deplored so raucously their imperfections.

It was not his fault that he was always in the minority. It was not of his choosing, this ceaseless attack upon established institutions. It was his misfortune that so much of his energy had gone into the thankless task of clearing away debris — theological superstitions and philosophical misconceptions and social conventions. He had never been satisfied with agitation: even in the beginning he had emphasized the Permanent in Christianity rather than the Transient, and his quarrel with Unitarianism was that it was a negative instead of a positive religion. He disliked professional critics, and warned the Garrison boys that "reform makes a poor profession for any one." He was a worker and an organizer; he was willing to compromise, he wanted to see results.

Too much of his energy had gone into the fight against slavery; that had come to overshadow everything else in his life, it had deflected him from scholarship and even from social reform; it had wrecked his plans. He had not wanted it so. He had kept clear of the anti-slavery movement as long as he could; he had tried his best to keep abolitionism in its proper place. But that was just the trouble: abolition insisted upon assuming its proper place, and in time he came to see that all other interests, all merely personal ambitions, must give way before this commanding reform. It was not, in itself, more important than spiritual or social reform, but he came to realize that nothing could be effected until this question of slavery had been settled, and settled right. He came to see that you couldn't emancipate the minds of men until you had emancipated their bodies, that you couldn't advance the cause of free labor until you had done away with slave labor. So much of his time had gone into anti-slavery! It was as an abolitionist, perhaps, that he was best known. That had not been his plan; but he was satisfied, now. It was an ephemeral fame, he knew that; the noise of agitation would soon enough be drowned out by the noise of war, and then the echoes of the anti-slavery fight would seem faint enough.

For all his learning and his many interests, he was a simple man, simple in his tastes and his habits, in his emotional and his intellectual reactions. There were no secret places in his heart, no hidden recesses in his mind. He was natural and unaffected, did not pretend to an understanding of music or of art, did not pretend to social graces. He liked "Nearer My God to Thee," and the story of the Nativity, he liked ballads and folk and fairy tales, he would rather hear "Brattle Street" or "Dundee" than an aria from an opera, he preferred an upland meadow to a formal garden, he liked country ways and country men, or thought that he did. He liked to walk the streets of Boston and see the bustle and excitement, see the children at play or the Negroes sitting on the stoops of their ramshackle houses, or the laborers unloading ships at the wharves. He liked the pleasant, intimate side of the ministry — prayers, parish calls, the baptism of children.

He was a sentimental man, easily moved to tears and to laughter. He was happy with children, and his failure to have children was the one great sorrow of his life that he came back to again and again. "All other disappointments," he said, "I count as small in comparison." He knew all the children of his parish, gave them pet names and spoiled them; one drawer of his desk was given over to toys, and whenever he went on a trip he carried a pocketful of candy. He was never too busy to write little Patience Ford, or his "Bettina" up in the New Hampshire hills; and of all his letters, none pleased him more than those from little Willie Apthorp, who drew bears up and down the margins of the pages. It was some satisfaction that he could list in his Journal sixteen children who had been named for him — one of them a girl, too!

For all his severity, his hatred of sham and injustice, he was womanly tender. He was affectionate and demonstrative, none of your New England reserve. He remembered birthdays, scores of them, and celebrated them all. "I wish you would tell me when you were born," he wrote to Frances Cobbe, whom he had never seen, "that I may keep the day as a festival. So I do with other dear ones." He was not satisfied with the assurance of love, but needed the outward signs — gifts and flowers and letters. "You forget to send the customary kisses," he wrote to Sarah Hunt, "but I will call tomorrow and take them." He was spoiled and petted, by men as well as by women; he was always looking for someone to comfort him; he was not afraid to tell people that he loved them.

He was sensitive, as easily hurt as a child, and as easily consoled. He imagined all sorts of slights, needed constant reassurance. He could never understand why anyone should dislike him, yet he took a curious, perverse pride in believing that he was the best hated man in the country. He could not stand disapproval or criticism. "I like good *plump* criticism," he told Higginson, but it was not so. He would never be persuaded that he was in the wrong, he would never believe that he had said anything uncharitable, he was saddened and hurt when friends rebuked him for his sarcastic words. "What you say about sarcasm and all that I by no means plead guilty to," he wrote Sam Jo May. "I wonder that you should bring this charge. I never wrote a line with any ill-will or sarcastic humor toward maid or man." And to Caroline Dall: "Faithful are the wounds of a friend . . . Today comes your note with its womanly tenderness and its manly rebuke. But while I thank you for your frankness, I by no means admit the justice of what you say." Whatever folks might think, he knew that he was generous, his intentions were good; but years later Howe was still rebuking him. "Dear Parker, do try to restrain that inborn spirit of destructiveness now that your whiskers are so gray — or else dye them. Come come, be a little less conscientiously and intellectually charitable and more emotionally and heartily so."

He had an immense capacity for friendship, but his closest friends were not his intellectual equals. It took time for men to appreciate him, they were inclined to look askance at that colossal energy, that passion, that want of reserve, that highhanded arrogance. Yet for all his irritating ways he was, in the end, irresistible. "How I want to hear you, how I want to see you," wrote Horace Mann from Yellow Springs, and Parker could say of Sam Jo May, "He loves me a little too well to see me quite as I am." Howe was devoted to him, and so was Garrison, and the younger men worshiped him. But his dearest friends were women. He aroused their maternal instinct, they were always wanting to take care of him. He was so boyish, so playful, so gentle with them, he was so eager for affection, he relied so on their appreciation and their criticism, and they didn't criticize too often.

Curious how he couldn't get along without people; he had such resources, such interests, yet he was the most gregarious of men. He liked to mingle with people, liked society, liked to have guests in for tea and for dinner. He was never sufficient unto himself, never sure enough of himself to get along. He had none of that cold aloofness that was an armor for Emerson. He was always getting up some convention or organizing some committee. He could never refuse any work, any lecture engagement, any reform movement. He was not meant for solitude, he did not have to commune with his soul, his spiritual reactions were always on tap.

Yet he was introspective too, in a superficial way. He thought overmuch about himself and his lot, he sympathized with himself, pitied himself, congratulated himself. He could never get over the wonder that the farm boy from Lexington had come so far in the world. He worked his emotions hard, he had too much imagination, he worried and nagged at experience and would not let it alone. In everything he was subjective, his theology, his criticism, his public reforms, even. He was forever analyzing himself, looking into the state of his soul and his mind; his Journal was one continual spiritual and intellectual inventory. He wrote of Wordsworth, "He knows the anatomy of his own mind as if he took himself to pieces," and, as so often, the criticism was autobiographical.

He was acquisitive — of emotion and experience, of learning, of people. He was always making up to himself what he had been denied in his boyhood. He was a gourmand for knowledge, he could never be satisfied. He wanted to do everything, to manage everything, he liked power, prestige, position. Things came easily to him, he had never really known defeat, or disappointment, he had always had his way, in the end. He was clever, and persistent, he wasn't easy to outwit or to discourage. He knew what he wanted of life, and he could always get the upper hand of life. There were things that he missed, but he didn't realize that, or he didn't have time to think about them.

He was adaptable, but he had a core of independence and integrity that nothing could affect. He took on the color of his surroundings, he could mingle with farmers or mechanics, with scholars, with men of the world. He could play with children and give fatherly advice to lovelorn maidens and baby his wife and speak arrogantly to every politician in the country. He was intellectually adaptable, too, as became a democrat; he could turn his hand to whatever work

came along — theology or literature, history or science, it
was all one to him. He was no specialist; a popularizer
could not afford to be a specialist. Yet whatever he did
was characteristic; no one could mistake those sermons or
speeches, they had a quality of their own. He had independence, he was curiously persistent, he never let go of
an idea or abandoned a principle. Once he had taken a
position you couldn't budge him, nor frighten him,
either.

He had courage and fortitude. Easy enough to have courage when there were men to applaud you and women to flatter you; easy enough to have courage when you were in the
swing of things, as in the fight against slavery. But it had
not been so easy earlier, when he had risked his career
over questions of theology, a young man, unknown and
friendless, flying in the face of respectable opinion in the
most conservative of institutions. It had taken courage to
meet those black looks, those biting remarks, at the Berry
Street Conferences. It had taken fortitude to endure the
misrepresentation, the odium, the social ostracism that he
had suffered, he and Lydia. Perhaps it would have been better if he had not fought back so hard; but he was a fighter,
he couldn't help that. There was fighting blood in his veins,
and he was far too conscious of it. He could never forget
Grandfather Parker, the muskets hanging there in his study,
the words of Lexington Common ringing always in his
ears. He had always been a fighter, he had carried the war
into the enemy's camp, and he had come away with the
honors of war. It might have been better if he had lost
some of those battles, it might have given him a sense of
the tragic, a greater humility. But he had not lost: religion,
slavery, reform, he had won his way every time.

He was much concerned with ideals and principles, as
became a transcendentalist, but he was not a doctrinaire
or a long-nosed reformer. He was high-spirited, bubbling
with excitement, boyish and playful. His letters spilled
over with boisterous humor, with wild flights of imagina-

tion: to Hannah went a hundred letters recounting the meetings of his fantastic society, "The Sirty," and when he
couldn't amuse others, he would amuse himself, in his
Journal. He had an unerring eye for the ridiculous, a terrible talent for mimicry and burlesque; he could puncture
any pompousness, expose any pretentiousness. His humor
was for the most part good-natured, lacked subtlety and
malice, but he could be malicious when he chose, and he
had a devilish keen thrust. Agassiz was so great a man, he
said, that if he and Nature differed, Nature must give way,
and when Pierce was elected he remarked that any man
was in danger of being made President now.

His good humor, his high spirits, extended to every
phase of his life. There was a vitality about him that was
contagious, it appeared in his energy, his emotions, his affections, his indiscriminate and insatiable curiosity. He
could not leave life alone, but must go out and embrace it.
Every book was worth reading, if only to discover its de-
ficiencies, every language worth knowing, every person
worth thinking about; when he went to Europe he did not
miss a cathedral or a university or a great man. Yet he was
not satisfied with the appearance of life, but needed to
know the reasons behind all things, the mechanics of nature
and of man.

He was right when he said that he had found an intense
delight in life. Who else had known such happiness in mere
living, such delight in experience, such leaping response to
every moment and every day, to every person, to every man-
ifestation of nature. To him life was an incredible, a perpetual miracle, and he never got over the wonder of it.
"When I recall the days of my boyhood and youth and
early manhood," he said, "I am filled with a sense of sweet-
ness and wonder that such little things can make a mortal
so exceeding rich." Nothing could restrain his happiness,
it burst through every situation, surmounted every disappointment; try as he would to strike an attitude becomingly
solemn or tragic, he was unable to do so. This was not any

sentimental optimism or a conscious determination to be happy, but a natural irrepressible joy in life.

His sermons were full of this joy, even Whitman did not have greater sensuous appreciation of the richness of life and of nature. It found expression in his letters, in his Journal, it burst through the hard crust of his philippics, the Webster oration, for example; it gave a lyrical quality to his prayers, and in his last Letter to his church he sounded the same note.

To me human life in all its forms, individual and aggregate, is a perpetual wonder; the flora of the earth and sea is full of beauty and of mystery which science seeks to understand; the fauna of land and ocean is not less wonderful; the world which holds them both and the great universe that folds it on every side, are still more wonderful, complex and attractive, to the contemplating mind. But the universe of human life, with its peculiar worlds of outer sense and inner soul, the particular faunas and floras which therein find a home, are still more complex, wonderful and attractive; and the laws which control it seem to me more amazing than the mathematical principles that explain the celestial mechanics of the outward world.

Nothing could change that thrill of living, that richness and goodness of life that he felt around him, the excitement of the moment and of the morrow and of the past. He awoke to every day with a sense of anticipation, and when the day was over he liked to look back on it and savor again the joy that he had known, and the disappointment too — it would never do to leave that out. He lived in the past, he rejoiced in the present, he looked eagerly to the future. Every Sunday was a new experience, and he never got jaded, he never longed for a rest, he couldn't end his vacations quickly enough, so anxious was he to get back to the Music Hall and to his friends and his work. He never got used to the excitement and fineness of it all: his own church, his own congregation, the thousands of people to hear him, the fine sermon that he would preach, the prayer of thanksgiving to Our Father and Our Mother God. Every lecture was a new challenge; he gave hundreds of them, but he could hardly bear to turn down one. The traveling was hard enough, yet it was something to know the hardship of traveling; the audience was sometimes unresponsive, but he liked to get that feeling, too, there was something in contrast. He wrote a dozen letters every day, and he poured himself into each one of them; he had a hundred friends, and when he thought of them his happiness was almost too great to bear. Life never palled on him, life never really disappointed him. He had little discrimination, but how ungenerous to discriminate, as if to say that God made some things that were not good. God was infinitely perfect, and Man was adequate to all his functions. When he thought of all this, he was saturated with felicity.

There was little time, of course, to absorb all of his experiences and assimilate them, little time for contemplation. He did not get the quintessence of things, only their flavor. He did not stop to analyze character, but delighted in a gesture or the glance of an eye; he did not stop to analyze experience, but took it all in and used it as best he could and hurried on to some new experience. His life was never finished and rounded and polished, nor were his sermons nor his books. He lived and worked breathlessly.

His optimism was instinctive as well as philosophical. He was hopeful not because his study taught him the doctrine of progress, but because he had faith in the Divine Order of things; he did not trust men because his transcendentalism taught him the doctrine of the Divinity of Man, but because his love of man gave him assurance of man's spiritual nature. He was optimistic, in short, because he could not help himself. Perhaps it was all a matter of physical energy, perhaps it was all something that came out of his own experience, his own triumph over life. No matter, what he had known and felt, others could know and feel, and it was essential for him to communicate his faith in life. He was not always successful, for his experience, after all, was limited. He had never known ecstasy or despair; he had missed tragedy. "Several times in my life," he wrote, "I have met with what seemed worse than death . . . Yet my griefs all turned into blessings; the joyous seed I planted came up discipline and I wished to tear it from the ground, but it flowered fair and bore a sweeter, sounder fruit than I expected from what I set in earth. As I look over my life I find no disappointment I could afford to lose; the cloudy morning has turned out the fairer day; the wounds of my enemies have done me good. So wondrous is this human life, not ruled by fate but Providence, which is Wisdom married unto Love, each infinite."

No, he could never understand despair or futility or surrender. He could not enter into the world of a Hawthorne or a Melville, he could never know even what Emerson knew after little Waldo died. So he did not face, realistically, the problem of evil, but evaded it, and it was a fatal flaw in his philosophic system. To the end he remained not so much hopeful as confident, buoyantly, aggressively, confident. Always, with him, the best was yet to be. "In estimating the phenomena of evil," he wrote, "my own faith says there is a perfect system of optimism in the world, that each man's life is to him an infinite good."

Here was the pattern of his life and his mind. It did not go into his Letter, but, for all its formality, the Letter was revealing enough, and it ended on a characteristic note: "This progressive development does not end with us; we have seen only the beginning, the future triumphs of the race must be vastly greater than all accomplished yet. In the primal instincts and automatic desires of man, I have found a prophecy that what he wants is possible, and shall one day be actual. It is a glorious future on earth which I have set before your eyes and hopes. What good is not with us is before, to be attained by toil and thought and religious life."

3

The Letter was finished. Nothing to do now but get well, here in Santa Cruz. It was a strange new world, Santa Cruz, tropical and lush, an island of lotus eaters, yet wretched enough, too. Parker was supposed to rest, but he could not rest; everything was so different, so exotic, he had to find out about it all, take notes on it, prepare sermons. He was up at five in the morning for a long ride on a pony, jogging slowly along the uneven roads through the parched, dusty countryside, through the straggling little villages where the children played naked in the streets, spinning their inevitable tops, and the women wandered slowly down to the spring for the day's water, the turkey buzzards floating in the air above. A queer place, tropical and barbaric for all the trim cultivation, the hills so carefully tilled, way up to the top, the whole island one vast sugar vat, one vast distillery. There was decadence everywhere, two thousand Creoles, twenty-three thousand Negroes, the Creoles living in the past, talking of their grandeur, the Negroes overcome with lassitude. There was death in the air, everything so hot and damp, everything so slow, it was torture for a Yankee to watch it all. The children did not romp and play, but walked sedately; even the animals were infected with the universal torpor, the ducks lying all day in the street, the cock walking as deliberately as a Dutchman, the pigs, "long-nosed, grave-looking animals," they looked as though they had been through a revival, Parker thought, and were preparing for the ministry.

Parker alone was busy, he was the only energetic person on the whole island. He found out all about the Creoles and the Negroes and the labor system, he could give you the particulars of island economy — so many sugar plantations, so many ranches, so many orange groves (wretched ones, too, not to be compared to those of Rome). He visited the churches and the cemeteries, talked with the ministers, found a Scotchman who knew the whole of Kant by heart.

He read up on the history of the island, and the genealogy, and solved the problem of the paternity of Alexander Hamilton, and wrote all about it to Charles Francis Adams back in Boston. His notebooks bulged with information, and the post had never carried so many letters.

No, Santa Cruz was not without interest, but the interest was almost morbid, and he was eager to get away. The food was bad, the climate insufferable — too hot, too moist, a perpetual Turkish bath. He had lost weight here, and his cough was as bad as ever. So off to St. Thomas, and then to England and the Continent. The very thought of it cheered him: Lyman would be there waiting for him, and Doctor Bowditch, and other friends, and there would be people to talk to again and things to see that were worth the time of even a dying man.

But the voyage proved hard on him, seven pounds lost, and his cough worse than ever. He was discouraged when he came to England, no visiting for him now, no sightseeing, nothing but rest and quiet. So he said, but he did not know what it was to rest, and it was all just like that first visit, fifteen years earlier. He went everywhere, saw everything, took sheaves of notes, called on all the leading men, and this time he didn't need to introduce himself and say, "I am an American, I have read your book," this time they were the ones who said to him: "We have read your books." All the scholars came to pay their respects to him. Martineau and the Reverend Tayler, whom he remembered from his previous visit, and Professor Rogers down from Glasgow, and Francis Newman. There were politicians, too: John Bright himself took him to the House of Commons, and Seward came calling. And there was Thomas Cholmondeley, nephew of the famous Bishop Heber, a shy young man anxious to do something for Parker, give him money, perhaps, if Parker would let him. But best of all was a visit from Ellen Craft, free now, and as grateful as ever. "I am as busy as a nail-machine," Parker said cheerfully, "and get little rest, there are so many friends."

But England was no place for a consumptive, so cold and

damp and smoky, and Lyman was anxious to get him off
to some dry climate. Lyman was in charge, now: "He
took command of me as soon as he arrived, and hoisted his
broad pennant, so I shall sail under his colors," wrote
Parker. So off they went to Paris, to consult a new batch of
specialists — Doctor Louis and Doctor Bigelow, who were
like the doctors in America in that they couldn't agree on a
course of treatment. But the visit to Paris was not wasted.
Sumner was there, waiting for him at the station, dear,
noble Sumner, "the finest sight I have seen yet in Europe."
They went riding all over the city until Sumner had to cry
quits, and then back in his rooms they found John Lothrop
Motley, ready to greet them, as aristocratic as ever.

But Switzerland was his destination now, the Apthorps
and the Hunts were waiting for him there, and best of all,
Desor. It was like being back in Boston, there were so many
old friends. "I was stivering along the road from Mon-
treux," he wrote, "eating grapes, and heard somebody call
out, 'Can you tell me the way to Boston Meetin' House,' and
behold, there was Fields, with a great handsome beard and
an umbrella." Soon he was with Desor at Combe Varin. A
wonderful place this, up in the Jura Mountains, great pine
forests towering behind Desor's chalet, vineyards below,
and in the distance the Val de Sagne, dotted with little
Swiss villages, and the whole panorama of the Alps crowding the horizon. Desor was as lovable as ever, the best
friend in the world, and what a collection of celebrities he
had gathered here: Hans Küchler, a Catholic liberal from
Heidelberg, and Charles Martin, a learned botanist, and
Doctor Schönbein who had invented gun cotton, and M.
Gressly who knew all about the habits of marine animals,
and Doctor Moleschott, Professor of Physiology at Zurich,
who gave Parker another overhauling. There was never such
a group before, and they sat around the dinner table drinking wine from the vineyards of Combe Varin and talking
science and philosophy by the hour. "Mr. Parker was of
all the most animated," Desor remembered, "and such was

his desire for information that he easily obtained from the guests communications upon the subjects most familiar to each."

It was just the place for a consumptive, too, the dry mountain air, the wonderful sunshine, and Parker gained back all the strength that he had lost, fattened visibly every day. He had so much energy that he took it out in chopping down trees, the forest wasn't safe from his ravages. He was busy, too, with his contribution to the "Album" that they were getting up: a memorial to him and Küchler, it was to be. He wrote a paper on "The Bumblebee's Thoughts on the Plan and Purpose of the Universe." He felt encouraged, up here, he began to plan for the future again, collected statistics on Swiss agriculture and industry, laid out a course of reading, mapped out his sermons.

Soon the summer was gone, and he had to decide on a warmer climate. Everyone was ready with advice — some urged Egypt, others Algiers, or the South of France. But Parker decided to go to Rome; the climate was good, he thought, he had friends there, and, best of all, there were libraries, churches, monuments, things to interest him. "He departed," said Desor, "full of hope, notwithstanding the apprehensions of his friends. . . . Such was his firmness of will that nothing could divert him from the project." But there was something more to it than the lure of libraries, and the memory of the past. "I had little confidence in Rome when I entered it," he confessed later to Desor. "I thought I would never leave it, but an inexorable fate, which I cannot tell you of more particularly, drove me on. I did not do as I would but as I must, and came here to receive the *coup de grace* which ends all my mortal troubles."

Everything went wrong, that winter in Rome. The weather played tricks on him, one cold, rainy day after another; he might as well have stayed at home. The Papal State was in turmoil that year, the shadow of war still hanging over the whole of Italy; visitors stayed away, and the hotel-keepers and the cabbies and the peddlers were beggared.

Things were not right in his own household either; there was a bitter quarrel between Hannah and Sarah and Eliza Hunt. The Hunts and Apthorps had taken rooms just below Parker, but Hannah wouldn't go into their quarters. "Do you know how demoralizing it is to associate wholly or chiefly with women — even with superior women?" Parker asked Lyman. "I shall be a little afraid of any more logical deductions from an assumed first principle of politics or morals which runs counter to common sense and common experience of mankind. The weak point of woman is not her intellect, it is her temper. I think there is no hatred so unforgiving as a woman's." But it was too late, now, to learn about the necessity of qualifying first principles. Too late to do anything, now, and he burst out to Lyman: "My journey to Europe *hygienically* is a terrible failure, and æsthetically it is equally so — this latter and a good deal of the former must be set down to the bitter hatred between —— and the three females . . . *Ubi Feminae ibi querulae.* I hope you don't know the devilish side of woman."

But it was not all unhappiness, even with the quarreling and the pain and the prospect of death; his spirit was buoyant still. Here was society to amuse him: half of Boston seemed to be in Rome that winter. Here was Doctor Appleton to take care of him, "no end to his kindness," and George Bemis of the Boston bar, and the Reverend Frothingham, chastened now, his wife dying of consumption; he came and read Parker some of his poems, and Parker was sorry for the hard things he had thought and said. Here was Sarah Hunt to coddle him and the Apthorps with their precocious little William who was here to study drawing — "Potamoussie," Parker called him; he was hardly more than a baby, but you could see already that he was a genius.

Rome was swarming with artists. William Story came to see him almost every day, and modeled a bust of him which Lydia thought an almost perfect likeness. Parker let Saulini do a cameo of him, but it didn't turn out so well, he thought, a little idealized, a little smooth. The eccentric Hattie Hosmer was there, a great pet of Robert and Elizabeth Browning, a genius among women, and her friend Charlotte Cushman, the most talented of actresses; almost every day they climbed three flights of stairs to see Parker. Then there was Miss Landor and Miss Stebbins and the lovely Louisa Crawford, sister to Julia Ward Howe; and the sculptor, Sidney Morse. Parker visited Morse in his studio and found him busy at a bust of Emerson; he tried his hand at modeling, and Morse told him that he was a born sculptor: those plowman's hands weren't so clumsy after all! There were authors, too. Hawthorne and Bryant had just left, but here was Harriet Beecher Stowe, having the time of her life, dashing about Rome in a coach, going to fancy dress balls, enjoying her emancipation from Puritanism. And here were the Brownings, of course: Parker had tea with them, and he made an immense impression on Elizabeth, he knew so much, he was so dramatic, so full of life.

Rome was endlessly interesting. Nothing could keep him off the streets; he made a topographical survey of the city, and wrote it all off to old Charles Ellis, just as if it weren't in the books. He bought all the books on Roman history that he could find, a whole shelf full of them, and began to take notes, and to write out his own version. He visited all the historic places, and saw that nothing had changed, except for the worse. He stayed out of the churches, ever so conscientiously, — damp, cold places, — but there was no ban on the bookshops, and he haunted them. No use buying books now, he knew that; but he couldn't resist the auction rooms, and he picked up such wonderful bargains, that winter! For years, now, he had been looking for a book by a Dutchman, Nieuwendt, on the "Existence of God," and here it was, at last, for fifty cents. "If I were a heathen," Parker said, "I should look on this as an auspicious omen."

But it was not an auspicious omen, and when Desor

came down to take charge of him, he was shocked to find how Parker had aged in these few months. Every day he grew worse, for all the tinkering of doctors and the tumbler of asses' milk that he drank every morning. He knew now that he was fighting a losing fight — the odds of ten to one were too much for him. "O, George," he wrote to Ripley, "it is idle to run from Death. I shrank down behind the sugar canes of Santa Cruz, Death was there too; then I sneaked into a Swiss Valley, there he was; and here he is at Rome. I shall come home and meet him on my own dunghill."

Rome had treated him badly, and he was discouraged. At home the atmosphere was heavy with quarreling, outside was rain and cold, and the spectacle of poverty and degradation and tyranny, and four times a day, one hundred and twenty steps to climb. He hadn't minded at first, but now it was all a nightmare, and he wanted to get away. He was reconciled to death, but not here, not in Rome. Desor thought that he was morbid on the subject. "I will not die on this accursed soil," he said, "I will not leave my bones in this detested soil." He determined to go to Florence, and, as always, he had his way. A *vettura* was hired; Doctor Appleton agreed to go along with them, and on April 22 they set out.

Then out of the Papal States. Away from the Holy City and the shining dome of St. Peter's, symbol of spiritual tyranny. Hasten, Parker, the joggling of the *vettura* is hard on a dying man, but harder still death in the shadow of the Palatine. Through Viterbo and Orvieto and Perugia, past the waters of Lake Trasimeno, racing with death. "Tell me when we pass the frontier," Parker said. "If I am asleep, wake me to tell it." And when they passed the frontier and Desor pointed out the gaudy new posts, all red and white and green, "he roused as if electrified."

It was enough. When he reached Florence he was ready to die. It was bad to leave Lydia this way, on foreign soil, but Hannah would take care of her. Frances Cobbe was here, she had hurried down to see him, sometimes he thought that she was Sally Russell, and that these flowers were lilies of the valley from the Russell garden behind his house. But he would rouse himself, he had to make an effort with Miss Cobbe, seeing her now after all these years. He had to explain that this wasn't the real Theodore Parker, this was just a dying man, the real Theodore Parker was in America and would flourish there. It was good to think of America and of his friends. "Tell the Miss Thayers that I would like to see them," he said, "that I went away in February 1859 and came back in July 1860. I should like to touch them and tread on Boston Common." He asked for a pencil, and, painfully, scratched off his last letter: "My dear John Ayers, So I shall still call you. Will you come over to-morrow and see us, just after your dinner time. Bring me a last year's apple if you can, or any new melon."

THE END

BIBLIOGRAPHY

THIS biography is based almost entirely upon the writings of
Parker and of his contemporaries: it was a remarkably articulate
and self-conscious group, and it left an historical record embar-
rassingly voluminous. The main body of Parker material is de-
posited in the library of the Massachusetts Historical Society —
some twenty volumes of letters, journals, and notebooks. The
Boston Public Library has a considerable collection of Parker
manuscripts and clippings: eleven volumes of sermons, letters,
clippings, and so on, collected by Rebecca and Matilda Goddard;
two volumes of letters and clippings assembled by Miss Caroline
Thayer; the Rufus Leighton scrapbook; a volume of material relating to Parker's South Boston sermon; a volume of clippings
and posters on the fugitive slave cases, and another on Anthony
Burns; several volumes of manuscript sermons, a day-book, a list
of lectures, and a two-volume manuscript index of the Parker
library. Here, too, are the William Lloyd Garrison manuscripts
which contain some of Parker's letters. Parker left his library
of some fifteen thousand volumes to the Boston Public Library:
the collection has been maintained as a unit. Mr. Lewis Gannett generously permitted me to use two boxes of clippings and
notes about Parker which had been collected by the Reverend
William C. Gannett.

Parker's writings have been collected in two editions. The first
was that edited by Frances Cobbe; "The Collected Works of
Theodore Parker," 14 vols. (London, 1863–1874). The editorial
work was not well done; there are some duplications, some omis-
sions, and the arrangement of material leaves much to be desired.
Not until almost half a century later did circumstances in the
United States justify a similar collection. In 1910 the American
Unitarian Association, tardily recognizing their debt to Parker,
brought out a fifteen-volume edition of his "Works" (Boston,

1907–1913), each volume with a separate introduction. Editorially this Centenary edition of Parker's "Works" leaves nothing to be desired, but no more than the Cobbe edition did it include all of Parker's writings. The translation of De Wette's "Introduction to the Old Testament," the "Trial and Defence," and the "West Roxbury Sermons," must be consulted separately: neither edition includes any of Parker's letters. A large number of Parker's sermons and lectures were published in pamphlet form only, others were never published.

There is an excellent bibliography of Parker, embracing not only his writings but books and articles written about him, in John Chadwick's "Theodore Parker, Preacher and Reformer" (Boston, 1900), and an even more extensive one edited by Charles W. Wendte in the fifteenth volume of the Centenary edition of his "Works." Neither of these bibliographies covers in any detail that large body of literature which deals only incidentally with Parker and his participation in public affairs. I see no reason for duplicating, here, the impressive list of critical and memorial articles, pamphlets, and reviews which Mr. Wendte has assembled: a few of the more valuable of the some two hundred titles will be mentioned below.

Parker has not lacked for biographers: there are three American biographies, two Swiss, an English, a German, and a French, to say nothing of a Bengalese. Parker has been fortunate in his American biographers, for each of the biographies supplements and complements the other two. The first was that written by John Weiss, "The Life and Correspondence of Theodore Parker," 2 vols. (Boston, 1864). Mr. Weiss was the choice of Lydia Parker who, in her zeal for the preservation of her husband's reputation, rather mismanaged his affairs. Parker himself asked Joseph Lyman to be his literary executor and expected that Frank Sanborn or perhaps George Ripley would write his biography. Weiss's volumes are ill-digested and wretchedly arranged, yet they are quite invaluable. Lydia Parker and Weiss were assiduous in collecting letters written by Parker to his friends, and this biography includes a large number of Parker letters which I was unable to find in the Parker manuscripts or elsewhere. The second biography, and probably the best, is that by Octavius Brooks Frothingham, "Theodore Parker, a Biography" (Boston, 1874). Frothingham had the advantage of close personal acquaintance with Parker and with many of his contemporaries, yet he wrote at a time when most of the controversial subjects that agitated Parker's generation had been settled, and he succeeded in presenting a picture that was at once sympathetic and objective. Frothingham was, indeed, the self-appointed historian of this chapter of American intellectual history, more familiar, perhaps, with the religious and philosophical aspects of transcendentalism than any other man: he had scholarly standards, learning, and literary ability. The most recent biography of Parker is that by John White Chadwick: "Theodore Parker, Preacher and Reformer" (Boston, 1900). Chadwick's interpretation is less personal and more largely theological than that of Frothingham; it is sympathetic, learned, and clear. No account of Parker biographies can omit Parker's own "Letter to the Twenty-Eighth Congregational Society, 'Theodore Parker's Experience as a Minister.'" I have spoken of this letter at some length in the final chapter of this book; it is necessary to say here that it is not only the best brief account of Parker's public career but also the most satisfactory intellectual history of the Boston of the forties and fifties of the last century that has ever been written.

Scarcely less important than this Parker material is the large body of literature produced by Parker's contemporaries, throwing light on Parker himself. It is almost impossible to list all of these books, and the more important ones will be listed below under the chapter bibliographies, but two sets of literary material are of such general value that they must be mentioned here. Of utmost value, for the whole of this study, are the writings and the Journals of Emerson. I have used the Riverside Edition, "The Complete Works of Ralph Waldo Emerson," 12 vols. (Boston, 1883–1894) and "The Journals of Ralph Waldo Emerson," 10 vols. (Boston, 1909–1914). Of only less importance are the "Works of William E. Channing," 6 vols. (Boston, 1843), and "The Life of William Ellery Channing," by his nephew William Henry Channing, 3 vols. in 1 (Boston, 1899).

Several books dealing in a general way with New England in the second quarter of the nineteenth century must be mentioned here as well as in the special chapter bibliographies. The indefatigable Frothingham has written half a dozen books of value: "Transcendentalism in New England," (N. Y., 1876), a book of learning and charm, too long out of print; "Boston Unitarianism, 1820–1850: a study of the Life and Work of Nathaniel Langdon Frothingham," (N. Y., 1890), and "Recollections and Impressions, 1822–1890" (N. Y., 1891). My own copies of these two books were formerly owned by James Ford Rhodes, and I have been interested and edified by his annotations. Mr. Frothingham has also written biographies of "Gerrit Smith" (N. Y., 1878) and "George Ripley," (Boston, 1882). Of greatest value is the "Memoir of Ezra Stiles Gannett," by his son William C. Gannett (Boston, 1875).

Information on Parker and his period also is furnished, largely or stingily, by the following biographies, autobiographies, and memoirs: Frank B. Sanborn and W. T. Harris, "A. Bronson Alcott, His Life and Philosophy" (Boston, 1893); M. A. DeW. Howe, "Life and Letters of George Bancroft," 2 vols. (N. Y., 1908); William Birney, "James G. Birney and His Times" (N. Y. 1890); V. I. Bowditch, "Life and Correspondence of Henry Ingersoll Bowditch," 2 vols. (Boston, 1902); Charles Francis Adams, "Richard Henry Dana," 2 vols. (Boston, 1890); "Autobiography, Memoirs and Experience of Moncure Daniel Conway," 2 vols. (Boston, 1904); James Elliot Cabot, "A Memoir of Ralph Waldo Emerson," 2 vols. (Boston, 1887); Van Wyck Brooks, "The Life of Emerson" (N. Y., 1932); "Autobiography, Diary and Correspondence of James Freeman Clarke" (Boston, 1891); W. H. Channing, R. W. Emerson, and J. F. Clarke, "Memoir of Margaret Fuller Ossoli," 3 vols. (London, 1852); "William Lloyd Garrison, 1805–1879: The Story of His Life Told by His Children," 4 vols. (N. Y., 1883–1889); Edward E. Hale, "Life and Letters of Edward Everett Hale," 2 vols. (Boston, 1917); Edward Everett Hale, "Memories of a Hundred Years," 2 vols. (N. Y., 1902); Mary T. Higginson, editor, "Letters and Journals of Thomas Wentworth Higginson" (Boston, 1921); and "Thomas Wentworth Higginson; the Story of His Life" (Boston, 1914); "Reminiscences of Julia Ward Howe," (Boston, 1899); Laura E. Richards and Maud Howe Elliott, "Julia Ward Howe, 1819–1910," 2 vols. (Boston, 1916); Samuel G. Howe, "Letters and Journals," 2 vols. (Boston, 1906–1909); "Letters of James Russell Lowell," edited by C. E. Norton, 2 vols. (N. Y., 1894); Horace E. Scudder, "James Russell Lowell, a Biography," 2 vols. (Boston, 1901); Samuel Longfellow, "Life of Henry Wadsworth Longfellow, with Extracts from his Journals and Correspondence," 3 vols. (Boston, 1896); "Life and Works of Horace Mann," 5 vols. (Boston, 1891); Anna D. Hollowell, "James and Lucretia Mott" (Boston, 1884); Wendell Phillips, "Speeches, Lectures and Letters" (*First Series*, Boston, 1863), (*Second Series*, Boston, 1891); Franklin B. Sanborn, "Recollections of Seventy Years," 2 vols. (Boston, 1909); Edward L. Pierce, "Memoir and Letters of Charles Sumner," 4 vols. (Boston, 1878).

One interpretation of Parker demands special mention: that of Vernon Louis Parrington, in "The Romantic Revolution in America, 1800–1860" (N. Y., 1927). It was Parrington who first attracted me to Theodore Parker; of all historians he best appreciates Parker's significance to American thought and character.

CHAPTER I

Parker's own account of his childhood, up to his eighth year, is published in the first volume of Weiss: it is not very satisfactory. There are scattered references to Lexington, his family, his boyhood, throughout his sermons and his letters, and brief mention in his "Letter to the Twenty-Eighth Congregational Society." The New York Public Library has a folder of miscellaneous material on Parker genealogy; a "Genealogy and Bibliographical Notes of John Parker of Lexington and his Descendants, 1635–1893," was published in Worcester, 1893. The most satisfactory genealogy is that in Charles Hudson's "History of the Town of Lexington," 2 vols. (Boston, 1913), a revision of the earlier one-volume edition published in 1868. This "History" gives, likewise, a good deal of detail about Lexington in the early nineteenth century. Additional material on Lexington and the Parker family can be found in "Lexington, Mass. Record of Births, Marriages, and Deaths, to January 1, 1898" (Boston, 1898); "Proceedings of the Lexington Historical Society," 4 vols. (Lexington, Mass., 1890 ff.), especially the volume of "Lexington Epitaphs," by Francis Brown, in the volume for 1905. The bibliography for the battle of Lexington is too extensive to list here; Parker's version of that battle can be found in his "Trial and Defence" (Boston, 1855) and in a letter from Parker to George Bancroft, published in the first volume of Weiss.

For Quincy, Concord, and Waltham, I have supplemented Parker's own fragmentary references with material from local histories: for Quincy, George Whitney's "Second Centennial Anniversary of the Town of Quincy" (Boston, 1840), and "Some Account of the Early History and Present State of the Town of Quincy" (Boston, 1827); for Concord, Lemuel Shattuck's "History of the Town of Concord" (Concord, 1835), and Margaret Sidney's "Old Concord, her Highways and Byways" (Boston, 1888); for Waltham, Charles A. Nelson's "Waltham, Past and Present" (Cambridge, 1879).

CHAPTER II

For Boston in the early 1830's see the material listed in Chapter VI, below and, "A Trip to Boston, in a series of Letters to the Editor of the United States Gazette" by . . . [E. C. Wines] (Boston, 1838). The account of Parker in Boston is taken from Parker's letters. For Watertown, see Convers Francis, "Historic Sketch of Watertown" (Cambridge, 1830), and George F. Robinson and R. R. Wheeler, "Great Little Watertown" (Watertown, 1930). There are a large number of Parker letters from the Watertown period, and subsequent letters to Francis refer frequently to the Watertown years. The manuscript "History of the Jews" is in the Boston Public Library. For Convers Francis, see references to Watertown, above, and the "Letters of Lydia Maria Child" (Boston, 1883): there are some further references in Vol. VI of the "Dictionary of American Biography" (N. Y., 1928, seq.).

There is an article on Parker as a student, by G. E. Ellis, "Some Reminiscences of Parker at Cambridge," the *Christian Register,* January 7, 1892. The Divinity School of Parker's day is described in John Ware, "Memoir of the Life of Henry Ware, Jr.," 2 vols. (Boston, 1849); O. B. Frothingham, "Recollections and Impressions"; the "Autobiography, Diary and Correspondence of James Freeman Clarke," and Andrew P. Peabody, "Harvard Reminiscences" (Boston, 1888). There are frequent references

to Andrews Norton in the letters of Parker and of his contempo-
raries; see also M. A. DeW. Howe, "Letters of Charles Eliot
Norton," 2 vols. (Boston, 1913); W. B. Sprague, "Annals of the
Unitarian Pulpit" (N. Y., 1865); and A. P. Peabody, above.
For Palfrey, see the "Dictionary of American Biography," Vol.
XIV, and G. B. Adams, "Life and Writings of Jared Sparks,"
2 vols. (Boston, 1893). Parker's articles in the *Scriptural In-
terpreter* can be found in the Boston Public Library.

Something of the history and character of Barnstable during
the period of Parker's brief visit there can be read in H. C. Kit-
tredge, "Cape Cod" (Boston, 1930), and in E. Pratt, "A Comprehensive History, Ecclesiastical and Civil, of Eastham, Well-
fleet and Orleans" (Yarmouth, 1844).

CHAPTER III

The account of Parker in West Roxbury is taken largely from
his own letters. Some additional material can be found in the
West Roxbury Magazine, published by a Committee for the First
Parish of West Roxbury, 1900, and in Francis S. Drake, "The
Town of Roxbury" (Roxbury, 1878). A selection of Parker's
"West Roxbury Sermons," edited by S. J. Barrows, was published
in Boston in 1892; there is an article by S. J. Barrows on "Theodore Parker's Early Sermons" in the *Magazine of Christian Literature* of June, 1891. For West Roxbury, see also Leonora C.
Scott, "Life and Letters of Christopher P. Cranch" (Boston,
1917), and George W. Cooke, "John Sullivan Dwight, Brook
Farmer, Editor and Critic of Music" (Boston, 1898). I have
used Parker's own copy of "A Critical and Historical Introduction to the Canonical Scriptures of the Old Testament. From the
German of W. M. L. De Wette," 2 vols. (Boston, 1843), with
some marginal annotations. Parker's account of his method and
purpose is set forth in letters to Ripley which can be found in
Weiss.

Two chapters of Weiss's biography are devoted to the Groton
Convention: here are printed Parker's comments on the Convention, and his speech. Some light on the Come-outers and Mil-

lerites can be found in Clara E. Sears's "Days of Delusion" (Boston, 1924) and Gilbert Seldes's "The Stammering Century" (N. Y., 1928). For the Chardon Street Convention see the article by Emerson in "Lectures and Biographical Sketches," Vol. 10 of the "Complete Works." The letter from Quincy can be found in "William Lloyd Garrison, the Story of His Life," vol. 2.

The literature on Brook Farm is extensive; the most satisfactory account is that by Lindsay Swift, "Brook Farm" (N. Y., 1900), with a bibliography. See also J. T. Codman, "Brook Farm, Historic and Personal Memoirs" (Boston, 1894); O. B. Frothingham, "George Ripley"; W. H. Channing, *et al.*, "Memoir of Margaret Fuller Ossoli"; T. W. Higginson, "Margaret Fuller Ossoli" (Boston, 1884); G. W. Cooke, "John Sullivan Dwight"; Newton Arvin, "Hawthorne" (Boston, 1929); Edward Cary, "George William Curtis" (Boston, 1894); G. W. Cooke, "Early Letters of George William Curtis to John Sullivan Dwight" (N. Y., 1898) and Hawthorne's "Blithedale Romance." The chapter on Brook Farm in Parrington's "Romantic Revolution in America" is excellent. For some of the lesser figures, the "Dictionary of American Biography" is invaluable, and E. A. and G. L. Duyckinck, "Cyclopædia of American Literature," 2 vols. (N. Y., 1856) useful. The literature on Brownson is extensive. His "Works" have been published in twenty volumes (Detroit, 1882–1887) and there is a three-volume biography by his son, Henry F. Brownson (Detroit, 1898–1900). Comments on him, for the most part critical, are scattered through the writings of his contemporaries.

For Bronson Alcott and Fruitlands, see F. B. Sanborn and W. T. Harris, "A. Bronson Alcott"; Clara E. Sears, "Bronson Alcott's Fruitlands" (Boston, 1915). The best appreciation of Alcott in our literature is that by Emerson in his "Journal," vol. 6, p. 170ff.

The history of the Transcendental Club can be pieced out from Emerson's "Journals," which note the meetings, and from Higginson's "Margaret Fuller" and the "Memoir of Margaret Fuller" by Channing, *et al.* There is something in E. W. Emerson, "Early Years of the Saturday Club," and in H. C. Goddard, "Studies in New England Transcendentalism" (N. Y., 1908). It is not easy to find anything on the Friends; there are scattered references in W. E. Channing's "Life of Channing," in

Chadwick's "Channing" (Boston, 1903), in Carlos Martyn's "Wendell Phillips" (N. Y., 1890), and in Parker's letters.

Essential for an understanding of transcendentalism are the essays of Emerson, particularly those collected in "Nature, Addresses, and Lectures" (Boston, 1892), and the essay on Transcendentalism by Parker, not published until 1876. Goddard's volume, mentioned above, is of some value; Goddard has written the chapter on transcendentalism for the "Cambridge History of American Literature," Vol. I (N. Y., 1917), and the chapters in Parrington are brilliant. Far more important than these, however, are the volumes of *"The Dial,* a Magazine for Literature, Philosophy and Religion" (Boston, 1841–1844) and Emerson's Journals. On the *Dial* and its successor, the *Harbinger,* see Clarence L. F. Gohdes's "The Periodicals of American Transcendentalism" (Durham, N. C., 1931) and Frank L. Mott, "History of American Magazines, 1741–1850" (N. Y., 1930). On Elizabeth Peabody and her bookshop I have used a manuscript thesis by Queenie Bilbo, "Elizabeth Palmer Peabody, Transcendentalist" (New York University, 1932).

CHAPTER IV

There is a large literature on the so-called Unitarian controversy. One volume of clippings on the reaction to Parker's South Boston sermon is in the Boston Public Library. For a general discussion of the Controversy, see "Unitarianism, its Origin and History: a Course of Sixteen Lectures" (Boston, 1890), lectures 5, 8, 9, 10; George W. Cooke, "Unitarianism in America" (Boston, 1902); George E. Ellis, "A Half century of the Unitarian Controversy . . ." (London, 1858); Joseph H. Allen, "Our Liberal Movement in Theology, chiefly as shown in recollections of the history of Unitarianism in New England" (Boston, 1892); Joseph H. Allen, "Historical Sketch of the Unitarian Movement since the Reformation" (N. Y., 1894); and Frank H. Foster, "A Genetic History of the New England Theology" (Chicago, 1907).

Emerson's essays on Nature, and the Divinity School Address, can be found in countless editions; his "Journals" for these years

— Volumes 4 and 5 — are indispensable. The exchange of letters between Ware and Emerson is published in Cabot's "Memoir of Emerson." W. C. Gannett's "Memoir of Ezra Stiles Gannett" has a great deal on the Unitarian controversy: here is reprinted his article on Parker and transcendentalism, which first appeared in the *Examiner* of March, 1845. The important sermons, articles, and pamphlets called forth by the quarrel between Norton and Ripley are listed in C. W. Wendte's "Bibliography," as are the more important articles on Parker's South Boston Sermon. See also the article by Ripley, "Philosophic Thought in Boston," in "Memorial History of Boston," 4 vols. (Boston, 1880–1881) Vol. 4 (Justin Winsor, ed.); and "Some Reminiscences of the Life of Samuel K. Lothrop," ed. by T. K. Lothrop (Cambridge, 1898). For the German background of Parker's thought, see the Appendix to Goddard's volume, and George Cross's "The Theology of Schleiermacher" (Chicago, 1907).

CHAPTER V

For the continuation of the Unitarian controversy, see references for Chapter IV; for the Hollis Street Council, Parker's article in the *Dial* for October, 1842. The details of the Hollis Street controversy can be filled out from "Proceedings of an Ecclesiastical Council in the Case of the . . . Hollis Street Meeting House and the Rev. John Pierpont . . ." (Boston, 1841). Some comments on the Great and Thursday Lecture are in O. B. Frothingham, "Boston Unitarianism," Chapter 3, and in his "Recollections and Impressions," and in Arthur Ellis, "History of the First Church in Boston" (Boston, 1881). Parker's "Discourse of Matters Relating to Religion" was published in Boston, 1842, the "Critical and Miscellaneous Writings" in the following year.

The trip to Europe can be followed in Parker's letters, many of which are given in Weiss and in Frothingham. Some anecdotes are taken from Carlyle's "Life of John Sterling," and Henry D. Sedgwick's "Life of Francis Parkman" (Boston, 1904) and the "Reminiscences of Julia Ward Howe."

CHAPTER VI

The literature descriptive of Boston is extensive. I have used the *Boston Almanac,* published annually from 1837 to 1860 (Boston, *v.d.*), and the sumptuously illustrated brochures published by the State Street Trust Company — some twenty of them (Boston, 1906 *seq.*). I am indebted to the following books: Mary Caroline Crawford, "Romantic Days in Old Boston" (Boston, 1923), and "Old Boston Days and Ways" (Boston, 1909); W. S. Rossiter, ed., "Days and Ways in Old Boston" (Boston, 1915); S. A. Drake, "Old Landmarks and Historic Personages of Boston" (Boston, 1900); Henry Cabot Lodge, "Early Memories" (N. Y., 1920); "The Education of Henry Adams" (Boston, 1927); Josiah Quincy, "Figures of the Past," ed. by M. A. DeW. Howe (Boston, 1926); "Life, Letters and Journals of George Ticknor," 2 vols. (Boston, 1876); Edward Everett Hale, "A New England Boyhood" (N. Y., 1903, and a new edition, with supplementary chapters, N. Y., 1920); Edward E. Hale, "Memories of a Hundred Years," 2 vols. (N. Y., 1902); Allen Chamberlain, "Beacon Hill" (Boston, 1925); Justin Winsor, ed., "Memorial History of Boston," 4 vols. (Boston, 1880–1881); A. B. Hart, ed., "Commonwealth History of Massachusetts," 5 vols. (N. Y., 1930), Vol. 4; and S. E. Morison, "Maritime History of Massachusetts" (Boston, 1921). For a picture of the underprivileged classes of Boston, see Norman Ware, "The Industrial Worker, 1840–1860" (Boston, 1924).

There are comments on Father Taylor in S. E. Morison, above, and an article by Allan MacDonald, "A Sailor among Transcendentalists," in the *New England Quarterly,* September, 1935.

The account of Parker's correspondence and his social relations is based, of course, upon his own letters. In addition see J. T. Sargent, "Theodore Parker in his Social Relations and Letters," the *Radical,* July, 1871; Eyre Crowe, "With Thackeray in America" (N. Y., 1893). The letter to Parkman is printed in an Appendix of Charles H. Farnham's "A Life of Francis Parkman" (Boston, 1902). In addition, see the "Letters and Journals" of Higginson, "Letters and Journals" of S. G. Howe, "Reminiscences" of Julia Ward Howe, "Recollections" of Frank

Sanborn, "Autobiography" of Conway, "Garrison: Life, Told by His Children," Pierce's "Sumner," Vol. 3, all listed above. Comment on Parker's prayers can be found in Julia Ward Howe's "Reminiscences" and in "Life, Letters, and Journals of Louisa May Alcott" (Boston, 1880). An edition of the "Prayers" was published separately (Boston, 1861), and selections are included in the Cobbe edition of the "Works," Vol. 2, and in the Centenary Edition, Vol. 13. The extract from Lowell is from the "Fable for Critics."

CHAPTER VII

There is an account of Parker's library by T. W. Higginson in the Annual Report of the Boston Public Library for 1883; this is reprinted in Vol. XV of the Centenary edition of Parker's "Works." My own account of the library is based upon an inspection of the books in the Boston Public Library: many of these books have Parker's marginal annotations. I used, likewise, Parker's own set of the *Massachusetts Quarterly Review*. There are some perfunctory remarks on this periodical in the volumes by Gohdes and Mott, noted above. Emerson's introductory address can be found in his "Miscellanies." There is an account of the origin of the Review in Cabot's "Memoir of Emerson," Vol. 2.

The essays discussed can be found conveniently gathered in Vol. VIII of the Centenary Edition of the "Works," ed. by George W. Cooke, and in Vols. 7, 10, and 12 of the Cobbe edition. The Centenary Edition contains several essays not included in the earlier collection.

A list of Parker's lyceum lectures, with notations of earnings, can be found in one volume of the Parker papers in the Massachusetts Historical Society. Parker's own letters from the lyceum circuit are revealing. Some references to Parker as a lecturer can be found in the "Letters and Journals of T. W. Higginson," in Frederick Gillett's "George Frisbie Hoar" (Boston, 1934), in Austin Warren's "The Elder Henry James" (N. Y., 1934), in Mary Tyler Mann's "Life of Horace Mann" (Boston, 1865), in the "Letters and Journals" of S. G. Howe, and in Emerson's

"Journals." There are some interesting reflections on Parker's scholarship in T. W. Higginson's "Contemporaries" (Boston, 1900), and some severe animadversions in an article by G. Prentice, "Theodore Parker," in the *Methodist Quarterly Review* for 1873, and in an article by D. P. Noyes, in the *Bibliotheca Sacra* for January, 1861. See also the tribute by Wendell Phillips, in "Speeches," *Second Series*. Some of the material presented in this chapter can be found in H. S. Commager's "Theodore Parker, Intellectual Gourmand," the *American Scholar*, Vol. 3, 1934.

CHAPTER VIII

For the reform movements of the forties and fifties of the last century the literature is large, but there is no satisfactory general account. Something can be found in most of the larger histories — that of McMaster in perhaps the most appreciative. There is an excellent chapter in J. T. Adams, "New England in the Republic" (Boston, 1926), and there are several chapters dealing with various phases of reform in Volume Four of the "Commonwealth History of Massachusetts." C. R. Fish's "The Rise of the Common Man" (N. Y., 1927) is disappointing; A. C. Cole's "The Irrepressible Conflict" (N. Y., 1934) is better, and the bibliography is excellent.

For the philosophy of reform, Emerson's works, and particularly his lecture on the "New England Reformers" is indispensable. See, in addition, the bibliography on transcendentalism cited above.

For Channing, the invaluable "Life of W. E. Channing," by William Henry Channing (Boston, 1880) which contains hundreds of letters; and the "Works" of W. E. Channing, cited above. J. W. Chadwick's "Channing" is better even than his biography of Parker. See also Elizabeth P. Peabody, "Reminiscences of Rev. William Ellery Channing" (Boston, 1880). Two essays by Parker indicate something of his appreciation of Channing: the sermon of 1842, published in pamphlet form, and the essay of 1848 which appeared in the *Massachusetts Quarterly Review* and is reprinted in both the Cobbe and the Centenary Editions of the "Works." For Abner Kneeland see, H. S. Commager, "The Blasphemy of Abner Kneeland," *New England Quarterly,* March, 1935.

Other phases of the relation of the Unitarian Church to reform can be found in the "Autobiography" of J. F. Clarke, the "Letters and Journals" of T. W. Higginson, the "Memoirs of Samuel J. May," by G. B. Emerson, S. May, and T. J. Mumford (Boston, 1873). There are some severe remarks by Phillips in his "Speeches and Lectures," *Second Series.* The last stage of the Unitarian controversy can be followed in Parker's letters, and in his final blast against the Church, "A Friendly Letter," and so forth, printed in Volume 12 of the Cobbe edition.

Parker's conception of the function of the minister is fully set forth in his sermon on "The True Idea of a Christian Church," which can be found in Vol. 3 of the Cobbe Edition and Vol. 13 of the Centenary Edition, and in "Theodore Parker's Experience as a Minister." Elaborations of the position set forth here are in the whole body of his sermons and letters.

CHAPTER IX

The history of the reform movement and of Parker's participation in it must be pieced out from Parker's sermons and lectures and letters, and from the biographies and autobiographies of Channing, Garrison, Phillips, Mann, Higginson, Howe, Clarke, Sanborn, Sumner, and Emerson, already noted.

For the anti-Sabbath convention, see "Proceedings of the Anti-Sabbath Convention, Held at the Melodeon . . ." (Boston, 1848), and a great deal of material in "Garrison: Life, Told by His Children," Vol. 2. For the temperance movement, see John A. Krout, "The Origins of Prohibition" (N. Y., 1925); George F. Clark, "History of the Temperance Reform in Massachusetts, 1813–1883" (Boston, 1888); W. G. Hawkins, "Life of John Hawkins" (Boston, 1859); and Carlos Martyn, "John B. Gough" (N. Y., 1890). For welfare work there is material in "The Life of Charles Loring Brace, Chiefly Told in His Own Letters," ed. by his daughter (N. Y., 1894) and Francis Tiffany, "Life of Dorothea Lynde Dix" (Boston, 1891). The movement for woman's rights can be traced in the "Letters and Journals" of T. W. Higginson, and in Alice S. Blackwell's "Lucy Stone" (Boston, 1930), and in the lectures of Phillips and the sermons of Clarke and of Parker. For the Peace Movement: Merle Curti, "The American Peace Crusade" (Durham, N. C., 1929) and his "Non-Resistance in New England," *New England Quarterly*, Vol. 2, are satisfactory. For educational reform, the "Life and Works of Horace Mann," 5 vols. (Boston, 1891), is invaluable. Gilbert Seldes, "The Stammering Century" (N. Y., 1928) and E. D. Branch, "The Sentimental Years" (N. Y., 1934) provide breezy accounts of the agitations of this period.

Parker's sermons on War can be found in Vol. 4 of the Cobbe Edition, and Volumes 9 and 11 of the Centenary Edition, of his "Works." His sermons on "The Mercantile Classes," "The Laboring Classes," "The Perishing Classes," "The Dangerous Classes," "The Material Condition of the People of Massachusetts," and "The Moral Dangers Incident to Prosperity," are conveniently assembled in Vol. 10 of the Centenary Edition and in Vols. 7 and 8 of the Cobbe Edition. Students should consult the whole of Volumes 9, 10, and 12 of the Centenary Edition for an understanding of the scope of Parker's reform program. The writings, not only of Parker but of most of his contemporaries, are impregnated with the philosophy of Progress.

For Howe, Garrison, and Phillips the books already listed, together with bibliographies in the "Dictionary of American Biography," should be sufficient. Laura Richards' recent biography of S. G. Howe adds nothing to her earlier studies. There is no good brief biography of Garrison, and no biography of Phillips that does justice to his character. Gilbert H. Barnes's "The Anti-Slavery Impulse" (N. Y., 1933) presents a bitterly critical interpretation of Garrison: I think it is a thoroughly mistaken one.

CHAPTER X

I do not think it necessary to list here even a part of the vast literature on slavery. There is an excellent bibliography of the anti-slavery movement in A. B. Hart's "Slavery and Abolition" (N. Y., 1906). This chapter is concerned only with Parker's view of the institution and with his philosophy, as distinct from

326

his active attack upon it. Two collections of Parker's anti-slavery sermons and speeches appeared during his lifetime: "Speeches, Addresses and Occasional Sermons," 3 vols. (Boston, 1852) and "Additional Speeches, Addresses and Occasional Sermons," 2 vols. (Boston, 1855). Volume 11 of the Centenary Edition, "The Slave Power," is edited by J. K. Hosmer; Vol. 12, "The Rights of Man in America," by F. B. Sanborn: these contain the more important speeches on slavery. The same speeches can be found in the Cobbe Edition in Vols. 5, 6, 7, and 8. Volume 2 of Weiss's biography contains a mass of anti-slavery material, so badly arranged that it will baffle even the most patient student. There is no satisfactory study of Parker's contribution to the Higher Law doctrine in American politics: that it was great cannot be doubted.

CHAPTER XI

The literature on fugitive slave cases is very large, and I can list only those volumes which contribute directly to an appreciation of Parker's activities. The Boston Public Library has one volume of papers and clippings, "Memoranda of the Troubles Occasioned by the Infamous Fugitive Slave Law, from March 15, 1851 to Feb. 19, 1856," and another volume of material on the Anthony Burns case. These volumes include a large number of the posters prepared by Parker. For particular fugitive slave cases I have consulted the *Liberator* (Boston, *v.d.*). The annual volumes of the *Liberty Bell* contain some useful material: Parker's contributions will be mentioned below. Many of the accounts of anti-slavery days published later have the value of source material. The more important of such contributions are the following: Thomas Wentworth Higginson, "Cheerful Yesterdays" (Boston, 1898), and his "Letters and Journals"; James Freeman Clarke, "Anti-Slavery Days" (N. Y., 1883); Samuel J. May, "Some Recollections of our Anti-Slavery Conflict" (Boston, 1869), and "The Fugitive Slave Law and its Victims" (N. Y., 1861); W. C. Gannett, "Memoir of Ezra Stiles Gannett"; C. F. Adams, "Richard Henry Dana," 2 vols. (Boston, 1890);

V. I. Bowditch, "Life and Correspondence of Henry Ingersoll Bowditch," 2 vols. (Boston, 1902); "William Lloyd Garrison: His Life, Told by His Children," 4 vols.; Edward Pierce, "Memoirs of Charles Sumner," especially Vol. 3; M. D. Conway, "Autobiography"; Henry G. Pearson, "Life of John Andrew" (Boston, 1904); Julia Ward Howe, "Reminiscences"; Henry Wilson, "The Rise and Fall of the Slave Power in America," 3 vols (Boston, 1874) especially Vol. 2; Maria W. Chapman, "Right and Wrong in Massachusetts" (Boston, 1839); S. G. Howe, "Letters and Journals," 2 vols; F. B. Sanborn's "Recollections"; T. J. Mumford, et. al., "Memoir of S. J. May"; Lewis Tappan, "Life of Arthur Tappan" (N. Y., 1870); S. T. Pickard, "Life and Letters of John Greenleaf Whittier," 2 vols. (Boston, 1894). Marion G. McDougall, "Fugitive Slaves, 1819–1865" (Boston, 1891) is an uninspired compilation, and Lorenzo Dow Turner's, "Anti-Slavery Sentiment in American Literature Prior to 1865" (Washington, D. C., 1929) an uninspired literary chronicle.

The story of the Craft rescue is fully told in Parker's own letters, especially in the letters to President Fillmore and to the Reverend Martineau, both of which are given in Weiss, Vol. 2. Further material can be found in Parker's "Trial and Defence." There is an excellent description in the "Life and Correspondence of H. I. Bowditch," where is printed Bowditch's manuscript history of the "Thirty Years' War of Anti-Slavery." There is some confusion in the accounts of the escape from the city.

For Parker's early interest in anti-slavery, see his "Sermon of Slavery" of 1841, and his "Letter touching the matter of Slavery," of 1847, both in Vol. 5 of the Cobbe Edition. There are several contributions to the *Liberty Bell:* the volume for 1843 contains "Socrates in Boston: a Dialogue between the Philosopher and a Yankee," and succeeding volumes contain anti-slavery poetry, and the issue for 1848 a challenge "Come and Do it Better." For the Latimer case, see Bowditch, and S. J. May, "The Fugitive Slave Law." This case inspired Whittier's "Massachusetts to Virginia." The case of the slave Joe attracted some attention: John Quincy Adams's participation in the protest can be followed in the Memoirs, Vol. XII (Phila. 1877); other material is in Bowditch, in Adams' "Richard Henry Dana," and in Henry Wilson, "Rise and Fall of the Slave Power," Vol. 2.

For the Shadrach case, Parker's sermons and letters are useful. His "Defence" contains a history of the case. To the *Liberator*, Vol. 21, he contributed "Another Chapter in the Book of Daniel." T. W. Higginson's "Cheerful Yesterdays" is valuable on this, as on other fugitive slave cases. The best account of the trial of the rescuers is in C. F. Adams' "Richard Henry Dana," where Dana's Journal from this period is printed. For Elizur Wright, see Frank P. Stearns, "Cambridge Sketches" (Phila., 1905). I have followed the Sims case in the *Liberator*, in Parker's sermons and letters, and in the "Defence." The most important of the sermons, "The Function of Conscience in Relation to the Laws of Men," "Speech at the Ministerial Conference," and "On the Boston Kidnapping" can be found in Vol. 5 of the Cobbe edition. In addition, see the comments in Emerson's "Journals," in the "Life," of Longfellow, Vol. 2, and in C. F. Adams, Dana, Garrison's "Garrison," Bowditch's "Bowditch," the "Letters and Journals" of Howe, the "Letters and Journals" of Higginson, Pierce's "Sumner," the speeches of Phillips, in "Speeches," *Second Series,* and Austin Bearse, "Remembrances of Fugitive Slave Law Days in Boston" (Boston, 1880). The account of the vigil at the Court House is taken from Bowditch and from the *Liberator*.

For Webster's part in the Compromise of 1850 and the reaction of New England, see Vol. 2 of G. T. Curtis "Life of Daniel Webster" (N. Y., 1870); H. C. Lodge, "Daniel Webster" (Boston, 1883), and Claude M. Fuess "Daniel Webster," 2 vols. (Boston, 1930). I have followed Webster's defense in "The Private Correspondence of Daniel Webster," Vol. 2 (Boston, 1856), and in the speeches contained in "The Works of Daniel Webster," 6 vols. (Boston, 1851). Whittier's "Ichabod" is familiar to everyone. For the Jerry rescue, see S. J. May, "Recollections of the Anti-Slavery Conflict," O. B. Frothingham, "Gerrit Smith," and Andrew D. White, "Autobiography" (N. Y., 1905). The letter from the boys of the Groton Academy is mentioned in William S. Robinson's "Warrington," in "Pen Portraits" (Boston, 1877). The Sumner election can be studied in Pierce's "Memoir," and Sumner's early rôle in the political struggle against slavery in Vols. 2 and 3 of the "Works" of Charles Sumner (Boston, 1874). Some light on Sumner can be found in the extracts from Longfellow's "Diary." Parker's "Speech at a Meeting of the Citizens of Boston to Consider the Speech of Mr. Sumner" is in Vol. 4

of the Cobbe edition, the "Discourse on Webster" is in Volume 12. The comment on Parker's speech by Dana can be found in Adams' "Dana"; that of C. F. Adams is in one of the unpublished letters.

For the Anthony Burns case I have used the *Liberator*, and Parker's own account in his letters and in his "Defence." One of the best contemporary accounts is "The Boston Slave Riot, and Trial of Anthony Burns . . ." (Boston, 1854). The best account of the attack on the Court House is in Higginson's "Cheerful Yesterdays." There is valuable material in the biographies and memoirs of Higginson, Howe, Phillips, Alcott, Bowditch. There is a history, "Anthony Burns," by Charles E. Stevens (Boston, 1856). The anecdote of Rufus Choate is from H. C. D. Scudder, "Echoes from Parnassus" (N. Y., 1928); that of the Reverend Gannett's reaction, from W. C. Gannett's "Memoir." The Journal of Emerson and the Diary of Longfellow reveal something of the contemporary attitude of moderate men. Lowell's comment on Cambridge snobbishness is from "The Letters of J. R. Lowell," edited by C. E. Norton (N. Y., 1894). Several of the sermons and speeches on the Burns case are worth reading to-day: perhaps the best of them are those of J. F. Clarke "The Rendition of Anthony Burns, A Discourse . . ." (Boston, 1854), and of T. W. Higginson, "Massachusetts in Mourning, a Sermon . . ." (Boston, 1854). Some phases of the Trial of Burns are reviewed in Phillips' "Speech on the Removal of Judge Loring," in "Speeches, etc.," *First Series* (Boston, 1863), and in Parker's "Trial and Defence." The anecdote of Lowell and Higginson is taken from Bliss Perry's "Life and Letters of Henry Lee Higginson" (Boston, 1921).

The whole story of Parker's trial can be followed in his "The Trial of Theodore Parker for the Misdemeanor . . . with the Defence," by Theodore Parker (Boston, 1855). The charge of Judge Hoar to the Suffolk grand jury is given in M. Storey and E. Emerson, "Ebenezer Rockwood Hoar, a Memoir" (Boston, 1911). The sneer of Hallet and Parker's reply is recorded in F. P. Stearns' "Life of George Luther Stearns" (Philadelphia, 1907).

CHAPTER XII

For Kansas and John Brown, see Eli Thayer, "History of the Kansas Crusade" (N. Y., 1899), the "Letters and Journals" of S. G. Howe, and of T. W. Higginson, and the "Recollections" of F. B. Sanborn. There is an excellent article on the colonization of Kansas by E. E. Hale, in the 1920 edition of "A New England Boyhood." See also T. W. Higginson, "A Ride through Kansas" (N. Y., 1856) and "The Reign of Terror in Kansas" (Boston, 1856).

Oswald Garrison Villard has said the last word on "John Brown" (Boston, 1911). Brown's relations with Parker and other eastern supporters can be traced in the volumes of Weiss and Frothingham, and in O. B. Frothingham's "Gerrit Smith," Sanborn's "Recollections," the "Letters and Journals" of Howe, and F. B. Sanborn's "S. G. Howe, Philanthropist" (N. Y., 1891). Parker's letter on John Brown is printed in the Centenary Edition, Vol. 14.

Parker's relations with the politicians of his day are revealed in Volumes 10 and 11 of the manuscript letters in the Massachusetts Historical Society collection. Many of these letters are printed in Weiss. The correspondence of Parker and Herndon is likewise in the Massachusetts Historical Society: the most important of the letters that passed between them can be found in Joseph Fort Newton's interesting "Lincoln and Herndon" (Cedar Rapids, Iowa, 1910). There is some controversy as to the origin of the famous phrase that Lincoln used in the Gettysburg address, but Herndon is authority for the statement that Lincoln took it from Parker, and this suggestion seems entirely reasonable. See William Henry Herndon, "Abraham Lincoln, the True Story of a Great Life," by W. H. Herndon and Jesse W. Weik (N. Y., 1901). There is a short article on this subject by J. W. Chadwick, "The Gettysburg Phrase" in *American Monthly Review of Reviews* for April, 1901.

The essays on Buckle, on Beecher, and on "The Material Condition of the People of Massachusetts," as well as the "Sermons to the Progressive Friends," can all be found in the Centenary Edition of Parker's "Works." The revival sermons are in the

Cobbe edition, Vol. 3, and in the Centenary Edition, Vol. 4. There are some cursory remarks on the Revival of 1857 in G. C. Loud's "Evangelized America" (N. Y., 1928).

CHAPTER XIII

The voyage to the West Indies and to Europe is told very fully in Parker's own letters and his Journal, both reproduced at length in the second volume of Weiss. Julia Ward Howe's "A Trip to Cuba" (Boston, 1860) has a description of Parker.

"Theodore Parker's Experience as a Minister" is published separately, and as an Appendix to the Weiss biography: it is included in both editions of the collected works.

Emerson's comment on Parker and Alcott is remembered in G. F. Hoar's "Autobiography of Seventy Years," Vol. 1 (N. Y., 1903). Julia Ward Howe's poem, The Poetaster, is in "Passion Flowers" (Boston, 1854). For Combe-Varin, see G. Prentice, "Theodore Parker," in *Methodist Quarterly Review*, 1873. I was unable to secure a copy of the *"Album von Combe-Varin"* (Zurich, 1861). The "Letters to a New Hampshire Girl" are printed in the *Boston Transcript* for July, 1897. The anecdote from Morse's studio is told in an article by Sidney Morse in the *Conservator*, July, 1890. My analysis of Parker's character and mind is based upon the whole of the material cited in this bibliography.

INDEX